NETWORKED POLITICS

A VOLUME IN THE SERIES

CORNELL STUDIES IN POLITICAL ECONOMY

edited by Peter J. Katzenstein

A list of titles in this series is available at www.cornellpress.cornell.edu.

Networked Politics

AGENCY, POWER, AND GOVERNANCE

Edited by **Miles Kahler**

Cornell University Press ITHACA AND LONDON

First published 2009 by Cornell University Press
First printing, Cornell Paperbacks, 2009

Printed in the United States of America

Library of Congress Cataloging-in-Publication Data

Networked politics : agency, power, and governance / edited by Miles Kahler.
        p.   cm. — (Cornell studies in political economy)
    Includes bibliographical references and index.
    ISBN 978-0-8014-4752-5 (cloth : alk. paper) — ISBN 978-0-8014-7476-7 (pbk. : alk. paper)
    1. Policy networks.   2. Social sciences—Network analysis.
3. International cooperation.   4. World politics—20th century.
5. World politics—21st century.   1. Kahler, Miles, 1949–   II. Series.
    H97.7.N48 2009
    302.3′5—dc22   2008044164

Cornell University Press strives to use environmentally responsible suppliers and materials to the fullest extent possible in the publishing of its books. Such materials include vegetable-based, low-VOC inks and acid-free papers that are recycled, totally chlorine-free, or partly composed of nonwood fibers. For further information, visit our website at www.cornellpress.cornell.edu.

Cloth printing   10 9 8 7 6 5 4 3 2 1

Paperback printing   10 9 8 7 6 5 4 3 2 1

Contents

Contributors

PETER COWHEY is Dean and Qualcomm Endowed Chair in Communications and Technology Policy at the School of International Relations and Pacific Studies, University of California, San Diego. He can be reached at pcowhey@ucsd.edu.

METTE EILSTRUP-SANGIOVANNI is University Lecturer in International Studies at the Centre of International Studies, University of Cambridge, and a Fellow of Sidney Sussex College, Cambridge. She can be reached at mer29@cam.ac.uk.

ZACHARY ELKINS is Assistant Professor at the University of Texas at Austin. He can be reached at zelkins@austin.utexas.edu.

EMILIE M. HAFNER-BURTON is Assistant Professor of Politics at Princeton University's Woodrow Wilson School of Public and International Affairs and the Department of Politics. She can be reached at ehafner@princeton.edu.

MILES KAHLER is Rohr Professor of Pacific International Relations and Professor of Political Science at the School of International Relations and Pacific Studies, University of California, San Diego.

MICHAEL KENNEY is Assistant Professor of Political Science and Public Policy at the Pennsylvania State University, Harrisburg. He can be reached at mck14@psu.edu

DAVID A. LAKE is Professor of Political Science at the University of California, San Diego. He can be reached at dlake@ucsd.edu.

ALEXANDER H. MONTGOMERY is Assistant Professor of Political Science at Reed College, Portland, Oregon. His website is http://www.reed.edu/~ahm.

MILTON MUELLER is Professor, Syracuse University School of Information Studies, Syracuse, New York, and XS4All Professor, Delft University of Technology, the Netherlands. He directs the Internet Governance Project. His e-mail address is mueller@syr.edu.

KATHRYN SIKKINK is a Regents Professor and a McKnight Distinguished University Professor of Political Science at the University of Minnesota Twin Cities, Minneapolis, Minnesota.

JANICE GROSS STEIN is the Belzberg Professor of Conflict Management and Director of the Munk Centre for International Studies at the University of Toronto.

WENDY H. WONG is Assistant Professor of Political Science at the University of Toronto. She can be reached at wendyh.wong@utoronto.ca.

HELEN YANACOPULOS is a Senior Lecturer in International Politics and Development at the Open University in the United Kingdom. She can be reached at h.yanacopulos@open.ac.uk.

Acknowledgments

A research network, founded on collegial cross-border ties between three countries and two continents, created this book. Three research institutions hosted conferences and provided financial support: the Institute for International, Comparative, and Area Studies (IICAS) at the University of California, San Diego; the Munk Centre for International Studies at the University of Toronto; and the Centre of International Studies at the University of Cambridge. The editor and authors are profoundly grateful for the hospitable settings at these three institutions that promoted lively intellectual exchange and furthered our aim of contributing to better understanding the role of networks in international politics. We thank the University of California Institute on Global Conflict and Cooperation and its director, Susan Shirk, for critical financial support of the initial project workshop and the final authors' conference and the Airey Neave Foundation (London) for its generous support of the project's United Kingdom activities.

The authors were perhaps the best critics of each other's work during the course of this project. Others who participated in this project also provided important insights and correctives that substantially improved the final publication: Lars-Erik Cederman, Ronald Deibert, Luc Girardin, Tim Jordan, Michael Kleeman, Nikos Passas, Rafal Rohozinski, and Phil Williams. Scott Bailey served as rapporteur for the first San Diego workshop.

At IICAS, Leslie Kamps, Melissa Labouff, and Diana Wilder gave invaluable support to the project and its two workshops at UCSD. Nina Boric, Penny Alford, and their team provided support and warm hospitality at the Munk Centre. Roger Haydon, executive editor at Cornell University Press, was particularly generous with his advice and support as the manuscript moved toward publication. Two anonymous reviewers for the Press supplied detailed and constructive comments on the book's structure and individual chapters. Peter J. Katzenstein, editor of the Cornell Studies in Political Economy, also offered extensive and valuable comments that were, as usual, those of a renowned scholar in international relations as well as an experienced series editor. The outstanding editorial skills of Lynne Bush, senior editor at the Institute on Global Conflict and Cooperation, were essential for final preparation of the manuscript.

NETWORKED POLITICS

1

Networked Politics

AGENCY, POWER, AND GOVERNANCE

Miles Kahler

A century ago, during an earlier era of globalization, large hierarchical organizations dominated the international landscape. Nation-states hardened their borders, built up vast militaries, and extended their rule over far-flung territories. The earliest transnational corporations extracted oil and other natural resources, processed their products, and marketed them across the globe. Even the adversaries of these dominant powers accepted their hierarchical view of politics: the Bolsheviks broke with more moderate social democrats and forged an organizational model for revolution and rule that would influence most of the coming century.

Although those hierarchical organizations have hardly disappeared from contemporary international politics, networks now challenge their central place. Cross-border networks are hardly new: traders, bankers, and political activists deployed networked organizations more than a century ago. Technological change, economic openness, and demands for transnational political collaboration, however, have created conditions for network proliferation in recent decades. Well before the terrorist attacks of September 11, 2001, open networks of nongovernmental organizations had been joined by diasporic networks and dark networks or clandestine transnational actors (CTAs), made up of criminal and terrorist groups.[1] Transgovernmental networks—

The author thanks two anonymous reviewers for Cornell University Press as well as Roger Haydon, Peter J. Katzenstein, and the authors in the Networked Politics project for helpful comments on earlier drafts of this chapter. He is very grateful to Jeremy Horowitz and Benjamin Graham for research assistance.
    1. The classic statement on transnational networks that link nongovernmental organizations and other international actors is Keck and Sikkink 1998. On dark networks, Raab and Milward 2003; on CTAs, Andreas 2003, as well as Kenney 2005 and 2007; diasporic networks are

international collaboration among agencies of national governments—are promoted as a form of international governance that is more efficient and adaptable than the bureaucracies of international organizations.[2] Networked regional organization in Asia is contrasted with other regional models dominated by more conventional institutions (Katzenstein and Shiraishi 1997). Cross-border production networks have come to dominate the most dynamic sectors of the international economy, such as consumer electronics and information technology (Borrus, Ernst, and Haggard 2000).

This new international landscape is reflected in a vocabulary of networks that is broader than international politics. Networks have become the intellectual centerpiece for our era. If the contest between markets and state hierarchies was an organizing feature of the 1980s, *network* has emerged as the dominant social and economic metaphor in subsequent decades. The scope of networks expanded to include economic organization and trade (Powell 1996; Rauch 1998; Rauch and Casella 2001), society as a whole (Castells 1996), as well as widening applications in the natural sciences (Barabási 2002; Newman, Barabási, and Watts 2006).

The widespread discovery of networks has also imposed costs. In contemporary international relations, *network* has too often remained a familiar metaphor rather than an instrument of analysis. This book introduces two approaches to network analysis and applies them to international politics: networks-as-structures and networks-as-actors. The first approach embraces a broad definition of networks, concentrates on their structural characteristics, and assesses the effects of network structure. The second discriminates between networks and other modes of organization, evaluating network success or failure in achieving collective ends. In deploying these two approaches, the authors emphasize the empirical leverage and new understandings generated by more systematic use of network analysis. Their research illuminates important sectors of international relations: international inequality, the emergence of the human rights movement, governance of the Internet, terrorist and criminal networks, and normative change.

Network analysis also contributes to a second aim of this book, which is to reexamine three theoretical debates in international politics: the relationship between structure and agency, competing definitions of power, and the efficacy of emerging forms of international governance. Agency and its exercise within international structures have been a perennial interest of theorists in international relations. Kenneth Waltz attempted to build a neorealist theory of international politics by abstracting a particular structural feature—the

described by N. Watts 2004 and Wayland 2004. Adamson 2005 links the literature on nonviolent networks to an examination of radical and violent transnational groups.

2. Transgovernmental cooperation—"sets of direct interactions among sub-units of different governments that are not controlled or closely guided by the policies of cabinets or chief executives of those governments"—was an important constituent of the original formulation of interdependence by Robert O. Keohane and Joseph S. Nye (1974, 43; 1977). Networks, however, were not a central analytical category in those earlier discussions. The revival of interest in transgovernmental networks is described by Eilstrup-Sangiovanni in chapter 10.

distribution of capabilities—from the domestic attributes of states (Waltz 1979). Constructivists, often influenced by sociological theory, have placed agent and structure, and particularly the relationship between states and their environment, at the center of their concerns (Katzenstein 1996; Wendt 1999). Network analysis delimits a field of international structures that shape and constrain agents. Most important, it also enables their empirical investigation. The characteristics and capabilities of new agents in international politics—networks defined as actors—can also be defined more precisely.

When applied to international politics, the lens of networks also forces a reevaluation of the concept of power. Power in networks depends on structural position in a field of connections to other agents as well as actor capabilities or attributes. Simple dyadic measures of international influence appear inadequate in a world of networked states. The power *of* networks also requires assessment. Networked collective action, whether transnational networks of activists or illicit combinations of criminals or terrorists, may demonstrate greater capacity than its organizational competitors.

Finally, networked politics points to new forms of governance in international relations, distinct from more familiar types of intergovernmental collaboration. The emergence of networks as a significant feature of global governance need not mean that they are substitutes for more familiar and formal intergovernmental institutions. Those formal institutions may themselves be embedded in networks. Governments may also choose to delegate to networks, bargain with them, or use them as a new means of collaboration. Networked governance incorporates and sustains older forms of governance as well as challenging them.

Insights from political analysis serve to enrich network analysis, a third aim of this examination of networked international politics. Politics asks how agents will behave if they are cognizant (or partially cognizant) of network structure and can act to manipulate that structure to their advantage. Network analysis has too often obscured or ignored questions of network power and power within networks, portraying networks as an antithesis of the hierarchical exercise of power that lies at the core of familiar political institutions. Under a political lens, networked governance, too often represented as inherently consensual, reveals distributional and status conflicts that are often resolved through the introduction of centralization and hierarchy, within or outside the network. These insights from political analysis serve to revise network approaches to international relations and to expand their scope.

Defining Networked Politics: Networks as Structures and Actors

Defined in simplest form, as any set of interconnected nodes, networks are ubiquitous. The nodes can be individuals, groups, organizations, or states (as well as cells or Internet users); the connections or links can consist of personal friendships, trade flows, or valued resources.[3] For social scientists, network analysis employs "concepts of location, or nodes, and the relations among these positions—termed ties, connections, or links—to argue that the pattern of relationships shapes the behavior of the occupant of a post, as well as influences others" (Smith-Doerr and Powell 2005, 380).

Two approaches to network analysis have been applied to international politics. The first takes networks as *structures* that influence the behavior of their members, and, through them, produce consequential network effects. This approach accepts the broad definition of a network as interconnected nodes, a concept that can be applied at different levels of analysis. The nodes could be intergovernmental organizations (IGOs), national governments, nongovernmental organizations (NGOs), or individuals. In this approach, network design is not intentional on the part of any actor or set of actors.

The second approach concentrates on networks as *actors,* networks as a specific organizational form that can be contrasted with markets and hierarchies. Networks in this approach are, most often, intentional or consciously organized. Membership boundaries are clear rather than being determined by simple interaction over time. The success of networked actors at collective and collaborative action is typically the outcome of greatest interest. Through such action, these networks also influence significant international outcomes.

Networks as Structures

In the structural approach to international networks, relational structures within the network or emergent attributes of the network systematically influence the actions of its nodes (members) and produce identifiable outcomes. Hafner-Burton and Montgomery (2006), for example, examine the effect of networks of intergovernmental organizations on interstate conflict. Ingram, Robinson, and Busch (2005) claim that IGO networks have discernible effects on trade flows, even when the IGOs in question are not dedicated to lowering trade barriers. In defining structure, this approach to international networks often relies on social network analysis (a mainstay of sociological research), on network economics, and on a new science of networks that has been applied to subjects that range from the spread of contagious diseases to the growth of the Internet to the metabolism of cells.[4]

The nodes in social network analysis can include individual members of ter-

3. "In its simplest form, a network is nothing more than a set of discrete elements (the vertices), and a set of connections (the edges) that link the elements, typically in a pairwise fashion" (Newman, Barabási, and Watts 2006, 2).

4. Summaries of social network analysis are given in Wasserman and Faust (1994), Scott (2000), and Hafner-Burton and Montgomery (chapter 2, this book). Network economics, used by Cowhey and Mueller (chapter 9, this book), is described in Shapiro and Varian (1999) and Shy (2001). The "new" science of networks is described by J. Watts (2004) and Newman, Barabási, and Watts (2006). Lake and Wong (chapter 7, this book) make use of its structural vocabulary.

rorist organizations or countries linked by trade and investment.[5] Like the even broader notions of network deployed in the natural sciences—a set of interconnected nodes—social network analysis emphasizes interdependent actors and relational data rather than individual agents and their attributes. The ties or links among the actors (nodes) create a structure (a persistent pattern of relations) that in turn serves to constrain actors or provide opportunities for action (Wasserman and Faust 1994, 4; Scott 2000, 2–3). Social network analysis provides both a toolkit of concepts and a methodology for empirical research.

Network economics also emphasizes structural attributes of networks, such as scale or degrees of hierarchy, and the implications of those attributes for efficient operation and policy intervention. The new science of networks has introduced the dynamics of network development into an approach that has too often relied on static snapshots of network structure. Attention to network evolution and growth has directed attention to new structural variants, such as small-world and scale-free networks (Watts 1999; Newman, Barabási, and Watts 2006).

These approaches to networks and their structure rely on networks with relatively large numbers of nodes: states, for example, linked through IGOs or trade. Viewed as structure, networks are not the result of conscious design on the part of agents, even though they are sustained by interaction on the part of the nodes. An individual node (state, individual, or other agent) confronts the networks as a structural given, its behavior constrained by network ties.

Networks as Actors

The second, and more familiar, approach to network analysis in international politics captures networks as *actors,* forms of coordinated or collective action aimed at changing international outcomes and national policies. Networks are not treated as an omnipresent feature of social life. Instead, they are a specific institutional form that stands in contrast to the hierarchical organization of states and to the temporally limited exchange relations of markets (Powell 1990; Thompson 2003). In the widely cited definition of Joel M. Podolny and Karen L. Page, a network is "any collection of actors (N≥2) that pursue repeated, enduring exchange relations with one another and, at the same time, lack a legitimate organizational authority to arbitrate and resolve disputes that may arise during the exchange." In contrast to markets, network relations are enduring; in contrast to hierarchies, recognized dispute settlement authority does not reside with any member of the network (Podolny and Page 1998, 59). This definition provides only ideal types; hybrid organizational forms can also emerge. For example, in corporate networks, hierar-

5. Sageman (2004) analyzes al Qaeda using social network analysis; Cao (2006) describes networks created by international economic exchange.

chies (individual corporations) that populate one level of analysis may be networked nodes at another level. Within those hierarchical corporate nodes, individuals also may be networked in ways that compete with formal organizational design.

Other efforts to distinguish networks from hierarchies offer less precision in defining the boundaries of networked politics: "fluidity" (Lin 2001, 38); "relative flatness, decentralization and delegation of decision making authority, and loose lateral ties among dispersed groups and individuals" (Zanini and Edwards 2001, 33); or "voluntary, reciprocal, and horizontal patterns of communication and exchange" (Keck and Sikkink 1998, 8). As the contributions to this book demonstrate, such features may characterize some, but not all, of the networks that have emerged as actors in international relations.

The network-as-actor perspective differs from the structural approach in incorporating links defined by exchange and created by agents; structure (beyond the existence of a network) has been less central to the interests of investigators. Instead, the relative advantages and disadvantages of networked organization, when compared to its institutional competitors, occupy a more prominent place. The nodes of these networked actors may be government agencies (transgovernmental networks in chapter 10, this book), human rights activists (Amnesty International network in chapter 7), terrorist organizations (the al Qaeda network in chapter 6), or other international actors. The structural approach to networks abstracts structure from the characteristics of network nodes; for networked actors, however, agent characteristics may transform the aims and the effectiveness of these networks. The networks-as-actors approach lacks a common methodology, such as social network analysis. Its empirical methods have been eclectic and largely qualitative. Identifying the network as a network is the essential first step; assessing its organizational advantages and disadvantages, particularly in promoting collective ends, follows from that identification.

Distinguishing these two approaches to networked politics and their particular analytic and explanatory aims reduces, but does not eliminate, the confusion that has often surrounded the use of networks in international relations. Both approaches require careful definition of network nodes and links. Levels of analysis must be carefully separated: network actors may themselves become nodes in higher-level network structures. Each approach also challenges the other. The structural approach highlights an absence of both rigorous analysis and structural variables in many accounts of network actors. The ubiquity of networks in structural analysis may disguise an absence of theoretical content, an inability to relate network structure to international outcomes with a plausible causal account. In the chapters that follow, each approach contends with these challenges. Networks-as-structure derive structural consequences by drawing on existing international relations theory. Accounts of networks-as-actors take structure seriously as a possible determinant of the success or failure of collective action.

As several of the authors illustrate, however, both approaches may be required for a complete explanation of certain international outcomes. Zachary Elkins (chapter 3) examines both a network structure and a set of network actors—transnational human rights networks—that have influenced the international diffusion of constitutional models. Peter Cowhey and Milton Mueller (chapter 9) describe both a network with a particular structure (the Internet) and networked actors that participate in Internet governance. National governments contemplating Internet governance choices must deal with both.

Structure and Agency: A Network Perspective

Both approaches to networked politics, networks as structures and networks as actors, illuminate the relationship between structure and agency in international relations. A structural approach to international networks typically assumes that agents within the network are not aware of its overall structure and do not act to influence or change that structure. In other words, the actor nodes of the networks may behave in a purposive way, but their actions are not directed to altering the structure itself. Governments that negotiate preferential trade agreements (PTAs), in the account of Emilie Hafner-Burton and Alexander Montgomery (chapter 2), are likely to pursue relatively narrow economic gains or perhaps ancillary foreign policy goals. The social power that inheres in their network connections is unlikely to figure in their motivations. The physical infrastructure of the Internet, designed decades ago, has evolved to display the characteristics outlined by Cowhey and Mueller: network externalities, economies of scale and scope, and elements of hierarchy. Individuals linking to the Internet each day, however, are unlikely to be aware of the network structure created by their links (apart from the ubiquity of certain hubs such as Google).[6]

Network analysis defines structure in a way that is measurable, allowing a more precise determination of the effects of structure on collective or systemic outcomes. Structure may be a redefinition in network vocabulary of familiar concepts from international politics, such as systemic polarization (Maoz 2006). Structural definitions may also be imported from other varieties of network analysis as a precursor to an investigation of the effects of network structure on international outcomes (Maoz et al. 2005). Hafner-Burton and Montgomery (2006), for example, have associated structural equivalence, a measure of the extent to which two actors share the same ties to the same ac-

6. On Internet structure, see Barbási 2002, 79–92. Zeev Maoz (2001) distinguishes between discretionary and nondiscretionary networks in international relations. His distinction resembles on certain dimensions the network-as-structure and network-as-actor categories. For Maoz, discretionary networks are "created as a result of a decision of units to form such a connection." Nondiscretionary networks result from "force of circumstances or by structural conditions beyond the control of units" (148).

tors in a network, and degree centrality, a measure of the strength and number of direct ties to an actor, with levels of international conflict. In their investigation of the networks formed by preferential trade arrangements, this measure is supplemented by strength of ties between two states, measured by the number of shared memberships in PTAs (Hafner-Burton and Montgomery, chapter 2). Network position may also influence domestic policy outcomes, such as economic policy convergence (Cao 2006).

David Lake and Wendy Wong (chapter 7) add a dynamic element to network structure by identifying the scale-free nature of the original Amnesty International human rights network. In scale-free networks, network connections follow a power law distribution: a large number of nodes enjoy few network links; a few nodes display many links. Networks with these properties are created by growth through a simple rule of attachment or network membership: new members will preferentially link to nodes that are already densely connected to other nodes (Barabási and Albert 1999). Lake and Wong argue that many activist networks-in-formation follow similar laws of attachment for new members.

Each of these structural accounts of networks and their formation assumes that networks emerge from the actions of their members (nodes). Networks and their structures are not, however, the result of intentional design by members. The large scale of many international networks renders this assumption plausible, as does a lack of empirical data, even for trained observers, on the actual structure and operation of many networks. Structure is often obscured by overlap and competition among networks. Governments negotiate PTAs and thereby construct a web of social interaction that produces persistent patterns over time. They also negotiate a host of other international agreements or join international organizations, actions that produce different and potentially competing networks.

Agents, Structure, and Normative Change

Many international networks are large, but not as large as the web of Internet users or the universe of all scholarly citations. In international relations, some awareness of network structure often seems a more realistic assumption. The introduction of such awareness may transform the relationship between network and agent. In four chapters that describe the network sources of domestic and international normative change, decision rules for network membership and efforts to influence network structure were consequential. In his description of the effects of international networks on the cross-border diffusion of constitutional models, Elkins (chapter 3) describes two distinct avenues of network influence on diffusion, one offering network benefits, another offering information about the policy being considered. Affinity with one or another network type was an important determinant of the ways in which networks influenced national outcomes. Agents did not influence the structure of networks in this case, but their choices over linking to particular networks influenced the domestic constitutional outcomes described by Elkins.

As described by Lake and Wong (chapter 7), the early history of Amnesty International (AI) and the international human rights network produced a network structure that both influenced human rights activists and was the target of their actions. Dominant human rights norms in this instance are an outcome of network structure. From an existing pool of normative understandings of "human rights," AI crystallized around one alternative: an emphasis on prisoners of conscience and, more broadly, civil and political rights. As activists linked rapidly (and cross-nationally) to this original core in networked fashion, AI's original normative choice gained dominance within the emerging human rights movement and within human rights discourse, at least in the liberal industrialized democracies. Similar to the constitutional principles that filter through Elkins's networks, dominant human rights norms were not determined by any single set of actors. Nevertheless, agent choices to link to a particular network ultimately produced a network structure that favored certain norms rather than others.

AI and the human rights network bridge the divide between networks as structure and networks as actors. Actors within the network (such as the AI secretariat) made strategic choices that influenced network structure, choices that were intended to confirm their position within the network and reinforce the attraction of AI's human rights alternative for prospective activist-members. When networks themselves are considered as actors, such design choices, often taken without full information about the outlines of an emerging network, are critical. The consequences—although not always the intended ones—determine the network's attraction for new members and for its effectiveness in organizing collective action.

In the cases of constitutional networks in Latin America and the nascent Amnesty International, network structure influenced competition between norms, in both cases by influencing the decisions of governments or individuals to affiliate to particular networks. In such cases, provision of information *about* the network is one means for actors to ensure their success *within* the network. In a third case of normative conflict and change, agent design played an even larger role. The campaign networks described in chapter 4 by Helen Yanacopulos—Jubilee 2000 (J2K) and Make Poverty History (MPH)—mobilized political support for norms of international justice that were politically suspect when the campaigns began. Both network structure and strategy differed from the constitutional and AI networks. The J2K and MPH coalitions were networks of networks. The "work" of networking was carried out by individual organizations that made up the coalition. The strength of individual network ties—wearing a colored armband or watching a Live 8 concert—was lower than the links established by AI's adoption of prisoners of conscience.

These networked coalitions were less centralized than AI, and member organizations resisted assertions of network leadership. Rather than aiming at normative change within the network or the broader justice movement, existing norms were wielded instrumentally to forge a networked political coalition and broaden its political appeal. Norm diffusion occurred from the network to the wider society. Loose networks of organizations, in which leadership nodes wielded limited influence, built only weak individual ties to the networks. This network structure was adequate for the political task at hand. Despite differences with AI in network configuration, both J2K and MPH coalitions were successful in organizing mass collective action and producing policy change, more clearly in the case of debt relief than in that of poverty reduction.

The Active Learning Network for Accountability and Performance (ALNAP), described by Janice Gross Stein in chapter 8, is a final example of network-induced normative change. Aid agencies, which provide a large share of the funding for humanitarian nongovernmental organizations, became increasingly concerned with the politically charged issue of accountability during the 1990s. Rather than wielding their budgetary clout to impose normative change on their NGO clients, the aid agencies chose a less costly route: networking with the NGOs. The network structure of ALNAP permitted a more gradual and consensual normative shift within the humanitarian community through a structure that incorporated both governmental and NGO actors and preserved the effectiveness of the larger network of organizations engaged in humanitarian relief.

Clandestine Networks and Structural Adaptation

In these cases, actor choices influenced network structure and international outcomes, though not always as intended. In two cases of clandestine and illicit networks, networked actors also changed network structure as they adapted to a hostile environment. Two clandestine networks—Colombian drug trafficking networks and the terrorist network centered on al Qaeda— investigated by Michael Kenney (chapter 5) and Miles Kahler (chapter 6) shared certain characteristics: transnational illicit activities, a willingness to use violence as an instrument, and unwanted attention from their governmental adversaries. Their environment was competitive in two respects: competition with government agencies that were seeking their suppression and competition with rivals who were seeking to displace them in the larger universe of drug-trafficking and terrorist organizations.

As Kenney describes, the effectiveness of drug-trafficking networks is highly correlated with adaptability to a harsh environment. Network structure influences survival: centralized wheel networks are more easily targeted by government agencies. Transition to decentralized chain networks—more "diffuse and self-organizing" and flatter in organizational design—enabled the Colombian drug-trafficking trade to continue despite law enforcement countermeasures. Kahler also associates shifts in al Qaeda's network structure with its changing environment of adversaries, particularly the United States and its allies, and competitors, the universe of violent Islamist groups. In this case, the environment was shaped in part by the purposive targeting by al Qaeda of the American "far enemy" rather than the "near enemy" (local regimes) favored by other Islamist activists. Unlike drug traffickers, al Qaeda could not be completely clandestine if it wished to accomplish its political aims. The more complex task of striking at the United States, coupled with a need for clandestinity, favored more hierarchy within the structure of the al Qaeda network. Hierarchy, like centralization in the Colombian drug networks, made al Qaeda more vulnerable to countermeasures by the United States and other state adversaries after 9/11. That crushing response imposed segmentation and decentralization on the network, a structural shift that weakened but did not eliminate its ability to conduct terrorist operations.

Network analysis allows empirical investigation of international structures that are both the products of purposive action and at the same time constrain that action. In this quest, the two approaches to networks complement one another and also share two shortcomings. The structural approach must accept that network nodes may become partially cognizant of the network's structure, even if that knowledge is imperfect. With that understanding, they will act to further their interests by changing network structure. Those who emphasize networks as actors must take structure seriously, connecting structure with the success and failure of collective action. Both approaches spend too little time considering the links within the networks and what those links convey, whether resources, information, or other content. In the contest between a view of network links as "girders" and their identification as "pipes," the former, structural view too often dominates over the latter, connectionist perspective.[7] Related to this neglect of the content of network links is an underspecification of network effects. The microfoundations of network consequences—how network position influences behavior and, through behavior, international outcomes, is too often neglected.[8]

Power and International Networks

A networked perspective challenges conventional views of power in international relations. At the same time, attention to the exercise of power refreshes

---

7. On this distinction, see Borgatti and Foster 2003, 1002–3; also Smith-Doerr and Powell 2005, 394.

8. For example, Ingram, Robinson, and Busch (2005) claim strong effects on trade from networked membership in social and cultural IGOs. Their explanation relies on the effects that membership may have at the level of citizens, without any demonstration of how citizens might be affected by such memberships (830).

network analysis by questioning its overly consensual and trust-laden view of networks. Rather than the narrowly dyadic and behavioral view of power common to international relations and political science, a structural approach to networks relates power *within* networks to network position, to persistent relationships *among* states rather than individual attributes *of* states.[9] Network structure inverts the neorealist view of international structure as a distribution of capabilities; capabilities in the networked view rely on connections to other members of the network. The perspective of networks-as-actors also undermines certain simple definitions of capabilities. Networking of agents may contribute to their relative success at collective action vis-à-vis international actors with different organizational designs.

Varieties of Network Power

Position within networks defines three distinct forms of power: bargaining power, social power, and the power of exit. *Bargaining* power or leverage is most familiar. A network node increases its bargaining power through links to network partners that are otherwise weakly connected or those that have few outside options.[10] States that are the sole link between clusters of highly connected states might gain influence as brokers within the network. Lake and Wong (chapter 7) describe leverage or bargaining power in the strategies pursued by Amnesty International within the human rights network. A powerful node in the human rights network, such as the AI secretariat, exercises influence through both this first face of power—leverage gained through the threat to sever links or promise network expansion—and through power's second face, setting the network's agenda through structural control of information. The Internet, a layered network of infrastructure and users, also presents structural features that permit the exercise of bargaining power. Power within the Internet derives from a network position that permits the exploitation of network structure. As Cowhey and Mueller (chapter 9) warn, assumptions of flatness and decentralization may obscure the hierarchy that emerges in networks. That hierarchy provides opportunities for those outside the network (governments) or agents within the network to exercise power.

Social power is a second variant of power within networks. In their analysis of PTA membership networks (chapter 2), Hafner-Burton and Montgomery argue that "social power is determined by the social capital created and accessed through ties with other states in the international system such as ties through mutual membership in PTAs." Their choice of degree centrality as an indicator awards greater social power to states that are more connected.

---

9. "A position's power—its ability to produce intended effects on the attitudes and behaviors of other actors—emerges from its prominence in networks where valued information and scarce resources are transferred from one actor to another" (David Knoke, cited in Smith-Doerr and Powell 2005, 380).

10. Bonacich 1987 makes a similar distinction.

Social power based on network position does not closely track other measures of power, such as military capability or economic weight. The United States, for example, is a middling power in the social network of PTAs; European states rank higher in the hierarchy of social power. Is social power fungible? Hafner-Burton and Montgomery argue that poorer and militarily less powerful states may offset their material disadvantages through the accumulation of social power. Nevertheless, increasing inequality on material dimensions has coincided in recent decades with convergence on measures of social power.

Manger (2007) produces a different assessment of the power consequences of PTAs, also based on network analysis: countries that negotiate more PTAs tend to reinforce their position by becoming ever more attractive nodes in the network. Low-income countries (originally less connected through PTAs) are threatened with exclusion from the benefits of economic integration provided by these trade agreements. Rather than compensating for other types of power, network power reinforces inequality in the international system.

Social power also measures influence within networks constituted by informational or normative links. Normative influence may increase as the number of links to other actors grows, a conclusion supported by the cases of AI and the constitution-making networks described by Elkins. Parallels between social power within dense international networks and soft power in international politics are close. Network centrality across several issue areas may serve as a candidate indicator of soft power. Investigating other consequences of social power, defined by network position, is an important direction for future research.

A final form of power within networks may set them apart from other organizational forms: the power of *exit* or delinking. On this dimension, many networks are closer to markets than hierarchies (and certainly states), which may attempt to constrain exit. The claim that networks are more consensual or that their design is the result of negotiation may in fact capture the importance of the exit option. If bargaining power is the power of nodes that serve as brokers and social power inheres to highly connected nodes, the power of exit is often wielded by less embedded nodes at the margins of networks. Strategic efforts within the network to exploit bargaining power may result in threats of exit by those who are its targets. The existence of outside options, therefore, becomes critical in assessing network power of this kind. The decision rules for linking to networks also determine the credibility of exit threats: if activists overwhelmingly attach to more connected nodes in an NGO network, the structural position and power of those organizational nodes is more likely to remain stable.

In a conventional imperial, hub-and-spoke network, for example, exit was constrained by coercion and by the absence of political space that was not colonized (exit from one empire risked capture by another). In the emerging AI network, incentives to join were necessary for the network's rapid growth, because prospective members could easily exit. Expert networks, whose central role in Internet governance is described by Cowhey and Mueller (chapter 9), often magnified the leverage granted by their professional standing through the existence of options outside the network. Although clandestine criminal and terrorist networks are more likely to exert coercion to prevent exit, their behavior suggests both the presence of competition for members among networks and the high reputational costs associated with obstructing exit.

Building Power within Networks

As agents within networks comprehend the power that inheres in network structure, they will attempt to influence that structure over time. Lake and Wong (chapter 7) claim such a long-term strategy on the part of AI's secretariat. Cowhey and Mueller (chapter 9) describe strategies of delegation that are deployed by governments that wish to reduce their vulnerability to the exercise of network power by other governments. Even in cases where such network-shaping activities are less apparent, such as the PTA networks studied by Hafner-Burton and Montgomery or the uncoordinated networks investigated by Elkins, pursuit of network power favors agent strategies that differ from those in conventional international politics. If social power is based on connectedness or centrality, then strategies of membership in international institutions may reflect more than simple calculations of interest in a particular organization or its benefits. The access that international institutions and agreements grant to larger networks may be as important as the individual agreement itself. For example, the trade benefits of a bilateral agreement with the European Union (EU) may be outweighed for a nonmember by access to the wider networks represented by the EU. In a networked world, unilateralism, which sacrifices the social power of networks, may appear less attractive as a strategy. If networks provide information that fosters learning, and if that learning can be biased in ways favorable to other agents in the network, international networks will become targets of influence by governments and other actors. As suggested by Elkins (chapter 3), power exerted in networks of this kind would be multiplied many times over, through replication of norms and practices in the domains of other states.

Building the Power of Networks: Scalability and Adaptability

Identification of power within the structure of networks calls into question conventional views of power in international politics. In the second approach, networks-as-actors, estimating the power of networks as international actors undermines standard views of capabilities. Political networks succeed as actors if they can promote and sustain collective action on the part of their constituent agents. For these authors, such success is often dependent on two features of networked organizations: *scalability* and *adaptability*.

Scalability, a concept based in the technical literature on networks, refers to the ability of political networks to grow rapidly at relatively low cost without altering the fundamental form of the organization. For both the transgovernmental networks analyzed by Mette Eilstrup-Sangiovanni (chapter 10) and the nongovernmental AI and justice networks, the ability to add new members quickly and at low cost was a significant organizational asset. The ill-defined membership rules of transgovernmental networks (TGNs) awarded them advantages in comparison to more formal intergovernmental organizations. New members were easily incorporated as issues were redefined or added to the agenda. Equally attractive was the ability to exclude troublesome prospective members who might force their way into an IGO. The relatively "loose coupling" that characterizes TGNs also permits members of these networks to opt out in particular instances without endangering the larger cooperative endeavor.

A more dramatic example of the benefits of scalability was the Jubilee 2000 and Make Poverty History networks that campaigned to redefine the policies of rich countries toward debt cancellation and development aid. As Yanacopulos demonstrates, the explosive growth of these networks, enabled by the weak network ties of their individual supporters, was critical to their political impact. Scalable networks were particularly suited to the campaign strategy—a clearly defined target for which mass mobilization provides a critical political resource. AI also aimed at a scalable network, but the strength of network ties among its activists was greater, as expected for an organization that aimed for longer run rather than episodic effectiveness. AI was also concerned with its power to define the normative content of the network, which could be undermined by growth that was too rapid for a clear definition of normative identity to take hold. The ALNAP network was in an even more tenuous situation, balancing between its governmental and NGO members and aiming for a new normative consensus on accountability. Its networked form proved a successful vehicle for this task, but paradoxically the network was centralized (centered on a relatively small number of nodes), not inclusive (restricted full membership), and nontransparent.

Finally, in contrast to open and licit political networks, clandestine networks are seldom scalable: growth may be desirable, but the cost of adding new members is high, risking suppression by government agents and the dilution of ideological identity (for networks in which identity is a core attribute). Al Qaeda's core established dominance of the network agenda by segmenting the original network of violent Salafists. It avoided penetration by its adversaries through establishing mechanisms, particularly training camps, for careful evaluation of prospective network members.

Adaptability of organizational form over the life cycle of a network is another key dimension of successful collective action. Networked organizations often demonstrate an ability to incorporate elements of hierarchy and centralization into their networked structure. In effect, they can become more or less "networked" as political demands shift or their environments change. As part of their organizational repertoires, successful network actors have developed an ability to hybridize with hierarchical forms.

Al Qaeda (chapter 6) and the Colombian drug cartels (chapter 5) both demonstrate life cycle adaptability, even though the structure of their networks moved in opposite directions. As the drug trafficking cartels adopted a decentralized chain network form, they also adapted through a strategy of learning enabled by the network form. Even in the clandestine world of drug trafficking, wider social networks and the network structure of the cartels encouraged information sharing and further promoted network adaptability under pressure. In its confrontation with the United States, and with more mixed success, al Qaeda adapted its networked organization by awarding more prominence to its hierarchical core rather than expanding its original role in the larger terrorist network: a broker between less connected parts of the network and a source of valuable resources for network members.

Over its life cycle, Amnesty International, a legal organization in an open political environment, displayed a changing mix of network and hierarchy. Its early network, crucial to the rapid expansion of its membership, eventually evolved into a conventional hierarchical organization. An "organizational paradox," it remained "hierarchical and heavily bureaucratic," and, at the same time, struggled to maintain its networked origins through an inclusive membership and volunteer base. Eventually—at the next stage in its evolution—it became one influential node in a much larger international human rights network. AI moved from "pure" network to a more hierarchical form and finally to participation as one (central) node in a larger human rights network. Its organizational transformation over its life cycle promoted both its own success and the successful adoption of the human rights norms that it espoused.

Scalability and organizational adaptation over time are associated with more effective collective action by networks in specific environments. Rather than offering explanations for network power under all circumstances, the authors suggest conditions under which network structure and characteristics diminish influence over international outcomes. Scalability was a distinct advantage for the justice networks that campaigned in democratic polities. Clandestine networks avoided scalability, occasionally embraced segmentation, and carefully selected prospective members. As Eilstrup-Sangiovanni points out, in situations requiring highly credible commitments, the adaptability of transgovernmental networks makes them a less attractive modality for international collaboration. Introduction of centralization within networks may increase efficiency, but it also provides a target for adversaries outside the network, as both the Colombian cartels and al Qaeda discovered. Such nuanced assessment of network attributes and their effects on network power are an important next step in analyzing the influence of networked actors in international relations.

Networks and International Governance

The role of networks in international governance has been poorly defined and oversold. As Mueller (forthcoming) notes, the analysis of networks and international governance has borrowed from such longstanding approaches to domestic policy analysis as policy networks and issue networks (Knoke 1990; Marsh and Smith 2000; Klijn and Koppenjan 2000). These networks were relatively stable sets of governmental and private actors that emerged in particular sectors of public policy. For some observers, these networks-as-structures were then transformed into a new organizational design for governance, potentially more nimble, innovative, and inclusive than hierarchical, bureaucratic modes of governance.[11] Networked governance in international relations has been touted as a panacea to the problems of cumbersome multilateralism and slow-moving and inefficient international organizations. Networks have been promoted for "their general virtues of speed, flexibility, inclusiveness, ability to cut across different jurisdictions, and sustained focus on a specific set of problems."[12] With both hope and alarm, nongovernmental networks have been pitted against states as rivals for international influence and possible substitutes in domains previously monopolized by IGOs and other more hierarchical forms of interstate collaboration.

Both imprecise definitions and unbalanced evaluations of networked governance require careful scrutiny. Networked governance has at least three different meanings:

(a) Governance through networks that emerge from state membership in formal IGOs (Hafner-Burton and Montgomery, chapter 2)
(b) Governance by transgovernmental networks (TGNs), cross-border networks of government agencies (Eilstrup-Sangiovanni, chapter 10)
(c) Governance that includes a role for private or NGO networks in particular issue areas (Cowhey and Mueller, chapter 9)

Each of these understandings of networked governance implies networks with different levels of agency; each implies a different role for state and nonstate actors. The last two imply a form of governance that can be compared to other modes of governance, such as those based on intergovernmental agreements or organizations. On the other hand, none necessarily implies that networks—whether structures or actors—will substitute for formal international institutions or national governments in global and regional governance.

Networks that emerge from formal international agreements or member-

---

11. For an analysis of network governance in the domestic context, see Scharpf 1993a; Reinicke 1998 transfers network governance to the international domain.
12. Slaughter 2004a, 167. For a more cautious assessment, see Raustiala 2002.

ship in IGOs, such as those described by Hafner-Burton and Montgomery (chapter 2) or Ingram, Robinson, and Busch (2005), are not designed by member states. They do not represent a challenge to conventional, formal international institutions; their existence is dependent on those institutions. The consequences of these networks are only beginning to be explored. Manger (2007), for example, poses one important question: how different network configurations of PTAs might influence the volume and direction of trade. Networks may influence IGO performance, since more networked IGOs may also be more effective. The social capital of these larger networks can be an important benefit of IGO membership. Formal agreements and membership in IGOs create new networks in international politics; how those networks might affect governance in the future and how their effects might reinforce IGOs in other domains are important questions for future investigation.

In the case of TGNs, network nodes are agencies of national governments. As Eilstrup-Sangiovanni (chapter 10) points out, changes in the international environment have made TGNs more appealing than IGOs, but only under certain circumstances. The choice of TGNs by governments is highly dependent on network structure and the value of certain network characteristics. In the cases of two TGNs, the Proliferation Security Initiative and the Missile Technology Control regime, and an IGO, the Chemical Weapons Convention, Eilstrup-Sangiovanni suggests that governments will delegate to TGNs in the face of uncertain environments, potential domestic political conflict, and, perhaps most important, when clubs of like-minded governments seek a flexible means to realize their convergent interests. In other circumstances, an IGO is both more effective and more politically palatable.

The Internet illustrates the role of nongovernmental networks in the governance of a strategically important transnational sector. Rather than a calculus of government choice between TGNs and ITOs, Cowhey and Mueller (chapter 9) frame their central question as a decision by governments to delegate to networked and often private entities in Internet governance. Conflicts over governance create a need for collective action in order to sustain the many benefits of a key global communications network. In two cases, standards setting and resource allocation (assignment of domain names), governments have delegated authority to nongovernmental networks. In the first instance, expertise was decentralized and networked; the transparency of the professional network produced the conditions for successful delegation. In the second, delegation was a more surprising outcome, since hierarchy was built into the characteristics of the network. Here once again, the networked agent, Internet Corporation for Assigned Names and Numbers (ICANN), was nongovernmental, expert, and transparent in its operations. As in the case of TGNs, the advantages of particular networked organizations, in this case expert networks, produced choices by governments to delegate authority over key dimensions of Internet governance.

Carefully defined, networked governance does not imply a field of conflict between governments and networked actors or an inevitable substitution of networks for conventional international agreements and institutions. TGNs are useful formats for intergovernmental collaboration, but only under certain conditions. Raustiala's (2002) argument for synergy and mutual support between IGOs, international agreements, and transgovernmental networks seems a more likely outcome than simple substitution. Nongovernmental networks may serve as the instruments of governments, through delegation, and as their collaborators. In some cases, governments and nongovernmental organizations may partner in a new, networked form of governance. ALNAP was just such as creation, serving the purposes of both aid agencies and their NGO clients.

The presence of networks within a governance arrangement does not mean that they are the *only* means of governance in a particular issue area (Mueller forthcoming). Networks have taken their place in a menu of governance modalities that also includes formal international institutions and hierarchy, the transfer of authority to dominant states for certain international purposes (Kahler and Lake forthcoming). As Eilstrup-Sangiovanni demonstrates for TGNs and IGOs, these modalities are deployed under different conditions, and their efficacy in advancing international collaboration necessarily varies. Formal international institutions can be designed to address particular problems of cooperation, and networked governance can best be assessed, not as an inevitable or universal solution to such problems, but rather as an important contributor to those solutions.[13]

Networked International Politics

The emergence of networks in international politics is hardly new, and investigation of cross-border networks is now decades old.[14] Analysis of networks in international relations has paralleled an earlier trajectory in the study of international institutions: first, international institutions were redefined as a category broader than formal international organizations; their significance to international relations was then established (do international institutions matter?); and finally, variation among those institutions and the effects of that variation became a focus of research. In similar fashion, networks are moving from the phase of definition and agreement on their significance to a more rigorous examination of the dimensions of their variation and the effects of that variation on consequential international outcomes.

13. Although their account omits network alternatives, the research strategy endorsed here resembles that suggested by Koremenos, Lipson, and Snidal (2001b).
14. Keck and Sikkink (1998) describe international campaigns with network characteristics in the nineteenth and early twentieth century. Cross-border economic networks can be discovered in even earlier periods.

Although two distinct approaches to networks—as structure and as actors —are represented in the following chapters, those approaches are complements in understanding international politics. Structural analysis requires renewed theorizing—drawn from international relations—to supplement the powerful analytic tools that it commands. Networked actors can no longer be viewed as a simple and omnipresent residual—neither hierarchies nor markets—but should be seen as carefully defined entities whose behavior and effectiveness must be based on network characteristics.

The empirical value of network analysis in international relations will drive its future trajectory, but its theoretical contribution should not be overlooked. Networks offer a means to investigate, in a more rigorous and empirically convincing manner, the relations between agents and structure in international politics. Networks force attention to dimensions of power that conventional views of international politics neglect. Networks are new contributors to international governance, ones with a roster of strengths and weaknesses that require careful evaluation.

The claims made by the authors in this book are ultimately claims of theoretical innovation and empirical utility—the value of network analysis as a tool for understanding international politics. Sidestepping grandiose claims about the transformative role of networks in world politics, we advance a claim that is more easily confirmed in the following chapters: a wide swath of international relations—encompassing trade agreements, the diffusion of constitutional ideas, transnational criminal activity, and Internet governance —cannot be understood without comprehending the structure, behavior, and consequences of networks and subjecting those networks to more rigorous analysis.

PART I

Networks as Structure

International and Domestic Consequences

2

Globalization and the Social Power Politics of International Economic Networks

Emilie M. Hafner-Burton and Alexander H. Montgomery

Despite unprecedented economic growth in recent years, economic globalization is causing growing inequalities within and between states (United Nations 2005). This idea is ubiquitous. Politicians everywhere campaign on it; nongovernmental organizations mobilize around it; and academics and intellectuals study it (Mazur 2000). Data corroborate the story. Trade liberalization might improve global economic prosperity, but it is also marginalizing the world's poorest countries, creating a global political economy that destabilizes weak states and spreads inequality among them (Wallerstein 1974; Nemeth and Smith 1985). Trade, from this point of view, is not just about money or goods; it creates power politics, making poor countries worse off, robbing them of the material capabilities necessary to defend their interests in an increasingly integrated world marketplace. A flood of recent protests and scholarship emphasizes that institutions such as the World Trade Organization (WTO) or preferential trade agreements (PTAs) such as the North American Free Trade Agreement (NAFTA) only aggravate the problem (Dowlah 2004). Meanwhile, economists are concerned that PTAs are at odds with the goals of the multilateral trade regime, diverting trade from more efficient to less efficient producers for political reasons and obstructing multilateral negotiations and initiatives (Bhagwati 1993; Schott 2004).

In this chapter we adopt a "network as structure" perspective to consider the rise and evolution of structural power inequalities in the international political economy; in it, we contrast inequalities in social power between states that result from relative possession of social capital due to density of ties through PTAs with inequalities in material power that result from relative possession of resources such as guns and butter. Our argument is a simple one. The globalization debate revolves around the consequences of increased trade and investment for inequality, both within and between states. That debate has focused mainly on material inequality. Examining the social networks formed by PTAs produces a different view of inequality, one which may redress in part the material effects of economic transactions. Trade is a set of transactions between agents that allocates information and material resources and, in the process, structures states' material roles in the global economy (Snyder and Kick 1979; Smith and White 1992). We argue that the formal organizations that regulate trade (PTAs), like other intergovernmental organizations (IGOs), generate informal social networks through joint membership. These networks give some states more social capital than others, structuring group relations and creating a social dimension of power politics that also shapes inequality (Hafner-Burton 2005; Hafner-Burton and Montgomery 2006).

PTAs are spreading rapidly—hundreds have already been notified to the WTO and more are being created. Are these agreements bad news, not just for global prosperity but also for global political equality? We do not adopt the standard economic refrain that a rise in absolute global economic prosperity offsets the importance of how those gains are distributed (Wolf 2004). Rather, we accept that the world economy is characterized by substantial distributional inequalities between states, generating material power politics and shaping development. But the increasing material gap between the poor and the rich is not the whole story, and international institutions are not uniformly making the problem worse, as some have argued, or better, as others think. Preferential trade arrangements such as NAFTA more and more govern economic exchange, shaping material power relations derived from sums of money or financial transactions—although there is some debate about whether these organizations have an appreciable effect on material wealth and power (Frankel 1998); yet the same PTAs also create and sustain social power politics created by group dynamics. Like other organizations (Ingram, Robinson, and Busch 2005; Hafner-Burton and Montgomery 2006; Dorussen and Ward 2008), these institutions form social network structures, creating ties between states. The distribution of these ties endows certain states with more social capital than others, creating social power relationships that significantly affect international politics, shaping issues like whether states go to war or use economic sanctions (Hafner-Burton and Montgomery 2005, 2008). While states' material power is determined by the relative size of their material capital, social power is determined by the relative social capital created by and accessed through ties with other states in the international system such as ties through mutual membership in PTAs.[1]

---

1. Our conception of social power is derived from a particular conception of social capital. Bourdieu defines social capital as "the aggregate of the actual or potential resources which are linked to possession of a durable network of more or less institutionalized relationships of mutual acquaintance or recognition" (1986, 248); power can be measured by looking at relative amounts of capital. Two schools of thought regarding social capital due to networks have

Unlike inequality in material power (as measured by potential military power or gross domestic product), inequality in at least one form of social power—that endowed to states by virtue of their positions in the international network of PTAs—has been falling dramatically since 1947. Elsewhere, we have examined the effects of this form of social power on outcomes of interest in the international system; in this chapter, we concentrate on comparing how the distribution of one particular aspect of social capital in the international system (centrality in the PTA network) has varied over time relative to traditional conceptions of material power. In doing so, we add nuance to the traditional debates over inequality and globalization; this broader view suggests that the net institutional effects of globalization on inequality may be less severe than traditional measures suggest, although it is middle-ranking countries rather than marginalized states that are closing the gap.

Our approach is different from but compatible with customary understandings of power. Scholarship on political economy has traditionally concerned itself with relative disparities in material power (Hirschman 1945; Gilpin 1987). International relations theory, however, has long recognized that disparities in social power also shape the landscape of politics; the recent rise of constructivism has recovered the insights of the English School, reemphasizing the role that social power plays in international relations (Bull 1977; Hopf 1998; Wendt 1999), while classical realists have long made the case that power arises from nonmaterial resources as well (Morgenthau 1948), and some liberal institutionalists have argued that "soft power" significantly affects international relations (Keohane and Nye 1977).[2] Through social network analysis, we offer a way of conceptualizing and measuring the role of social power relationships in international relations created by the increasing institutionalization of interstate interactions. This method of analysis can help to explain why mutual membership in international organizations in general or preferential trade agreements in particular fails to have a consistent effect on politics, such as militarized disputes or economic sanctions (Russett, Oneal, and Davis 1998; Mansfield and Pevehouse 2000; Hafner-Burton and Montgomery 2008): the socially significant effects of membership can only be measured by aggregating across the effects of all ties rather than by just looking at mutual membership. Social network studies have found that although mutual membership is rarely a significant predictor of behavior, both social power and competition between groups due to membership patterns are strong predictors of belligerent behavior (Hafner-Burton and Montgomery

---

since developed (Portes 1998); the idea that structural holes (gaps in networks between important actors) are sources of capital (Burt 1992), and the idea that centrality is a source of capital (Coleman 1990). Following Bourdieu and Coleman, we take the latter definition as our basis for measuring social capital and therefore social power derived from PTA network membership.

2. Soft power is defined as a residual category to hard power; by contrast, social capital (and social power) is positively defined.

2005, 2006, 2008; Dorussen and Ward 2008). Consequently, the social network approach to power politics offers both a robust and nuanced perspective on how institutions shape violence and coercion.

In this chapter, we map how the distribution of this type of social power compares with material power over time. Both sources of power, material and social, generate inequality: the distribution of social ties in the international system created by PTA membership advantages some states over others just as the distribution of material capabilities does. Yet while material inequalities between states are high and rising, inequalities in social power derived from PTA membership have been on the decline from the beginning of the contemporary trading system that began after World War II. Standard analysis of the global economy demonstrates that trade is dividing the world into groups of winners and losers, conferring more material resources on some states than others; a social network view of power in the global economy reveals that the apparent losers are not at a complete loss for power. Economically disadvantaged states are making up for relative disparities in material power through rising social power in the network of PTAs, which gives them some new advantages. Although trade is dividing the world into haves and have-nots, PTAs can be a vehicle of social power for states otherwise disenfranchised materially by globalization, although the "middle" states benefit most; while the distribution of social power through PTAs may be more equitable, it is far from a level playing field.

Our three aims are (1) to identify the type of social power created by the network of PTAs and distinguish it from standard concepts of material power in international relations—relative economic clout and military strength; (2) to generate empirical indicators to measure this concept that can be widely applied to the study of political economy; and (3) to trace the evolution of structural inequality in this type of social power between states over time. We first introduce social network analysis as a framework of investigation. We then consider how PTAs create social power discrepancies through networks. Next, we define our network concepts of social power and our indicator of social capital from PTAs (*PTACentDegree*, or the degree centrality of a state in the PTA network) as well as material capital (*GDP* and *CINC*, or Correlates of War Composite Index of National Capability), using them to create specific measures of state inequality generated by the network of agreements. Finally, we analyze the evolution of structural inequality over time and show that the political economy is actually characterized by two opposing trends: rising material inequality between nations accompanied by a decline in social inequality, both of which influence international relations.

Social Network Analysis, International Political Economy, and Intergovernmental Organizations

This book considers the role of social networks in world politics—social structures made up of actors that are connected through various ties ranging from terrorist and criminal networks to transnational human rights networks. Social network analysis (SNA) is not only a research focus on networks—it is a research methodology distinctive to the social and behavioral sciences that is inherently concerned with such networks. It is possible to study networks without employing SNA, but it is not possible to employ SNA without attention to networks. Like rational choice, SNA is not a unified set of theories but rather a framework for analysis based on a set of primary assumptions and formal tools that can be applied to an assortment of subjects. At the most abstract level, SNA concerns relationships defined by linkages among units, such as people, institutions, or even states. The underlying difference between SNA and standard ways of analyzing behavioral processes is accordingly the use of concepts and indicators that identify associations among units rather than solely focusing on the attributes of the units (Wasserman and Faust 1994).

SNA concepts and indicators are relational. They describe the connections that associate one actor to another and cannot be reduced to the traits of an agent; relationships are not properties of agents but of systems of agents (Scott 2000). SNA research is thus grounded by three principles: actors and their behaviors are mutually dependent rather than autonomous; relational ties between actors are channels for the diffusion of resources, whether material or nonmaterial; and persistent patterns of associations among units create a social structure within which actions take place that provide occasions for or restrictions on behavior (Wasserman and Faust 1994).

SNA has been only sporadically applied to international relations in general or to intergovernmental economic networks in particular (Hafner-Burton, Kahler, and Montgomery forthcoming). Historically, it has been used to explain global economic stratification (Snyder and Kick 1979; Rossem 1996), transaction flows in the international system (Brams 1969), and international trade (Nemeth and Smith 1985; Smith and White 1992).[3] The latter two studies used blockmodeling to investigate world systems theory, which claims that states are in more or less fixed structural relationships with each other and can be divided into core, periphery, and semiperiphery. By dividing states into discrete groups based on their relationships with others, both papers found that there was some mobility between groups, and that the number of groups was greater than that predicted by world systems theory. However, much of this literature has been ignored or marginalized.

---

3. More recently, it has been applied to democratic networks (Maoz 2001) and alliances (Maoz et al. 2005) as well. See Hafner-Burton, Kahler, and Montgomery forthcoming for a review of SNA applications in international relations.

Recently, a few scholars have begun to acknowledge that international organizations (IOs) create social networks among their members and that these networks shape politics in very significant ways that are different from conventional understandings of what IOs do.[4] For example, we (2005, 2006, 2008) use SNA to study the relationship between IOs and conflict. We argue that conflicts between states are shaped not only by material power but also by relative positions of social power created by institutional memberships and characterized by significant disparity. Membership establishes hierarchies of social capital in the international system, making certain policy strategies more practical or rational. Dorussen and Ward (2008) emphasize a different aspect of social network analysis, arguing that networks are conduits for information that affect the propensity of states to engage in conflict, while Kim and Barnett (2007) look at the effects of communication networks on conflict. These perspectives are only just developing and most concern themselves with the effects of organizational networks on various behaviors; we complement and extend these approaches by investigating the distribution of the variables that these studies have identified as empirically significant.

The Power of Social Networks

Thinking about power in the international political economy as a matter of social networks is not obvious. Markets, after all, involve the exchange of material resources between parties. Political discussions around globalization and inequality concentrate on relative disparities in material attributes of relevant actors, whether states, corporations, or people. It is these material components of power—the size of a national economy or the wealth of a population—that matter most to individual consumers and voters and so garner the most rhetoric and debate. What, then, is "social" or "networked" about the power politics of global inequality?

Our social network approach to power politics in international relations is similar to traditional theories of power politics in important ways, but also differs on crucial points. First, although many international relations (IR) theories already treat power as a relational attribute, most traditional empirical approaches to studying the concept derive power relationships from the attributes of individual states instead of from ties between states. Second, they unnecessarily favor the material over the social content of state networks, ignoring, for example, information. Third, social power—which we define as power that originates from social capital formed by ties with other states, rather than material capital formed by resource capabilities—is not a simple

4. The number of articles using social network analysis to study international institutions has increased dramatically since 2000 (K. Kim and Barnett 2000; J. Kim and Barnett 2007; Beckfield 2003; Ingram, Robinson, and Busch 2005; Hafner-Burton and Montgomery 2005, 2006, 2008; Dorussen and Ward 2008).

derivative of material power; it operates in tandem with material forces but is not entirely dependent on them. In both cases, capital forms the basis for power; disparities in capital between actors lead one actor to have power over the other. Finally, social power gained through networks relates to all three of the "faces of power" (coercion, agenda setting, and identity/interest alteration).

First, power in international relations is already thought of in relational terms, but usually only references network concepts implicitly. Realists have long understood that power has both material and social dimensions: "Power may comprise anything that establishes and maintains the control of man over man. Thus power covers all social relationships which serve that end, from physical violence to the most subtle psychological ties by which one mind controls another" (Morgenthau 1948, 11). Structural realists argue that the power in the international system depends not on individual states but rather is an emergent property of the distribution of capabilities among all states: "Power is estimated by comparing the capabilities of a number of units" (Waltz 1979, 98). What matters is not how much money or how many guns a state acquires; what matters is the distribution of these resources relative to all other states. Power relationships are not properties of states but of systems of states. Consequently, although our most basic understanding of power is not usually described in SNA terms, it is in every way grounded in the same defining principles of network analysis: that actors and their behaviors are mutually reliant, not independent; that relational ties between actors are conduits for the diffusion of resources, which include but are not limited to material resources; and that lasting patterns of associations among units create a social structure within which actions take place that provide occasions for or restrictions on behavior (Wasserman and Faust 1994). However, social network analysis looks not at the distribution of a unit-level variable (capabilities of individual states), but rather at the distribution of an interaction-level variable (ties between states).

Second, social network analysis includes social as well as material power in its considerations; not just material capabilities and trade flows but social ties between states and the social capital that flows from them are included in network analysis. Although Waltz is implicitly materialist, other realists (such as Morgenthau) are not; social conceptions of power are compatible with traditional realist notions of power, and, increasingly, with some constructivist notions as well (Goddard and Nexon 2005). This is not to suggest that social power matters as much as material power; such a statement would be nothing more than a conjecture, likely to be true in some circumstances but not in others. However, the core of international relations theory acknowledges that social sources of power matter, even if it does not tell us how much or when, while research into the behaviors of agents of all kinds, including animals, children, and firms, show that relative social connectedness is a crucial factor in cooperation and conflict behaviors.

Third, social power is not necessarily determined by material power. All states occupy positions of material and social power in the international system, but positions of material power, which are established by the distribution of wealth, do not determine positions of social power, which are established by the distribution of ties with other states.[5] States with privileged material resources relative to other states do not necessarily acquire advantaged social network relations, much in the same way that not all rich children are popular and all poor children outcasts. The relationship between material and social forms of power is an empirical question, not a theoretical one to be deduced a priori.

Fourth, like material power, social power has several "faces," giving an agent various capabilities to coerce another agent to do something they would otherwise not do (Dahl 1957), to prevent grievances from being aired through setting or shaping agendas and deciding who sits at the table (Bachrach and Baratz 1962), or to manipulate the desires, interests, and identities of another agent (Lukes 1974). Advantaged social network positions provide a state various capacities to coerce another state to do something they would otherwise not do—the first face of power. In the same way that a materially powerful state can use or threaten military force to intimidate another state into taking certain actions, forcing governments to withdraw from captured territories, a socially powerful can bully another state through naming and shaming or isolation into doing what they want, signing onto human rights agreements they had no intention of joining, or helping to overturn regimes, or bring states to the bargaining table. Bad reputations and threats of social isolation or ridicule among a network of states are weapons; they may operate in much the same way as threats of military or economic coercion, imposing costs on target states that would otherwise not be there. The denser a state's social ties to other states, the more influence and therefore power they have to manipulate reputations and even potentially cut other states' ties. And in some cases, bad reputations may lead to material coercion as well. In general, however, it is our view that the direct costs imposed by tools associated with social power are apt to be lower than those imposed by most material weapons in the first face of power, but that they can matter in ways that shape politics nonetheless; they may be more "usable" than material weapons as well.

The same logic applies to the second and third faces of power. The ability of a state to shape who gets to speak and who is silenced is affected by a state's capacity to mobilize support for its positions; a state's density of ties with other states through social networks assists in this mobilization. A state's ability to

5. Material power can also result from material ties, for example, from trade relations between states. Yet power relations measured in this way usually end up being reduced to stocks of capital, not flows. If a state has power over another due to their mutual trade, this results from one state having a lower dependence on that trade than the other—in other words, the discrepancy in GDP, not trade, is what gives that state material power.

define interests and identities in the international system (such as the attempts by the United States to define certain states as rogue, outlaw, or evil) is a function of how many other states are listening; the more ties a state has to a broad audience in the international system, the more conduits it has through which such actions can be taken, and the more likely it is that such identity manipulation can take place. We believe that in the second and third faces, social power is likely to be both more "usable" and more effective than material power.

The Social Network of PTAs

States form social networks through membership in international institutions—in this case, PTAs. Mutual memberships create *ties* between states and, although the strength of these ties increases with additional joint memberships, they do not necessarily create positive or negative bonds between states. These ties define states' relative positions in social hierarchies in the international political economy. Like the balance of military or market power, these positions are state characteristics that are measured (and have their effects) relative to other states, shaping the conditions under which certain strategies of action become rational. Table 2.1 summarizes our social network concepts and measures as they compare to material concepts and indicators standard in the literature.

A state's structural position relative to other states in the system places external constraints and pressures on it, while a state's power enables it to take action. Both concepts have long been staples of international relations theory; both structural realism (Waltz 1979) and world systems theory (Wallerstein 1974) argue that state action is constrained by outside influences due to a state's material position in the international system and enabled by a state's material capital—measured by the monadic measures *GDP* or *CINC*. For realism, a state's position is determined by the distribution of material capital

Table 2.1. Concepts and indicators

Concept	Level	Material measures	Social measures (PTA network)
Capital	Monad	GDP, CINC	PTACentDegree
Power	Dyad	GDP_i/GDP_j or GDP_i-GDP_j $CINC_i/CINC_j$ or $CINC_i-CINC_j$	$PTACentDegree_i/PTACentDegree_j$ or $PTACentDegree_i-PTACentDegree_j$
Structural Similarity	Monad	Great Power Status	PTA Group Membership
Inequality	System	GDP Inequality = StDev(GDP)/ Avg(GDP) CINC Inequality = StDev(CINC)/Avg(CINC)	PTACentDegree Inequality = StDev(PTACentDegree)/Avg(PTA CentDegree)

relative to other all states. Inequality in the overall distribution can be measured by any standard inequality measure; we use the standard deviation of a measure divided by its average to produce the system-level measures *GDP Inequality* or *CINC Inequality*. Certain systemic configurations and balances of power are more or less likely to lead to conflict than others. For example, a system configuration with only two great powers is thought to be more stable than one with three or more great powers; when the balance of power between two states is roughly equal (that is, both have about the same material capital), conflict is more likely between them, although it is most likely when one power is slightly ahead (Mearsheimer 2001). By contrast, world systems theory argues that a state's position in the system (core, semiperiphery, or periphery) depends on ties—in particular, economic flows and military treaties among all of the states in the system. These ties flow among states in the core and between states in the periphery and the core, but not among states in the periphery (Snyder and Kick 1979; Rossem 1996; Borgatti and Everett 1999).

SNA derives states' social positions and power from the ties between nodes in a network. However, instead of using material ties, as does world systems theory, social network analysis uses social ties. We focus here on social ties between states that are created by common PTA membership.[6] Although many social network studies of international organizations only determine whether or not a tie exists between two nodes, information on the strength of a tie can be used to perform a more in-depth analysis of the structure of a network. In the specific case of the social network formed by PTA membership, the number of shared memberships measures the strength of a tie between two states. A state's social capital is an attribute that a state possesses by virtue of its direct relational ties with other states (although this can be weighted by the social capital of the other states)—a concept we measure with the monadic *PTACentDegree;* the more countries a state is connected to and the more strongly a state is tied to those others, the more social capital a state possesses. This measure has been found to significantly affect conflict propensity among states; for example, an increase from the mean to the maximum increases the likelihood that a state will initiate economic sanctions by a factor of ten (Hafner-Burton and Montgomery 2008), an effect as substantively significant as democracy; differences in the same measure also increase the likelihood of militarized disputes (MIDs) (Hafner-Burton and Montgomery 2005).

As with material capabilities, in order to measure the inequality of the distribution of social capital, we use the standard deviation of a measure divided by its average to produce the systemic measure *PTACentDegree Inequality.* Finally, states with more social capital relative to others can exert more social power, which can be measured by the difference or ratio between two states'

6. Where the focus of the debate is on economics-related inequality, PTA-generated ties are most appropriate (Hafner-Burton and Montgomery 2008); elsewhere, we and others have used IGO-generated ties. For a discussion of the problems associated with using noninstitutionalized ties, see Hafner-Burton and Montgomery (2006, 8).

social capital. The distribution of social ties in the international system, like the distribution of material capabilities, is uneven; some states have very strong ties to many other states, while others have weaker ties to only a few. The distribution of ties determines states' structural positions relative to each other in the international political economy; states with similar patterns of ties are placed into structurally similar positions—a concept we measure as *PTA Group Membership*. As with realism, the number of states in a given social group can significantly affect their conflict propensity; for instance, a greater number of states in a social group empirically correlates with belligerent behavior (Hafner-Burton and Montgomery 2006, 2008); in particular, moving from the mean number of states to the maximum increases the propensity of a state to initiate sanctions by a factor of 2.5.

Our variables, PTA Group Membership and PTACentDegree, are derived from the strength of ties between states, which we measure as the number of PTAs that two states have in common.[7] We start by deriving a general measure of mutual membership in PTAs. We incorporate all trade institutions in the sample, excluding PTAs composed of other PTAs such as that between the European Union and Gulf Cooperation Council, but do include nonreciprocal arrangements such as the Cotonou arrangement and the numerous EU arrangements with individual states outside of the EU.[8] We treat all memberships as symmetrical and equal since co-membership in any of these institutions is a mutual affiliation that not only reflects social ties between states but also causes and reinforces such ties.

For the PTA Group Membership variable, we start by calculating a measure of distance (a measure of dissimilarity) by taking the sum of the differences between two states' memberships with every other state. Note that these states do not have to belong to the same PTAs as long as they share the same number of memberships with other states; for example, if two states belong to two different bilateral PTAs with the United States and no other PTAs, the distance between them would be zero. We then use the distance measure to divide the international system into structurally equivalent clusters (a group of states a short distance from each other and a larger distance from other states). Hierarchical clustering starts with each actor in a separate group and then increases the distance level using the clustering criteria until the desired number of clusters or the desired level is reached. We use average-link clustering because it produces more homogeneous and stable clusters than other methods.[9] Here we set the number of clusters to be proportional to the num-

---

7. All social network attributes were calculated using the SNA package in R (Butts 2007; R Development Core Team 2007).

8. We exclude the General Agreement on Tariffs and Trade/World Trade Organization.

9. See Wasserman and Faust (1994, 381) on different clustering criteria. For example, single-link clustering puts together the two clusters with the smallest minimum pairwise distance, and tends to create more heterogeneous, less stable clusters. Complete-link clustering, by contrast, merges two clusters with the smallest maximum pairwise distance in each step. Average-link clustering strikes a balance between the two.

ber of states in the system in order to be consistent with previous work that tests the hypothesis that states that inhabit larger clusters are more prone to conflict.[10]

An actor with high social capital, in social network terms, can be either the recipient of many strong ties or a recipient that has exclusive ties to certain actors; an actor with more social capital than another can exert more social power. The appropriate measure to use depends on whether higher social capital comes from being linked to actors with a great deal of social capital, any actors, or actors without their own social capital. For example, bargaining leverage may be increased if actors have connections to otherwise weakly connected actors,[11] while being connected to strongly connected actors may increase the resources a state can draw on, as is the case for many former European colonies. As a default assumption, we treat all actors as equal, since it is unclear whether being connected to strong or weak actors would be more likely to affect conflict (or, for that matter, what weight should be put on the centrality of an actor). The formal measure for the sum of all incoming ties in social network analysis is called *Degree Centrality*.[12] We then define PTA-CentDegree to be the sum of a state's ties to all (n) other actors in the system through PTAs.

To measure inequality in all of our measures across time we tested two different metrics, Gini and coefficient of variation (Firebaugh 1999). The coefficient of variation is simply the standard deviation of a measure divided by the mean. These two measures of inequality are generally highly correlated to our social network measure; for PTACentDegree, the correlation is 0.92. Due to the high correlation between our two metrics, we only plot the coefficient of variation. In our analysis section below, we examine the distribution of PTACentDegree and the amount of social mobility across the groups in the international system over time.

Evolution of the Network

We use these SNA tools to trace the historical evolution of social power generated by the network of PTAs over time. Our objective is to refocus analytical attention away from the standard worldview that regards states as independent users of PTAs toward a worldview that understands states as embedded in an interconnected set of organizational associations that structures world

---

10. Another method of measuring the fragmentation in the international system, network polarization, has been proposed by Zeev Maoz. This method, complementary to our measures, requires ties to be dichotomized, and offers a systemwide measure of polarization based on the overlap between cliques of states (2006).

11. See Bonacich (1987) for a generalization of centrality measures and conditions under which ties to weakly connected actors may be a source of centrality.

12. See Wasserman and Faust (1994, chapter 5) on centrality.

politics by endowing members with PTA social capital (PTACentDegree) and placing them in different PTA groups in the international system (PTA Group Membership). As we will illustrate, this analytical shift has implications for the ways in which we understand the structure of the international political economy, as well as its effects on states' behaviors.

We focus our attention on the postwar period, 1950–2000, as the vast majority of PTAs were created during this time. We begin by mapping inequality at the global level and then turn our attention to the experience of a dozen politically prominent states.

PTACentDegree Inequality from 1950 to 2000

Global levels of inequality in PTA social capital have declined over time (see figure 2.1). Since social power is simply relative social capital, a decrease in inequality of social capital also represents a decrease in inequality of social power from PTAs. The figure illustrates four continuous trends. First, the number of states in the international system has increased dramatically during the latter half of the twentieth century; dozens of new states have come into existence, as old empires fell and colonization waned.[13] Second, the number of PTAs has grown exponentially since the end of World War II as nation-states have proliferated and postcolonial relationships have evolved through market ties. The international system at the end of World War II was sparsely populated by trade institutions; fifty years later, the number of PTAs has radically outpaced the growth of states and the world economy is characterized by dense networks of organizations.

Third, while states and PTAs have proliferated, the inequality in the distribution of social capital as measured through PTACentDegree (plotted against the right-hand axis) has declined over time. As more and more states belong to more and more PTAs, their associations are distributed increasingly evenly over the long term, although inequality in institutional ties has been on the rise since the 1990s, reflecting similar trends in IGOs and international nongovernmental organizations (INGOs) (Beckfield 2003). The temporary increase in the 1970s is due to a number of agreements created in that period between individual countries and the European Community (EC), which rapidly increased the centrality of EU states. Note that many former colonies are represented in these agreements, suggesting that former empires are shaping the distribution of social power through PTAs (and not necessarily in a way that benefits the most marginalized). The general trend, though, suggests that a growing number of states are gaining social capital, measured by PTACentDegree, in the international network of PTAs; most belong to multiple agreements and most share ties with many other states. It also suggests

13. We measure the number of states in the international system in accordance with the Correlates of War Project (2005).

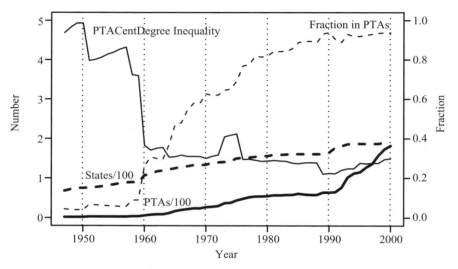

Figure 2.1. Population of PTAs and states (divided by 100), PTACentDegree inequality (left axis); fraction of states in PTAs (right axis), 1947–2000

that world trends of social power have been bumpy, as the pattern of decline is nonmonotonic.

Finally, the fraction of states participating in at least one preferential trade agreement has rapidly increased over time; since the mid- to late 1980s the fraction of states participating in preferential trade agreements has consistently exceeded 90 percent. Even if PTA social capital is somewhat unevenly distributed, most states have been able to enter into at least one agreement.

These trends tell us something very different than standard perspectives about globalization and inequality. Although in individual cases states that have a great deal of social capital from PTAs also possess high levels of material capital, our measure of social capital is not at all correlated with traditional material measures of capital. For economic power, we use GDP. For military power, we use the standard Correlates of War (COW) measure of a state's combined index of national capabilities, or CINC.[14] Using all observations in the dataset from 1950 to 2000, PTACentDegree is correlated 0.13 with GDP and 0.04 with CINC.[15] Not only is our main measure of social capital from PTAs unrelated to material capabilities, but the distribution of this social capital and therefore this kind of social power is also very different from the distribution of material power.

14. We use version 3.02 of the National Material Capabilities dataset (Singer, Bremer, and Stuckey 1972).

15. Correlation with the total amount of trade of a country is higher, but still not very significant (especially considering an expected connection between trade institutions and trade), at 0.37.

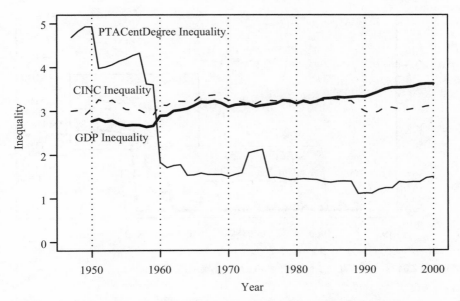

Figure 2.2. Comparison of material (GDP, CINC) and social (PTACentDegree) inequality, 1947–2000

We compare social inequality from PTAs with material inequality derived from GDP and CINC in figure 2.2. As can be seen, while inequality in the distribution of PTACentDegree has more or less steadily decreased over time, GDP and CINC inequality have grown even while material inequality in energy and capabilities has mostly held steady. Moreover, since 1960 the general level of inequality of material power has been much greater; for both measures, the standard deviation is always multiple times the mean for these quantities. This is not to say that PTA social capital is equitably distributed, that large differences do not exist, or that these differences do not have significant implications for world politics; but rather that social and material capital and therefore power do not correlate well with each other and are very differently distributed.

World-level indicators can be misleading because they smooth out the important relative variations that determine dyadic power relationships and shape international relations. Figures 2.3a and 2.3b add caution to optimism. Here, we plot the logarithm of PTACentDegree of a dozen politically prominent states in six panel years: 1950, 1960, 1970, 1980, 1990, and 2000. For these figures, we have chosen a sample of states that have been in existence since before 1910 (and existed at the beginning of every one of our years), that contains the great powers, and has at least one representative from every major region: Brazil (BRA), China (CHN), Ethiopia (ETH), France (FRN), Iran (IRN), Japan (JPN), Mexico (MEX), Russia (RUS), Thailand (THI),

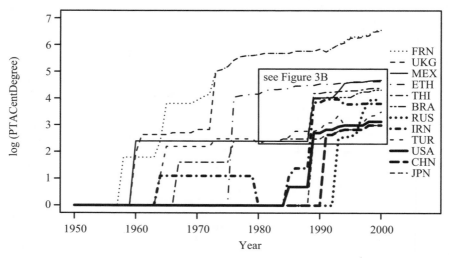

Figure 2.3a. Logged PTACentDegree for twelve prominent states, 1950–2000

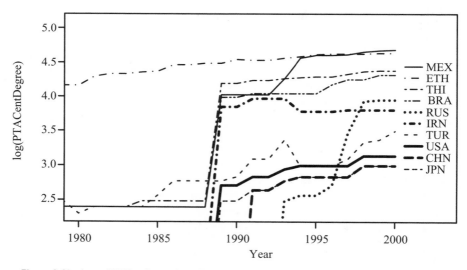

Figure 2.3b. Logged PTACentDegree for ten prominent states (excluding Britain and France), 1980–2000

Turkey (TUR), the United Kingdom (UKG), and the United States (USA). Figure 2.3b illustrates a small subsection of the same plot in order to better illustrate recent trends.

Figure 2.3 illustrates four historical trends. First, PTACentDegree rankings in the PTA network exhibit hierarchy. Differences in relative PTACentDegree between the top few rich core states (such as France or the United Kingdom) and poorer developing states (such as Mexico or Turkey) and impoverished underdeveloped states (such as Ethiopia) have remained steadily high over time. Differences in *PTACentDegree* among the rest of the world have waxed and waned. Yet the inequality in PTACentDegree created by the PTA network looks very different from inequality created by relative disparities in military power or markets: the United States has ended up near the bottom of the distribution in 2000, while Ethiopia, Mexico, Thailand, and Brazil have settled into a grouping above many developed countries, with the latter three demonstrating a radical increase in PTA network centrality since the end of the cold war. This suggests that PTAs organize the international political economy in ways that are not only derivative of material power.

Yet historical ties have had an enormous influence on PTA network formation—in particular, the legacy of empire has had dramatic effects on these networks. Ethiopia's dramatic increase in centrality in the mid-1970s is due to a single agreement: joining the Lomé agreement in 1976, which connected it with a large number of other former European colonies as well as the states of the EU itself. Ethiopia's relatively high centrality today is not exclusively due to Lomé and its successors; it has subsequently signed a number of other PTA agreements as well. However, the weight of this agreement has significantly affected the distribution of PTA network centrality; it took until the late 1990s for Mexico to overtake Ethiopia.

Second, this process of convergence has not been uniform over the course of history. States' evolution of relative PTACentDegree derived from the PTA network has increased in fits and starts (with the exception of France). Moreover, PTACentDegree is clearly not proportional to military or economic attributes. Third, certain groups of states trend together over time. For example, France and the United Kingdom enjoy the highest relative PTACentDegree available to any state in the international system, a degree of political influence that is not derived from their market or military capabilities alone. Since the 1980s, both states have held high relative PTACentDegree in the network of PTAs. The United Kingdom initially had a great deal of PTA social capital due to its separate agreements in the 1960s, yet the rising social capital associated with EC membership due to an increase in agreements with the Community as a whole in the mid-1960s led to a temporary decline relative to the value of France's PTACentDegree in 1970. Once the United Kingdom joined the EC, its PTACentDegree increased again accordingly.

Finally, and perhaps most surprisingly, the non-European great powers have consistently failed to connect to large numbers of states through PTA networks. The United States, Japan, and China have been at the bottom of the list, and Russia has only recently surpassed Turkey and Iran in centrality. Although the networks of these powers, like many others, showed a dramatic increase at the end of the cold war, they still are relatively isolated. This may be best explained by realist theories; many great powers prefer economic autarky in order to preserve their security.

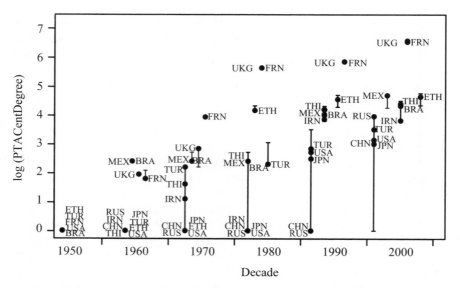

Figure 2.4. PTACentDegree of PTA groups in the international system for each decade, 1950–2000

PTA Group Membership in the Late Twentieth Century

Although PTACentDegree inequality is generally on the decline, the groupings of countries due to PTA ties in the international system is relatively stable, as can be seen in figure 2.4, which looks at snapshots of group membership at the beginning of each decade since 1960. Vertical lines connect states in the same group and indicate the maximum and minimum centrality of each group; groups are dispersed evenly around the beginning of each decade so the groups can be visually differentiated. In 1960, the United Kingdom's separate agreements with its former colonies pulled it into a different group than France and its agreements, while the Latin American Free Trade Association grouped together Mexico and Brazil. By 1970, Turkey, Thailand, and Iran had signed a few small agreements, while the benefits of EC membership are apparent with the French group (really, the EC states) far ahead. By 1980, the United Kingdom and France had nearly identical agreements with other countries, while Ethiopia formed another group all related by Lomé. Turkey's agreements were with sufficiently different partners by this time for it to break away from the bottom group of states, while Mexico, Brazil, and Thailand's agreements were similar enough (and small enough) to be classified with the rest of the laggards. The latter three, along with Iran, increased their ties to similar countries and pulled away from the bottom group by 1990; the remainder of the countries in the sample finally began signing a significant number of agreements by 2000.

The membership of the groups indicates a significant amount of hierarchy and splintering in the international system of PTAs; the EC has clearly formed a group apart since the 1970s that has been continually increasing in centrality in the PTA network, while boosting the centrality of groups of states that sign agreements with it such as Ethiopia and other former colonies. Smaller groups of advanced developing countries have followed, forming their own internal networks with each other. The largest and most diverse group still includes the laggard countries (including several great powers) that have yet to sign any agreements at all; it is no surprise, therefore, that studies find a relationship between group size and conflict.

Social Network Effects

PTAs, like international institutions of all kinds, do more than reduce transaction costs and lengthen the shadow of future cooperation; they also form social network structures, creating various distributions of ties between states that endow some with more social capital than others, creating social power relationships that are not derivative of material capital. They also partition states into potentially diverse (and quite large) groups of hierarchically organized states. This exercise is more than conceptual; states' social network positions significantly affect politics, shaping, for instance, conflict and aggression between states by making certain policy strategies more practical or rational than others.

For example, a recent study shows that PTAs, by themselves, have no influence on whether members choose to sanction one another; the social network positions they create, however, do shape sanctions behavior, significantly increasing the likelihood of sanctions among members. The more social capital from PTAs a potential initiator has, the more likely it is that sanctions will occur. The influence of PTACentDegree on sanctions onset is sizeable. When the initiating state is extremely central, the probability that sanctions will take place is ten times greater than under average conditions (Hafner-Burton and Montgomery 2008). Similarly, large differences in PTA degree centrality also have been shown to increase the likelihood of militarized disputes (Hafner-Burton and Montgomery 2005). By contrast, dyads that share a greater number of total IGO memberships are somewhat more likely to engage in militarized disputes, but large differences in IGO degree centrality (i.e., when large discrepancies in social capital due to IGO membership exist, creating an asymmetry of social power) created by the broader network of international organizations lead to less frequent MIDs. Dyads where two states have radically different IGO degree centrality values (called *Prestige* in that study) are four times less likely to engage in dispute behavior than dyads in which both states have similar values of IGO degree centrality, which is quite a substantial influence when compared to the effect of such state attributes as democracy and dependency (Hafner-Burton and Montgomery 2006).

This book seeks to introduce two approaches to network analysis as they apply to international politics and to use those approaches to reexamine major debates about the relationship between structure and agency, power and emerging forms of governance. Our chapter contributes to these goals (1) by identifying how the social network of PTAs structures the international political economy, emphasizing the types of social power created and distinguishing them from concepts of material power; (2) generating empirical indicators to measure these concepts in methodical ways that could be useful for studies of international institutions and political economy more broadly; and (3) mapping this structure globally as it has evolved over time.

Our social network approach is not intrinsically realist, liberal, or constructivist in orientation. Rather, it provides systematic empirical tools useful for analyzing all kinds of structural conjectures that take group aspects of international relations—informational and psychological—seriously, including insights from all three traditions. Nor does our approach argue against standard ways of thinking about international institutions, which focus on the individual attributes an institution has to offer—such as dispute resolution mechanisms or voting procedures—and how those attributes affect politics. We simply aim to demonstrate that international institutions also create social networks that place states in various structural positions of power, and that these positions, like dispute resolution mechanisms, can and do shape politics, sometimes in meaningful ways.

The insights to be gained from this kind of approach to studying politics are many. We have added some nuance to the debate about whether trade liberalization is creating more inequality. In response to the critics of globalization, many economists argue that liberalization may be creating inequalities but that the gains in overall global welfare outweigh concerns about distribution because even the poor are, or will be, better off. Our argument suggests, rather, that poor states may also be making up for relative disparities in markets through rising social power in the network of PTAs, and that trade agreements can sometimes be a vehicle of power for states otherwise disenfranchised materially by globalization. The implication of this argument more broadly is that power relations in the political economy are more than a matter of markets; they also emerge from social networks created by the institutions that govern them. Scholars need to engage with this aspect of politics because research is beginning to show these networks matter for political outcomes, just as the size and strength of material resources do. More generally, however, the social network approach taken here offers tools to grapple with many aspects of international relations broadly, providing methods to study complex interactions that give rise to power differences.

3

Constitutional Networks

Zachary Elkins

Constitutions are famously unoriginal documents. Legend has it that some Latin American constitutions in the 1800s shared not only the same provisions but also the same typographical errors. How is it that the most fundamental governing laws of states—documents that often symbolize the independence and sovereignty of such countries—come to be mere reproductions? Through international networks, of some sort, is the short answer. But we do not have a clear sense of what these networks look like or how they operate. Moreover, we do not know anything about the welfare consequences incurred when a state's constitutional choices are highly dependent on those of neighboring (or otherwise connected) states. Institutional convergence, if not globally then locally, is one possible outcome. Indeed, widespread adoption of certain policies or practices in the form of temporal and regional clusters has been at least one motivation for scholars to investigate the patterns of interdependence and influence among states and actors. Aside from such macroeffects, however, networks may have important implications for the quality of the institutions of the "importing" state itself. Indeed, one can imagine two distinct possibilities. Network forces may either push governments to adopt suboptimal or inappropriate institutions designed for the needs of others, or allow governments to adopt institutions superior to those they have the resources or knowledge to engineer for themselves. The welfare question, then, is whether networks are responsible for a state's squeezing into ill-fitting, but fashion-

I thank the participants at workshops in Toronto and San Diego for their insightful comments and suggestions. I am especially indebted to Miles Kahler and Kathryn Sikkink for steering the chapter and to Michael Kenney, David Lake, and Kurt Weyland for their comments on earlier drafts.

able, institutions or whether they channel to the state the most functional and efficient ones available?

My objectives in this chapter are, first, to develop a taxonomy that helps us understand the various effects of international networks on constitutional reform.[1] Given the impressive diversity in the usage and meaning of the "network" label, I adopt an explicitly plural approach, one that incorporates views of networks as structures that condition the decisions of actors as well as networks as agents in their own right. My second objective is to identify the likely welfare consequences of constitutional reform associated with various network processes. The differences in welfare effects imply that policy coordination (either among states or by international organizations) is desirable in cases in which network structures are likely to lead to suboptimal policy outcomes.

The Constitutional Setting

In this chapter I focus on constitutions in the narrow sense. In some work on political institutions, the term has taken on a broad meaning such that it has become shorthand for political institutions more generally (e.g., Persson and Tabellini 2004). However, nearly every country has a written document that is identified as its "constitution" or "basic law."[2] When nominal identification is not possible, one can sometimes identify the "constitution" functionally, given a clear hierarchy of laws. Constitutions are those documents that are either "highest" law (in that they trump other law) or are entrenched (in that they are harder to abrogate or amend than are other laws).

This refinement in terms helps us speak more precisely about the typical participants in constitutional reform as well as its setting—a setting that is qualitatively distinct from that of institutional reform more generally. Such contextualization might help to avoid the tendency in the analysis of institutional reform to speak anthropomorphically of the motives and beliefs of "countries" and "states." Constitutions are typically collective documents, written increasingly by either special assemblies or by an existing representative body (i.e., the legislature). If the set of actors doubles as a legislative assembly and there are no provisions for the assembly to disband following the promulgation of the document, the drafting process can become a highly political affair. As one can imagine, the degree to which actors are invested in the outcome of the drafting process affects the degree to which they are sensitive to network influences, as opposed to domestic political pressures.

The scope of participation in constitution making can vary as well. Occa-

1. This paper builds on a conceptual framework introduced in earlier work (Elkins 2003).
2. Roughly 95 percent of states since 1850 have operated with such a document (Elkins and Ginsburg 2006).

sionally—especially if we include authoritarian constitutions—the document can be the product of a small cadre of authors. At the other extreme, some constitutions have involved the public, at least symbolically, in the drafting process itself. In the Brazilian constitutional assembly in 1987–88, citizens were encouraged to submit proposals prior to the deliberations in the assembly. The result was a towering collection of boxes awaiting the assembly before its opening session, and an extraordinarily long and, at times, convoluted constitutional text at promulgation. Apart from participation, the extent to which the drafting sessions are public matters as well. In the recently completed constitutional reform in Burma, the military government not only excluded the opposition (which won 80 percent of seats in the prior election) from the process, but it also convened the assembly in a heavily guarded venue several hours from the capital.[3] It goes without saying that the debates were not broadcast on Burma's version of C-SPAN, as many democratic constitutional assemblies now are. Certainly, there are advantages to privacy in these sorts of occasions. For instance, scholars have noted that the relatively cloistered setting of the U.S. constitutional convention in 1787 discouraged grandstanding and allowed participants sufficient freedom to speak openly and change their mind without fear of charges of inconsistency (Elster 1995). For present purposes, the scope of public involvement likely affects how, and the degree to which, international networks matter. One implication, for example, is that members of advocacy networks (Keck and Sikkink 1998) would have a more prominent role in a setting that encourages public participation or at least oversight, whether or not their suggestions are influential.

Issues of timing might affect the scope and character of constitutional networking as well. Unlike institutional reform that runs on a more predictable schedule, replacing or amending constitutions is a sporadic affair. Timing is often outside the control of actors, as the window of opportunity for constitutional reform often depends on cataclysmic events (wars, economic crises) or other dramatic shifts in the political landscape. Constitutional change is, therefore, less predictable and more difficult to place on the national agenda. With respect to networks, these episodic moments of change mean that constitutional deliberations are often isolated events rather than widespread (and simultaneous) international affairs. Sometimes, of course, the replacement of a constitution in one country can trigger a replacement in another, in which case an international network of actors can build momentum. Witness, for example, the move for reform under way in Bolivia and Ecuador, re-

---

3. The Burmese process is notable not only for its degree of exclusion but also for its seeming endlessness. The military government announced the formation of a national convention to revise the constitution in 1992. In July 2006 the chairman of the organizing committee announced that the document was 75 percent complete. In the spring of 2008 the Burmese authorities decided that it was complete and scheduled a referendum for May 10, 2008. Even though a disastrous cyclone threw the country into chaos threatening thousands of lives, the military went ahead with the referendum, in which voters not surprisingly ratified the draft.

forms that have been cued by an important constitutional change in Vene-
zuela in 1999. For the most part, however, constitution writing is not concur-
rent across countries. Accordingly, network exchanges are often a matter of
historical learning rather than active simultaneous interactions.

Network Approaches

As is clear from the contributions to this book, scholars have come to think
of networks in two fundamentally different senses. We might think of the two
approaches, following Kahler (chapter 1) and Sikkink (chapter 11), as *network-as-structure* and *network-as-actor.* I am interested in exploring, at least at the
outset, constitutional networks in both senses of the term. That is, in how institutions evolve as a function of a state's position in a social network, and how
actors (state and otherwise) that are organized in a transnational network
shape the character of a state's constitution. At the risk of reproducing the typology sketched elsewhere in this book (see Kahler, chapter 1, and Sikkink,
chapter 11), it is illustrative to revisit the conceptual distinction in the case of
constitutions.

Despite sharing the network label, the two approaches differ markedly with
respect to their assumptions, unit of analysis, and general line of inquiry.
Those entering from the *network-as-structure* perspective are concerned with
how actors (whether they be individuals, organizations, or states and other
political jurisdictions) respond given both a certain set of relationships (ties)
with other actors and the characteristics of the network structure itself. In this
framework, the focus is on the behavior of the actor, conditional on its linkages with other actors, not on the collective behavior of actors with their
linked peers. On the contrary, those entering from a *network-as-actor* perspective are interested in how the structure of relationships among actors allows
them to act collectively. In that sense the network is no longer just a way of
describing relationships among actors, but an actor unto itself. A fundamental difference stems from the degree of coordination among nodes in the network. In the network-as-structure approach, units are often influenced by the
behavior of other actors in the network, but their behavior is typically not coordinated. In the case of network-as-actor, the very reason that they are linked
is precisely so that they can act jointly.

In the interest of clarity, it is instructive to disclose the two exemplars of institutional research that influence these characterizations. With respect to
networks-as-structure, I have in mind the extensive empirical literature on
policy diffusion. In that literature, diffusion is conceived as a general set of
mechanisms characterized by a certain "uncoordinated interdependence"
(Elkins and Simmons 2005), in which network ties among states influence
states' adoption or nonadoption of policies. The essential notion is that the
adoption of a policy in one state (usually a neighboring or otherwise related

state) alters the probability that another state will adopt, but that the states do not coordinate their behavior. The paradigmatic case of the network-as-actor mode is the advocacy network described in Keck and Sikkink (1998), in which rights activists constitute a transnational entity that shapes the ways in which policies are conceived and implemented.

Identifying the two exemplars is useful if only to illuminate a further distinction between the two modes of network research, as least in the context of political and institutional reform (although I suspect that the distinction has broader relevance). The distinction has to do with the position and status of the unit of analysis. In the diffusion perspective, the nodes of the network are responsible for the reform itself. That is, they are on the supply side; they are the states and jurisdictions *producing* policy. In the network-as-actor approach, at least in the paradigmatic case of advocacy networks, the nodes in the network are on the demand side. They are consumers (or perhaps targets) of the policy that organize in a particular network structure to shape the policy product.

We should be careful not to overdraw differences between the two approaches. Studies will not always fit neatly into one category or the other. Common to the two approaches, on the other hand, is a focus on the particular set of relationships among actors (the network) and an understanding that the influences over the behavior of actors in one jurisdiction do not stop at the border. A network approach to constitutions—within *either* theoretical approach—assumes that an analysis that posits constitutional outputs as a function of purely domestic political negotiation is largely incomplete.

A Typology of Constitutional Networks

These conceptual and analytic distinctions are helpful in categorizing and developing the various network influences on constitutional reform. Within these broad categories, we can think of network effects in a variety of ways. In diffusion studies alone, I have counted over thirty distinct mechanisms that we might classify as network-as-structure mechanisms. I have argued elsewhere that it is conceptually and normatively useful to think of diffusion mechanisms in terms of the motivations of actors (Elkins 2003; Simmons and Elkins 2004; Elkins and Simmons 2005). The critical distinction, in my view, is whether the foreign model tells actors something about the utility of the policy/institution itself, or whether the model alters the ancillary benefits associated with, but external to, the policy. Conceptually, this distinction cleanly and, I believe, almost exhaustively classifies the mechanisms/processes that are at the root of policy diffusion. Combined with a distinction between coordinated and uncoordinated action between nodes, this distinction with respect to motive helps us conceptualize the various *network* influences on constitution making.

Four important subtypes of network processes implied by the two dimen-

Degree of Coordination

	Uncoordinated	Coordinated
Instrumental	Adaptation	Dependency
Functional	Learning	Cooperation

Motives

Figure 3.1. A typology of network effects

sions are mapped in figure 3.1. These are general analytic categories that themselves encompass a set of mechanisms. I describe a representative set of each of these mechanisms in some detail in the section that follows. Those that we might consider part of the diffusion/network-as-structure framework are arrayed in the left column. Those in the network-as-actor framework are located in the bottom, right cell. The top-right cell—call it dependency—includes transnational exercises in constitutional reform that involve a set of hierarchical, coercive relationships.

As figure 3.1 depicts, we can think of diffusion mechanisms as one of two kinds: those for which another's adoption alters the value of the practice (thus implying instrumental motives for imitation), and those for which another's adoption imparts information (thus implying functional motives for imitation). Each of these two broad classes, which I term *adaptation* and *learning*, comprises a set of varied mechanisms. A comparison of two well-known social psychology experiments on social influence captures the essential distinction. In Solomon Asch's experiments on conformity (1951), subjects involved in very straightforward visual tests ignored their own judgment, instead choosing to follow the clearly flawed judgments of others. Subjects had instrumental motives to conform to the observed behavior of their peers. Specifically, they preferred to minimize the discomfort of dissenting from a public norm over getting the answer right. Muzafer Sherif's experiments (1935), on the other hand, demonstrated conformity in visual tests that were more private, but involved a high degree of uncertainty. Subjects were asked to judge the distance between two electrokinetic flashes of light in a viewer—a distance almost impossible to judge given the lack of any reference points. In these experiments, the answers of others served as a useful anchor for the subject's own answer. In Asch's case, then, subjects conformed *despite* their better judgment; in Sherif's case, subjects conformed *to better their judgment*. The basic difference in these two processes of social persuasion is one that runs through mechanisms of diffusion and divides the two classes in both analytic and substantive ways. Below, I identify and describe three important mechanisms within each class as examples. The three examples described are not exhaustive nor do they operate to the exclusion of any other. Indeed, when one process of interdependence is in operation, it is possible and even likely that other mechanisms will be as well.

Adaptation

In this class of mechanisms, the policy decisions of one government alter the conditions under which other governments make their decisions. Typically, the decisions alter the utility of the policy for others. In this sense, one can think of these decisions as producing externalities—externalities that subsequent adopters must factor into their decision calculus. Thus, actors influenced in this way act *instrumentally* in that they are less focused on the direct benefits of the policy itself. One can imagine any number of mechanisms that might fit under this class. I identify three critical ones below: *cultural norms, support groups,* and *competition.*

Cultural Norms. Norms may be understood as common practices whose value to an actor stems largely from their prevalence in a population. We can think of them almost like network externalities, since the benefits of adopting rise as a direct result of the number—or proportion—of others that adopt them. But exactly what kinds of benefits accompany increases in prevalence? In terms of norms, the predominant benefit is reputational. Joining a growing majority of other actors confers a degree of legitimacy or, in the case of a negatively valenced practice, *cover* from criticism.

The logic behind these factors follows very closely the "tipping," or "threshold," models that Schelling (1978) and Granovetter (1978) have described. The basic intuition is that most actors are highly sensitive to the number, or proportion, of other actors that have adopted the policy. The idea of "thresholds" or "critical mass points" is a useful (although not necessary) device with which to understand the process. Consider an example from Granovetter (1978). An individual faces the decision of whether to participate in a riot. Arguably, the probability that one would participate in a riot increases as the number of participants increases (the logic being that the greater the number of participants the greater the immunity from apprehension).[4] There is

4. Corroborating experimental research from social psychology substantiates the principles of the tipping model. For example, Asch's (1951) work on conformity showed that individuals were much more likely to trust their own information when they had just one or two confederates siding with them. Some safety in numbers is also evident in the Milgram (1975) experiments on obedience.

a certain level of participation, a threshold at which an individual will decide to participate in the riot. Presumably, these thresholds will be different for different individuals. For example, Schelling speculates that, in any given decision, roughly 5 to 10 percent of the population will commit to one choice or the other, regardless of what others decide to do, and the rest are highly dependent, but to different degrees, on the choices of others.

One can imagine countless examples of such threshold behavior. Schelling's (1978) absorbing book runs us through everything from professional hockey players' use of helmets to seminar attendance. What is common to these examples is that an increase in the number or proportion of adopters confers a certain degree of legitimacy, or immunity in cases of illicit practices, upon the potential adopter. My contention is that this dynamic describes the way social norms function with respect to constitutional reform. Consider the case of rights policies. There one sees that a country's propensity to maintain a policy that is viewed negatively in the international community—say, the death penalty—decreases as the proportion of countries with that policy decreases. There are only a small number of countries (e.g., the United States) whose threshold for world approbation is so high that they have, at least to date, resisted the wave of changes. The death penalty is but one example. Other political, civil, and human rights—both subscriptions to, and violations of—should work the same way.

Of course, the tipping effect can go in the opposite direction as well. That is, actors may be tempted to opt out of a practice once a certain number of others have adopted it. This will occur if there is some fear of crowding or a desire for uniqueness. One may imagine that this dynamic occurs with "isolate" nations such as Libya or Cuba. However, while isolate nations may be more comfortable with their uniqueness, it is not necessarily the case that they seek it. Cuba under Fidel Castro, for example, found itself alone only after the cold war. Until then, Castro sought a much more central position in the international community and actively promoted a "tip" in the opposite direction than that which occurred in 1989. Gaddafi's Libya, for its part, has moved away from the margins in recent years, at least with respect to the west.

Support Groups. The number of participants, or adopters, can confer credibility or immunity on a practice. There are other ways—apart from reputation—that the number of users alters the incentives for adoption. As economists who study industry standards have found, users derive practical benefits from a strong network of other users (Katz and Shapiro 1985). The simplest case is that in which the number of users directly increases the value of the product, as in the case of a telephone network in which the greater the number of individuals who subscribe, the more people there are with whom one may communicate. A well-known example of this phenomenon is the story of the QWERTY keyboard. Because of the positive network externalities associated with following the QWERTY standard (that is, access to the growing number of QWERTY typists), typewriter manufacturers failed to adopt more efficient keyboards (David 1985).

However, one can imagine a set of more indirect benefits arising from a strong network of users, benefits that are critical to the choice of institutions. One of these is the increase in technical support. It is well known that consumers of everything from automobiles to computer software are drawn to the technical support benefits accompanying a large network of users. For example, in the social sciences, particular statistical software applications become predominant in part because of the enormous advantages of add-on program code and fixes developed and shared by their large communities of users. Forces of this kind are equally strong in the development of economic and political policies. Policies to regulate capital flow or rules to regulate the powers of the legislature and the president are not especially easy for a government to design and maintain on its own. It is extremely helpful to have a community of users, preferably one with skills and knowledge, who are committed to refining and improving the practice. Adopting countries desire pools of expertise that they can draw on for policy enhancements and ancillary policies. In the case of Brazil (2003), I have shown that these sorts of externalities are important to constitutional delegates faced with designing an electoral system and balancing power between the executive and legislature. Pragmatic policymakers considering political reform are cognizant that they are joining a network of other users on which they will depend for advice and support on maintaining these very same institutions. Like that for cultural norms, the mechanism in the technical support argument follows very closely the dynamic that Schelling and Granovetter set forth in their tipping models. That is, each government will have a certain threshold of the number (or quality) of users, below which it will not be likely to adopt a policy.

Competition. Competition over scarce resources introduces another diffusion mechanism that alters the payoffs of policies for governments. Essentially, one country's adoption of a political or, more likely, economic policy can have a very strong effect on its competitiveness, whether that be for foreign capital, direct loans, a contract to host the Olympics, or any investment or honor. Simmons and Elkins (2004) make this argument with respect to transitions to liberalization in the capital account, current account, and exchange rates, but the same is true of market-enhancing institutions embedded in constitutions. If we assume that governments are interested in attracting capital investment, and we assume that weak protections for property rights or a lax commitment to customary international law increase the price of investing in a country's market, then it is easy to see how the one country's adoption of these constitutional provisions will disrupt the competitive equilibrium of other countries. By strengthening property rights, the price of a country's investment products dips and lures investors away from investments in other countries with higher costs. Ceteris paribus, a government would prefer more investment at home, and so there is some pressure to adopt strong property rights provisions as a result of similar moves elsewhere. Of course, there are clear costs to providing strong property rights, especially the forfeiture of sovereignty, which may predispose a government to restrict rights absent competition. Competitive forces will necessarily compete against these motives. Competition is not commonly considered a type of diffusion or network structure, per se, but it shares the essential qualities that characterize more ideal-typic instances of diffusion.

Learning

The second broad class of diffusion mechanisms concerns the exchange of information or, from the perspective of the adopter, *learning*. In a critical sense, these approaches are quite different from those discussed above. In learning processes, another actor's adoption does not alter the conditions of adopting. Rather, the action provides information about such conditions, including the benefits and drawbacks of adopting. Learning processes, therefore, are utility clarifying, not utility producing.

The premise behind such explanations is that the actions of others are more instructive to the individuals than are their internal drives or needs. The work of social psychologists has done much to substantiate this premise in the last fifty years. Among others, Festinger's (1950) theory of social comparison and Merton's (1968) work on reference groups are prominent statements of this doctrine. Bandura's (1977) social learning theory has been especially useful to diffusion scholars. In Bandura's model, individuals are not equipped with internal repertoires of behavior. Except for the most basic reflexes, actors are almost fully dependent on external models for understanding the consequences of certain actions. Of course, we must assume that governments learn from their own country's constitutional experience as well. In this respect, we should not expect constitution-making bodies to differ from other organizations (see Levitt and March 1988 for a summary of organizational learning theory with respect to direct experience). Indeed, my analysis (Elkins 2003) of the Brazilian constitutional assembly in 1988 confirms that such self-analysis is a large part of the deliberative process. Those same data, however, demonstrate that the experiences of other countries also constitute important lessons for constitutional framers.

How does social learning operate in the context of constitutional design? Under the best of circumstances, policymakers in nation-states learn in the same way social scientists might. That is, they recognize a problem in the organization or execution of service delivery, develop some basic theory about how to solve the problem, review the various solutions available, and attempt to ascertain the effectiveness of these solutions. Such is the "laboratory of democracy," where California can learn from Wisconsin's welfare experiment or from Oregon's health care trials. The same process occurs at the international level. Westney's (1987) account of policy borrowing in Japan during the nineteenth century demonstrates this sort of active learning.

What is interesting about learning, from a diffusion perspective, are the numerous ways it can go wrong. The worldwide constitutional laboratory turns out to be a confusing environment, and inefficiencies develop as a result of some predictable biases and limitations in the learning process. The fundamental problem with social learning at this level is that constitutional actors often have difficulty assessing the consequences of other constitutions. Lawmakers are "cognitive misers" (Fiske and Taylor 1991) as much as anyone else. As boundedly rational actors, they rely on a set of cognitive heuristics to make sense of these sometimes complicated constitutional choices. I describe three important learning patterns (or, rather, biases) that cognitively constrained constitutional engineers follow: information cascades, learning and availability, and learning and reference groups.

Information Cascades

In situations of the greatest uncertainty, actors may have no other information than the knowledge of whether others have adopted the constitutional provision. In this case, framers may reason that they should take advantage of the accumulated wisdom of prior assemblies. The logic is the same that one would use in choosing between two restaurants that are equal in many obvious characteristics: a common decision rule is to choose the restaurant with more patrons. The trouble, of course, is that aggregated decisions can point to what appears to be a clearly optimal restaurant (or constitution, as it were) even if these decisions are the result of a few and important choices by early adopters (who may or may not have had good information).

We can call this sort of problem an *information cascade*. Bikhchandani, Hirshleifer, and Welch (1998) develop a model of this process, which demonstrates that the choices of an entire sequence of actors can depend exclusively on the decisions of the first two or three actors. This can be true not only if the actors are initially indifferent about the choice but also if they are predisposed against the choice of the first three.

Thus, it is conceivable that information cascades will produce convergence toward one constitutional choice even in situations in which actors know nothing other than who has adopted what policy. Of course, in reality actors may try to gather more information than simply who has adopted what provision. Specifically, they may hope to draw inferences about the effectiveness of the various provisions. Again, however, lawmakers are limited by the data available to them, their resources to undertake analysis, and their own cognitive faculties. These limitations encourage a process of learning characterized by a dependence on highly selective samples of policy models. Below, I describe two processes that have predictable diffusion effects: learning from *available* models, and learning from those in one's *reference group*.

Learning and Availability. Individuals often have difficulty retrieving a full sample of information and tend to base their decisions on only those instances that are available to them (Kahneman, Slovic, and Tversky 1982; Weyland 2004).[5] The result is that the choice set of policymakers will be limited to the policies of states that are immediately accessible. Actually, these highly available models bias the learning process in a number of ways. One way, of course, is that the more available the model, the more likely it will be included as a data point in the analysis of alternatives. As such, these models will also be amenable to less scientific methods of analysis by constitution makers who, seeking to legitimate predispositions or conclusions they already hold, introduce these cases as representative examples in a less deliberate, more rhetorical forum.

Another way that a policy's availability can affect an actor's decision is through increased familiarity. Taste—whether it be for food, music, art, or constitutions—is often acquired rather than inherited and individuals have a tendency to prefer laws familiar to them. Such attraction might stem in part from a strategy of risk reduction: familiar choices may appear to be safe choices. However, it is also probable that familiarity breeds appreciation and shapes tastes. As such, surrounding oneself with highly available examples of policy can lead to an appreciation, or at least tolerance, for that constitutional provision.

Thus, a policy's availability can distort the learning process and increase its chances of adoption in another country in a number of ways. In the international arena, which constitutions will be more available than others? One clear expectation is that the experiences of those governments with which one communicates and interacts will be most available. Indeed, the idea that communication among actors transmits ideas is one of the prevailing assumptions in the broad diffusion literature (Rogers 1995). However, it is also likely that the policy of prominent nations will be highly available and, consequently, lawmakers will tend to weight those cases disproportionately. For example, it is likely that for many democratizing countries the United States will be the most available case of presidentialism. So, while the performance, however measured, of presidential systems may be poor in the sample at large, that performance may appear highly functional to those who have difficulty retrieving less-well-known (and less-well-performing) cases of presidentialism.

The most available constitutional models may be those espoused by states who have achieved economic success, or appear poised to do so. Decision

---

5. Kurt Weyland (2004) links this and other cognitive heuristics to diffusion in a very useful framework.

makers will understandably be drawn to such models, sometimes drawing lessons from single cases without any attention to issues of sample size and representativeness. For example, they observe a short period of tremendous success or failure and make projections for the policy based on those early high or low marks. Enthusiasm over the initial success of a single program— for example, the fiscal program Domingo Cavallo designed for Argentina in the early 1990s—can fuel fad-like adoptions. Similarly, a year or so of abject failure can lead analysts to soundly reject any program of its kind. Long-term trends or low-profile cases—both of which are less "available"—will have less of an impact.

Learning and Reference Groups. Actors may pay more attention to some policy models more than others because they are more available. However, they may also prefer policy models from countries that are similar to theirs. In fact, a reliable finding in the voluminous literature on diffusion and social influence is that entities that share similar cultural attributes tend to adopt the same practices.[6] This is true not only of individual behaviors such as teen smoking (Coleman 1961) and voting (Huckfeldt and Sprague 1995) but also of collective behavior with respect to corporations (Davis and Greve 1997), nonprofit organizations (Mizruchi 1989), subnational states (Walker 1969), and indeed nations (Deutsch 1953). Why is this so? One reason is that imitating similar individuals is one of the simplest and most effective cognitive heuristics in the calculation of utilities. Actors negotiating a complex set of political choices regard the actions of actors with perceived common interests as a useful guide to their own behavior. A growing number of political scientists suspect that such shortcuts allow the mass public to negotiate a complicated political world (Brady and Sniderman 1985; Lupia and McCubbins 1998), and it is likely that the same sort of process describes the reasoning of leaders making difficult policy decisions. Rosenau (1988, 359; 1990, 213) posits just such a process, suggesting that decision makers have a strong "cathectic" sense of whom their nation should look like and model their government accordingly.

So which countries are likely to be relevant reference groups? For constitutional designers, the easiest way to identify appropriate reference groups is to compare their visible characteristics. Some of the more visible and defining national characteristics are geographic and cultural: the country's region, the language its citizens speak, the religion they practice, and the country's colonial origins. It follows, then, that lawmakers will align their country's policies with those of geographically and culturally proximate nations.

---

6. As Rogers (1995, 274) states, "The transfer of ideas occurs most frequently between individuals . . . who are similar in certain attributes such as beliefs, education, social status, and the like."

Cooperation

The bottom-right cell in figure 3.1 subsumes a set of network mechanisms in which the actors—either states, experts, or interested constituencies—act collectively in the drafting or advocacy of constitutional law. Generally, the nodes in these networks are nonstate actors who are involved in constitutional design from the demand side. The paradigmatic case is the advocacy network as described in Keck and Sikkink (1998). In the case of constitutional reform, advocacy networks work in much the same way that Keck and Sikkink describe. Indeed, the policy issues in the Keck and Sikkink study—human rights, the environment, and women's rights—are, at least since 1945, central constitutional issues. Rights, more generally, are a natural focus of advocacy networks that are involved in constitutional design, given the orientation of these actors and the large role that rights continue to play in written constitutions. Every constitution currently in force incorporates *some* individual rights (Elkins and Ginsburg 2006). However, which rights are provided and the relative restrictions on these rights varies. Some eighty-six different rights have found their way into constitutions since the promulgation of the U.S. document in 1789 (Elkins and Ginsburg 2006). The provision of rights across time demonstrates some obvious time trends, with the traditional "negative" rights, such as those enshrined in the U.S. Constitution, common to constitutions throughout the last two hundred years. Modern constitutions, at least those written since World War II and the Universal Declaration of Human Rights (UDHR), have included positive rights as well (a practice that Sartori [1962] and others have decried as excessively aspirational). It is quite plausible that, in an environment of active human rights networks, the menu of rights in any given constitution will vary according, in part, to lobbying from rights networks. Lake and Wong's (chapter 7) hypothesis that Amnesty International's favored rights have enjoyed special billing is worth investigating in the context of constitutional design, in which each new assembly is a statement of the relative importance of certain rights.

Alas, networks of activists dedicated to the other political institutions that dominate constitutional debates do not seem to have materialized. In the early part of the twentieth century a number of international societies organized for the promotion of both list proportional representation and preferential voting electoral systems evolved in certain countries in northern Europe. These clubs had very little staying power, not to mention mobilization strength. Electoral system design is a rather technical issue, albeit with enormous effects on representation, and networks whose membership is based on the mass public are likely to be rather thinly populated. David Farrell's (2001) quip in the preface to his primer on electoral systems speaks volumes in this regard: "Pity the poor graduate student who must spend his Friday afternoon dwelling on the details of the droop quota."

From the supply side (that is, the side of state actors responsible for crafting political reform), we can point to a number of cooperative networks. There is, of course, a well-developed international force of legal scholars, political scientists, and other specialists who are employable in such situations. These are members of the "epistemic community" (Haas 1992) who decide both what issues should be raised in a constitution and how these issues should be addressed. In Dahrendorf's (1990) model of state development, the constitutional moment is the "hour of the lawyers," and certainly constitutional assemblies swarm with them. In the United States, the American Bar Association is probably the most active participant in international constitutional design, this despite the fact of the rather domestic character of its principal mission. Some political scientists have played central roles in constitutional design (e.g., Juan Linz, Larry Diamond, Arturo Valenzuela, Arend Lijphart, Matthew Shugart, and John Carey). Andrew Reynolds's (2006) intriguing paper describes the "dirty hands" of our colleagues in some depth. It is difficult to assess the impact of such knowledge-based experts on constitutional reform. Certainly some had direct roles in crafting or shaping constitutions (e.g., Larry Diamond on Iraq's Transitional Administrative Law). Many of them report that, although accorded respect, their testimony went largely unheeded (Reynolds 2006). Furthermore, as we would expect from members of the social scientific community who are actively engaged in research, constitutional consultants are not usually activists. Scholars may be responsive to requests for expert testimony, but given their typically overflowing research agenda they are less likely to be active members of an agenda-setting advocacy group.

Dependency

Given the large variation in power across states, one should expect that hierarchical links among countries would play an important role in constitutional design. Certainly, large lending organizations and hegemonic powers are known to extract concessions with respect to institutional and economic policy reform in exchange for economic or military support. Constitutional design, however, is qualitatively different from structural adjustment in that the former often occurs during moments of intense nationalism and eternal optimism regarding the future of a reconfigured state. Such aspirational moments make concessions to foreign powers unlikely.

Nevertheless, international organizations have developed what are effectively standards for *some* aspects of constitutions (e.g., rights) if not others (e.g., electoral systems). The United Nation's Universal Declaration of Human Rights is a prominent, and probably the most influential, example. Since the inscription in 1948 of its thirty articles, the content of new national constitutions has unmistakably changed (Elkins 2003). The UDHR, for many, represents a convenient menu of rights options—very few countries order items *not* listed on the menu and, increasingly, a great many order every single dish.

Hierarchical influences on constitution making are not always so indirect. Indeed, never is it more obvious as in the case of the constitution drafted during the occupation of the country by a foreign power. In these cases, such as Japan's 1946 constitution and Iraq's 2005 constitution, one would expect that occupying powers would exert substantial influence.

To what degree do occupying states shape the constitutions of their host states? In what follows, I summarize analysis reported elsewhere (Elkins, Ginsburg, and Melton 2008) that suggests that, whatever influence occupiers have on their hosts, the resulting constitutional document bears only a modest similarity to that of the occupying country. To begin with, a majority of occupations do not result in new constitutions. Of the 107 occupations identified in the analysis, forty-two resulted in new constitutions. Given that the median lifespan of all constitutions (seventeen years) is remarkably short (Elkins, Ginsburg, and Melton 2007), it is mildly surprising that existing constitutions would survive the occupation. Whether survival results from the occupying powers' indifference to domestic politics or their deference to local interests is unclear. In the case of Japan, General Douglas MacArthur and the U.S. government insisted on a new constitutional framework, a demand that came as a bit of a surprise to the Japanese. The Japanese reading of the Potsdam Declaration suggested that they could get by with better enforcement of their venerable Meiji Constitution, not its revision and certainly not its replacement (Moore and Robinson 2002, 51). On the other hand, constitutional revision seemed to have the air of inevitability in the Iraqi reconstruction. Transitions to democracy have come to be marked by constitutional change, and it is hard to imagine a U.S. occupying force after 9/11 celebrating a democratic transition without a new slate of fundamental laws.

When host states write a new constitution under occupation do they reproduce the political structure of the occupying power? One can begin to understand this by comparing the content of occupation constitutions to that of the operant constitution of the occupying country, as well as to other available models. Elkins, Ginsburg, and Melton (2008) do so by calculating similarities among constitutions based on a subset of ninety-two variables from the Comparative Constitutions Project.[7] With respect to the Japanese case, the authors compare the MacArthur-commissioned product to the seventy constitutions in the sample that were written in or before 1946, some going back as far as 1789. Strikingly, of the seventy constitutional models in the sample, the 1946 Japanese constitution is most similar to its predecessor, the 1889 Meiji Constitution. If MacArthur and company were aiming to reorient fundamentally the political structure in Japan, it is clear that that did not occur. On

---

7. Elkins and Ginsburg 2006.

the other hand, signs of U.S. authorship are evident as well. After the German 1924 constitution, the Chilean constitution of 1925, and (surprisingly) the Mexican document of 1825, the U.S. Constitution bears the strongest resemblance to the Japanese document. Together, these data suggest the persistence of a local constitutional tradition together with a heavy dose of guest writing.

Turning to the Iraqi 2005 constitution, we again see what appears to be a rather local affair, but this time with no evidence of the occupier's input. In that case, the U.S. document (at least the rights component) bears almost no resemblance to the Iraqi. Of the 534 cases in the data, the U.S. Constitution ranks 422 in terms of similarity to the Iraqi constitution, with a correlation of -0.62. The constitutions most similar to that of Iraq are all relatively recent documents from the developing world, with fourteen of the top twenty most similar ones in Africa, the Middle East, and Central Asia. Of course, much of this has to do with trends in rights provisions. Nonetheless, these findings lead us to be more cautious in assuming the direct imposition of constitutional ideas under conditions of dependency. Even in the extreme case of formal occupation, constitutional design (or at least the results thereof) bears signs of local craftsmanship.

Consequences of Networked Design

If network processes have any causal power (and countless studies attest that they do), then they are worth studying if only for historical reasons. However, just as any medicine that actually works is likely to have equally strong side effects, so too should networks. We have already shown that network-as-structure processes (specifically, diffusion) *may* lead to convergence in policies across the world. Indeed, such an outcome itself prompts researchers to investigate diffusion explanations. However, we have also observed that convergence is only one of several possible outcomes. Conditional (or channeled) convergence is equally probable and even increased heterogeneity, the opposite, is possible. Convergence, then, may or may not follow directly from diffusion.

How do network mechanisms shape societies and how are these societies better or worse off for them? Consider, for now, only the uncoordinated set of network processes (diffusion). It seems natural to speculate about such effects since diffusion very clearly causes states to veer off their normal course. Indeed, mechanisms of diffusion are intriguing (and likely consequential) because they imply that governments are making choices that they would not make if left to their own devices. For some, these "detours" suggest a state subordinate to, or at least constrained by, events occurring outside its borders. Such is the inference of those who speculate about the effects of globalization more generally (but see Evans 1997). However, diffusion, as we conceive it, does not necessarily imply a *weakened* state dependent on external forces. Undoubtedly, diffusion processes imply that external factors influence the decision making of states. However, these mechanisms assume a state responding independently to these factors. Adaptation or learning may influence a state's decisions, but it seems unreasonable to conclude that the state has been eclipsed by these forces.

States, then, may be clearly *autonomous,* but still veer from their normal course in response to external forces. These "detours" from a state's domestic trajectory may well portend important consequences for the quality of state policies. In particular, I see two interesting possibilities. Policy detours may mean that governments adopt suboptimal or inappropriate policies designed for the needs of others. Alternatively, detours may mean that governments adopt policies superior to those they have the resources or knowledge to engineer for themselves. These are two equally plausible possibilities with very different implications. We might lean toward the first conclusion, if only for our cultural preference for creativity and originality over imitation and conformity. However, the second conclusion appears equally plausible, especially after a number of scholars have begun to burnish the image of imitation, emphasizing its utility as a cognitive shortcut for problems whose answers are not always obvious (e.g., Lupia and McCubbins 1998). Imitation, in this light, is not slavish. It is an efficient and effective mode of behavior for policymakers. Thus, we see two distinct possible outcomes. I suspect that, to some extent, these outcomes will depend on the particular mechanism of diffusion, in particular whether such mechanisms are characterized by adaptation or learning.

Why should differences between these sets of mechanisms matter? Consider two factors. First, actors driven by a shift in payoffs (*adaptation*) may or may not develop practices that are suited to their needs. By definition, the actors' focus is not on the merits and outputs of the institutions themselves but on the ancillary benefits associated with adoption of the institution. When their focus shifts from the direct benefits of the policy to these externalities, states are in position to trade off the utility of the policy itself for utility derived from the externalities. In the case of *learning,* however, actors are focused squarely on the merits of the institution. In fact, the desire for a more efficient set of institutions is the very motive for their search through the foreign database of policy alternatives. Admittedly, some of what we call *learning* is hardly scientific. Indeed, some scholars may prefer a more general label for such mechanisms, say "information motives," that does not imply a studied, deliberate decision process. Nonetheless, even through cognitively constrained methods of research, actors may be successful in approximating the results of a more sophisticated methodology. Also, their motive of *improving* their institutions suggests that they will more often than not do better for themselves by searching internationally than they would if left to their own devices.

A second factor that distinguishes the welfare effects of these two sets of processes is the level of commitment associated with the adopted institution. Arguably, institutions work best when there is a firm commitment to their installation. Part of this commitment involves the "internalization" of the principles undergirding the reform. Actors internalize the principles and rationale of the reform when they accept and understand the need for reform, as well as the logic of the reform. Accepting the rationale and the logic of the reform leads to a certain degree of commitment to implementing the reform and seeing it through. This process of internalization is less likely to occur if actors are focused on the instrumental benefits of reform than they are its direct benefits.

Some examples might clarify these effects. Consider a straightforward case of competitive adaptation. In the last thirty years, developing countries have raced to sign a series of bilateral investment treaties (BITs) with capital exporting countries. The treaties—which protect foreign direct investment through a set of guarantees that in turn compromise the sovereignty of host states—seem to result from a process of competition for capital among developing countries (Elkins, Guzman, and Simmons 2006). This sort of "race-to-the-BITtom"[8] effect demonstrates very clearly the trade-off between instrumental network benefits and direct policy-specific benefits. Of course, the benefits of increased investment may well be worth the costs in sovereignty to the developing state, at least in the short term. In the long term, however, as BITs become universal and no longer privilege investment locales, the instrumental benefits of a BIT evaporate while the sovereignty costs remain. This suboptimal outcome is a general result of most adaptive mechanisms when the network benefits are orthogonal to more direct goals of public policy. When adaptive mechanisms—whether in the form of competition, support groups, or cultural norms—are aligned with the direct benefits of institutional designs, the direct benefits of policies will only be reinforced.

In many cases, adaptive and learning mechanisms operate simultaneously (albeit sometimes in opposite directions) and the welfare consequences of the two forces are quite apparent. Consider, for example, the development of welfare policies in U.S. states following the devolution of welfare policies to the states under the Temporary Assistance to Needy Families program. Under this legislation, designed to "end welfare as we know it," states were encouraged to experiment with different methods of transitioning citizens off welfare rolls. As Volden and Cohen (2006) show, this devolution of policy to states did lead to something resembling a laboratory of public policy in which states—albeit in a bounded manner—emulated the policies of states whose experiments had demonstrable success. Equally important, however, was the adaptive effect that the variation in the generosity of the policies had on

---

8. Rob Franzese is responsible for this playful summary of the findings in Elkins, Guzman, and Simmons 2006.

neighboring states. Fearing that they would become magnets for citizens seeking comparably generous welfare benefits, states tended to match the restrictions and cuts that neighboring states placed on benefits (an effect similar to the race to the BITtom). Adoptions elsewhere, therefore, triggered both adaptive and informational mechanisms, with the former pushing states toward goals clearly at odds with the state's more direct policy preferences.

These two examples suggest that some sort of coordination will be desirable in order to avoid the drift to suboptimal outcomes. Such coordination could be organized either horizontally (by states acting together) or vertically (by superordinate jurisdictions or organizations). In the case of BITs, a multilateral solution—provided that countries could solve the collective action problem—seems to be a natural antidote for *apparently* suboptimal bilateral treaties. In the case of welfare policies in the U.S. states, the tendency for states to compete to repel welfare recipients might be appropriately solved by federal intervention. Moreover, although I argue that learning mechanisms do not imply the distortions in outcomes characteristic of adaptive mechanisms, it may well be that severely bounded forms of learning would benefit from international coordination as well. The case of constitutional engineering demonstrates that even in more deliberate environments, learning is subject to the same cognitive limitations that characterize less-studied decision making (Elkins 2003). When learning is channeled (and, thus, impaired), some coordination, instruction, or at least information dissemination is appropriate. Accordingly, the efforts of international organizations to encourage best practices or consult with constitutional assemblies to adapt foreign models effectively makes good sense.

Therefore, we can expect diffusion to have very different implications for social welfare according to the particular mechanism at work. Identifying the mechanisms of diffusion, in this sense, takes on more importance than a simple accounting of historical sources. Indeed, understanding the path to institutional reform tells us much about the probable performance of the reform. With the widespread adoption of democracy and market reforms, albeit with very different degrees of success, such distinctions become increasingly important.

A principal goal of this essay is to identify a useful set of concepts and mechanisms for the empirical investigation of constitutional networks and their effects. A sharper conceptualization is useful analytically, especially in a field in which all-encompassing terms such as "globalization" come to mean everything and, thus, nothing. Analytical precision in this realm is helpful in building theoretical claims about the origins of institutions. This goal is certainly important; I agree wholly with Rustow's (1970) remarks in the context of democratization research that "history is too important to be left to historians." However, in addition to (or perhaps because of) its importance to the political trajectory of states, networks have more than simply historical implications. Networks almost certainly alter the functionality and performance of a state's institutions. The theoretical distinctions I have described go *some* distance toward understanding the direction of such effects. Certainly, the study of these implications should be pushed in more nuanced directions and by more scholars.

PART II

Networks and Collective Action

4

Cutting the Diamond

NETWORKING ECONOMIC JUSTICE

Helen Yanacopulos

Jubilee 2000 (J2K) and Make Poverty History (MPH) have been two of the most high-profile collective action coalitions to emerge over the last decade.[1] Both were intentionally set up to raise awareness around economic justice issues, as well as to increase political pressure on key policymakers on debt cancellation, trade justice, and increasing development aid. Both coalitions have been influential actors in world politics during the last decade. In this chapter, I examine how these two coalitions have been agents of change. The organizational form of J2K and MPH, specifically the *network-of-networks* form, has been successful in bringing together existing organizations such as non-governmental organizations, trade unions, and church-based groups for the purposive aim of collective action.

The key question motivating this chapter is, How did the J2K and MPH coalitions structure themselves to appeal to a wide range of organizational members and publics? To answer this question, we need to examine the evolution of J2K and MPH and see why they should be seen as a type of network. The mechanics in forming the two coalitions—mainly the framing of the issues—was vital in their structure and therefore the relation between the frame and the structure will be explored. Finally, these two coalitions were specifically formed to mobilize collective action and challenge power holders through various means. Thus, my third aim is to look at the influence of these two groups along with their efficacy and place in international governance.

---

1. In this chapter, J2K and MPH are defined as coalitions—an organizational form that is a type of network with higher degrees of formal ties and formal membership, as well as core steering committees and (formal and informal) secretariats.

Networking Economic Justice

Both J2K and MPH originated in the United Kingdom and both scaled up to become international coalitions. In both cases the coalitions were set up with a high-profile mass mobilization campaign in mind. The distinction between coalitions and campaigns is rarely made and it is essential to separate the two. Both coalitions were formed in order to increase political pressure, in the case of J2K around debt cancellation, and in the case of MPH around debt cancellation, trade justice, and increasing development aid. Although the debt cancellation campaign had a time frame between 1998 and 2000, the coalition did not have an end date, and it still exists in the form of the Jubilee Debt Campaign. Similarly, the MPH campaign was intended to run over the course of 2005, and the MPH coalition is still in existence. The purpose of high-profile campaigns is to provide a form of public education and to mobilize people around an issue; campaigning can be part of an advocacy strategy that may support an organization's other work, such as lobbying (Fowler 1997, 14). Campaigns require clear and simple messages and objectives with the aim of mobilizing mass support by using the media to put pressure on decision makers.

The J2K coalition originated through the coalescing of academics and activists in the mid-1990s around the idea of mobilizing public opinion in order to cancel all the unpayable debt of poor countries by the millennium. In 1994, Ann Pettifor and Ed Mayo of the Debt Crisis Network started working with others to build a coalition. In 1997, the Debt Crisis Network merged with the International Confederation of Free Trade Unions, various Christian church-based groups, and a large number of UK-based international NGOs such as Christian Aid and Oxfam, and the J2K coalition was formed.[2]

The J2K UK coalition had over seventy UK-based member organizations and networks, and other coalitions developed in other countries at the same time. The Jubilee International network was composed of sixty national debt cancellation coalitions (most using the Jubilee name). Ann Pettifor, the director of J2K, wrote in her report to the Second Assembly in October 1998: "Although we [J2K UK] are not an official international secretariat, we are recognized as one of the central information points for Jubilee 2000 campaigns everywhere" (Randle 2004, 3).[3] During the 1997–2000 period, the Ju-

2. For a detailed account of the organizational structures of J2K UK, see Clark 2003.
3. The J2K UK coalition was chaired by the then director of the UK charity Christian Aid. Both the steering group and board were elected in July 1997 by the First Assembly and elections took place annually. The assembly was the main decision-making body; while anyone could attend, only those representing organizations could vote or be elected to sit on the board (Randle 2004, 6). Although there were no formal dispute mechanisms, the president and the chair of the board informally dealt with disputes as they arose (27). There were frequently tensions among the secretariat, the board, and the members of the network, generally arising from issues such as fund-raising and decisions taken by the secretariat. J2K UK was intentionally not allowed to publicly raise funds, as some key members thought that this would compete with

bilee International network had a presence in almost all continents. Coordinated actions meant that there was a very successful public campaign. One of the main achievements of both the national debt cancellation coalitions and the international network was that they utilized a network-of-networks strategy. This ability to utilize existing networks of members was essential in scaling up and scaling down the actions of both the national coalitions and the international network quickly and effectively.

During the three years of the debt cancellation campaign to 2000, there were significant international outcomes: the largest petition ever submitted to the G7 up to that time with over twenty-five million signatures,; there were mass mobilizations of millions of people across the world; and debt cancellation was put on the agenda of the G7/G8. In the United Kingdom, the J2K coalition organized a human chain of seventy thousand people that circled the G7 meeting in Birmingham in 1998. During the 1999 Cologne G7 meeting over one hundred billion dollars of highly indebted poor country debt was "forgiven."[4] What was a fairly complex issue became a very public issue, mostly through the organizational structures of the UK J2K coalition and the international network.

After the end of the debt cancellation campaigns, the UK J2K coalition, with a reduced staff and secretariat, continued its lobbying work, providing information and analysis to its members as well as to other J2K national groups. However, the UK J2K coalition was one of a number of groups involved in a meeting that took place in 2003. This meeting was attended by twenty people from ten campaigning NGOs, representatives of the Trade Justice Movement, as well as what was now the Jubilee Debt Campaign. The result of this meeting was that a letter was sent to Prime Minister Tony Blair emphasizing the opportunities for action in 2005 on issues of increasing aid, trade justice, and debt cancellation.[5] By early 2004 interest in the group had grown and the umbrella network for UK NGOs, British Overseas NGOs for Development (BOND), as well as the Stop AIDS campaign had joined the

---

their own fund-raising efforts and would have a long-term negative impact, so J2K UK was dependent on contributions from members. The tensions between the secretariat and the board and membership were outlined by one of the J2K founders who stated that because the secretariat existed before the network, "the staff never really behaved like the secretariat, but acted more like the staff leading a membership-based pressure group" (19). When one member organization was asked whether disaffected members of J2K could quit, she answered that there was a "powerful reason for organisations not pulling out, namely that to do so would go down very badly with one's own supporters and do one's own image a lot of damage" (27).

4. G7 leaders meeting in Cologne in June 1999 agreed in principle to an "enhanced" Highly Indebted Poor Country (HIPC) initiative that would cancel an additional $45 billion of the bilateral and multilateral debt owed by the qualifying countries. This was to be added to the $55 billion already proposed through the Paris Club of bilateral creditors ($30 billion) and the HIPC initiative of $25 billion (Donnelly 2002, 165).

5. The year 2005 was an opportune one for the United Kingdom as the G8 summit was being held in Scotland, the United Kingdom was chairing the Commission on Africa, and it also held the EU presidency. It was thought that the UK government could be more influential with mass support.

group. By spring 2004, forty groups and networks established the Make Poverty History coalition with an interim steering group, and they agreed to a formal structure and terms of references for a co-ordination team and assembly.[6] The focus of this new coalition was a mass campaign during 2005.

MPH followed a similar organizational structure to J2K in that it was comprised of NGOs, church groups, trade unions, and large networks. It was also a coalition that was set up with a primary function of running a campaign. The MPH campaign was launched in London in January 2005 by Nelson Mandela and during the course of the year the UK MPH coalition had over 540 organizational members.[7] Similarly to J2K, MPH coalitions emerged in many countries as did an international MPH network.[8] In April 2005, twenty-five thousand people attended an all-night vigil in Westminster, and 250,000 people marched in Edinburgh on July 2 before the G8 meeting. Half a million people signed up on the MPH website and over eight million white wristbands (the emblem of MPH) were given away or sold during 2005 in the United Kingdom alone. Finally, the Edinburgh march corresponded with the Live8 concerts that were viewed by over three billion people.

The MPH campaign ended in 2005 but the coalition continues and has an extensive membership list of individual organizations as well as large network members such as the Jubilee Debt Campaign, Trade Justice Movement, UK Aid Network, Stop AIDS campaign, the UK Trade Union Congress (TUC), and BOND. The UK MPH coalition, along with the MPH international network, is also part of a much broader coalition—the Global Campaign Against Poverty, also known as GCAP.[9] GCAP was launched in January 2005 at the World Social Forum in Porto Alegre, Brazil, and the national coalitions belonging to GCAP represent more than 150 million people globally in more than eighty countries.[10] The national groups decide their own priorities, but the aims of the international coalition are "to pressure government to elimi-

6. UK MPH was highly decentralized and had a consensual management structure. An evaluation of the MPH campaign found that "regardless of perceived imperfections, the general consensus was that the ways of working delivered results" (Martin, Culey, and Evans 2006, 4). This same evaluation found that there were problems in resolving tensions and taking strategic decisions, as the ad hoc structure placed heavy demands on those centrally coordinating the coalition (what might be called an informal secretariat) (ibid., 4).

7. Although the network had a broad membership base, not everyone was allowed to join. For example, the Stop the War coalition was not granted membership because of its perceived radical views.

8. Not all coalitions call themselves Make Poverty History. For example, the U.S. coalition (and campaign) was called ONE.

9. GCAP has over one hundred national members and there is a clear organizational structure with voting rights biased toward southern regions (http://www.whiteband.org/resources /DocumentAndFile/standup/files.2006-09-28.1138175303). Additionally, between 2005 and 2006, GCAP supporters have taken 53.5 million actions demanding an end to poverty. In October 2006, GCAP claimed the Guinness World Record for the GCAP-organized Stand Up Against Poverty, in which, in one coordinated movement, 23.5 million people in more than one hundred countries around the world rallied during one day (http://www.whiteband.org/ GlobalPages/AboutGcap/en).

10. http://www.whiteband.org.

nate poverty and achieve the Millennium Development Goals [through] Trade Justice, Debt Cancellation, and a major increase in the quantity and quality of aid."[11] Just like the UK's MPH, the white wristband has also become the symbol of the GCAP international coalition. To scale this up even further, GCAP is part of what has been broadly called the "global justice movement," a loose collection of groups and individuals that oppose corporate globalization and aim at what has been termed "economic justice."

Networks as Agents

In the introductory chapter, Kahler offers us two different approaches to networks, networks as structures and networks as actors. The J2K and MPH coalitions most clearly fall into the networks-as-actors approach, formed as a result of desired collective action focused on changing national and international policies through mass mobilization in order to have the maximum impact in the campaigns they fostered. How did these coalitions structure themselves in order to appeal to a wide range of organizational members and publics? To start, it is essential to look at what makes J2K and MPH coalitions. The network-of-networks approach to mobilizing support was certainly one of the strategies of these groups, and framing was a key tool in building coalitions.

Before exploring this strategy, we need to distinguish between different terms used for collective action groups—mainly network, coalition, and movement. J2K and MPH have been called all three and it is important to distinguish what kind of collaborative organizational form they adopted. The term *network* describes a loose organizational structure comprised of voluntary nodes (members) that link to each other and to a core (secretariat) and have come together for a particular purpose. However, while the term network is generally recognizable and is used to describe the J2K and MPH structure, the more precise term for both is coalition. This distinction has been explored by Khagram, Riker, and Sikkink (2002) in their work on transnational advocacy networks, where they distinguish between these three forms. To summarize, transnational networks are the most informal type of configuration, bringing together nonstate actors with shared values and involving, dense exchanges of information and services across country boundaries; their primary aim is to exchange and use information (Khagram, Riker, and Sikkink 2002, 7). Transnational coalitions involve linking members across boundaries to coordinate or share strategies to publicly influence social change, and they require a greater degree of formal contact between members to strategize how to develop a campaign to achieve their aims. Transnational social movements have supporters with a common purpose that can

11. http://www.whiteband.org/Lib/take_action/get_involved/Lib/docs/en_action guide.pdf.

generate sustained social mobilization to publicly influence social change. They mobilize their constituents for collective action through the use of protest or disruptive action and have a high level of transnational collective identity (Khagram, Riker, and Sikkink 2002, 7–8).[12]

These distinctions help identify the organizational form of J2K and MPH as transnational coalitions. In the United Kingdom, both J2K and MPH brought together nonstate actors with shared values that exchanged information and services across boundaries. Additionally, members of J2K and MPH shared strategies with the specific aim of publicly influencing social change. Both J2K and MPH successfully resisted setting up an international secretariat, but in both cases one existed de facto.

Although one problem in the studies of networks has been a lack of precision, it is difficult to make real world networking structures fit neat typologies. These types of organizations can be messy and there are a variety of potential problems in researching networks/coalitions/movements. One such problem is visually graphing these organizational forms when they involve different types of organizations and different scales of networks within networks. Another problem is that while membership information is available for networks belonging to a coalition, this membership changes over time. The key concern in addressing the question of how the coalitions were structured to achieve their collective action aims leads the researcher toward qualitative data analysis instead of network structure analysis. Finally, linking the progression between the different coalitions—J2K, MPH, GCAP—and their place within the relatively recent global justice movement is difficult, particularly as coalitions may morph and join other coalitions. There is both an organizational and temporal path dependence that is challenging to graphically depict.

The Frame of Justice

The process of framing has been well utilized in the transnational advocacy network literature and dates back to the work of Goffman (1974, 1986). Framing is a system of interpreting, understanding, and responding to events. In the context of TANs, the elements of framing include the definition of an issue as being a problem, articulating a blame story, suggesting a solution, and motivating a moral appeal around this problem. Keck and Sikkink (1998, 27) argue that a causal story must be established, so that responsibility for an injustice is obvious and that "the causal chain needs to be sufficiently short and clear to make the case convincing." Frames are not stagnant, but are continuously negotiated. Thus, frames must be broad and inclusive to allow for mass mobilization.[13] In the case of the J2K and MPH coalitions, the importance of

---

12. For a further discussion of this, see Bandy and Smith (2005, 3–4).
13. For more on frames, see Goffman (1986) and Benford and Snow (2000).

framing cannot be overstated as a strategy; the importance of the justice-based frame was essential in building the network-of-networks coalition structure.

J2K's successful reframing of debt as a justice issue contributed to its success in attracting members and supporters (Yanacopulos 2004, 723); similarly, MPH learned from the debt campaign as well as the trade justice campaigners that the message of justice instead of charity spoke to more people. For J2K, the biblical principle of the jubilee (the freeing of slaves and forgiveness of debts every fifty years) was based on ideas of justice. During the two-year period before the J2K coalition started in the United Kingdom, there was a great deal of planning. Ann Pettifor, the director of J2K, recounts the early days of analysis and framing of the debt issue:

> Analysis is something that can build a coalition, and the analysis was not accidental. The analysis was worked on for two years. The working out of the analysis is like diamond cutting. You look at a diamond for two years if you're a diamond cutter. And when you cut it, you cut the problem in such a way as to maximize the reflection of the problem, enabling a lot of people to see themselves in the analysis. When you've done that, you then test the way you've cut this diamond is actually attracting light, is actually reflecting light, is actually credible.[14]

The issue was framed, or "cut," to allow the maximum number of organizations to see themselves in the problem. Thus, the shared goals were developed by the UK campaign—"cancel the debt by the year 2000 in a fair and transparent process for the poorest countries."[15] Before this, debt rarely entered public debate as it was always seen as a complex economic issue; in shifting the focus to injustice, J2K focused on the message that people in developing countries were paying more on the debt than they were paying on health or education. A member of J2K USA argues that the issue of debt was difficult to reframe because ordinary citizens (which the campaigns were appealing to) were ambivalent about repayment, feeling a moral obligation to repay their debts, and expecting the same of others (Collins, Gariyo, and Burdon 2001, 136). Where the campaigners succeeded was in their emphasis on the oppressive nature of the debt as well as its effects on the development of people in those countries owing the debt.

In the mid-1990s publics had to be convinced that debt cancellation was an important goal, and most people had not given debt much thought. Collins et al. (ibid., 136) write "as a global issue, unpayable debt presents more complex challenges than, for example, the banning of landmines. The suffering of those wounded by landmines is vividly clear. . . . As a global public policy issue, debt has proved more difficult." One reason for this is that debt reflects the fundamentally unequal economic and power relations between North

14. Interview conducted March 5, 2003, London.
15. Interview conducted March 5, 2003, London.

and South—debt is more about structural issues that are difficult to convey and challenge (Collins, Gariyo, and Burdon 2001, 137).

MPH benefited from the experience of J2K and also adopted the justice frame. In looking back, it seems obvious that justice would be the focal point of the MPH campaign, as there is a great deal of overlap among the activists in both coalitions. In a sense, J2K (and the trade justice movement) had already done the work on reframing for MPH. MPH also relied on a similar organizational structure to J2K and, arguably, MPH was the natural progression from J2K.

Why was it necessary to shift the focus from charity to justice? One factor has to do with the explanation of the root causes of poverty—mainly that the poor are poor because they are unlucky, victims of their government and corruption. Victimhood inspires a sense of empathy and pity, something that has been used as a fund-raising mechanism for decades. Lu (2000, 262) suggests that charity results from the mistaken conception of distant injustice as "misfortune." An alternative explanation of poverty would be that international structures have caused and perpetuate poverty, and that it is difficult for developing countries and the people who live in them to break out of this poverty. It is an injustice that there is poverty in the world and the way to deal with the injustice is to focus on justice as the message.

Although this was an effective strategy for building a coalition with a broad appeal, it was not problem free; the way that different coalition members have interpreted the frame has led to different courses of action. Thus, the very reason behind the success of these coalitions is also a contributing factor to the fractures and fissures that have occurred. This was most pronounced in the Jubilee International network where a division developed between what became Jubilee South and the remaining national coalitions.[16] Ideological differences became evident and Dot Keet attributes these differences to northern activists still being motivated by "charity," by

> people in rich countries [who want] to alleviate the suffering of the "helpless poor" elsewhere. This may be sincere but it will not end the suffering of the poor as long as it does not tackle the multiplicity of causes of that suffering, which include the roles of their own governments, banks, and other lenders, as part of the sources, and not only the "solvers," of the crisis. (Keet 2000, 466)

Another illustration of the divisions in the international network occurred after the G7 promised 100 billion in debt relief at the G7 summit in Cologne in 1999. One part of the network issued a press release stating that this was a good thing, whereas another part of the network proclaimed this as a defeat,

---

16. The deep divisions that emerged within the J2K international network became evident during the July 1998 meeting in Rome; the formation of Jubilee South—an alternative coalition to J2K—occurred at a conference in Guateng, South Africa, in November 1999, which divided the unity of the network (see Nelson 1997; Collins, Gariyo, and Burdon 2001; Keet 2000).

as not all the debt was being cancelled.[17] The primary divisions revolved around two key points. One was that a debt campaign should not have an end date of 2000 because the North will move on to something else, will have "done debt." The second divisive issue was around debt *relief,* which was seen as a form of charity, and debt *cancellation,* which was based on the principle that debt was not just. A final divisive point within the international network was one of ownership, with criticisms that J2K was a northern campaign imposed on the South.[18]

The MPH coalition also benefited and suffered from the broad and inclusive frame of justice. During the Live8 concerts in July 2005, viewers were repeatedly told that making poverty history was not about charity but about justice. Yet, viewers were shown images of Africa as a helpless continent (relying on pity), instead of more structurally based explanations of why Africa was getting poorer (Yanacopulos and Baillie Smith 2007). Inside the coalition, there are two different assessments of the actions taken in 2005 (Glennie 2006, 258). One group, composed of politicians and those close to them, was pleased with the progress made in 2005. The musician and organizer of the 1985 Live Aid and 2005 Live8 concerts, Bob Geldof, has been quoted as supporting "the G8 agreement 'On aid, ten out of ten. On debt, eight out of ten' while characterizing the G8's language on liberalization as 'a serious, excellent result on trade.'" However, activists were disappointed and frustrated with the lack of progress made by such a high-profile and well-supported campaign: "The policy experts advising the Make Poverty History coalition unanimously agreed that the G8 deal had not met the minimum demands on aid or debt and even the then UK finance minister, Gordon Brown, agreed that the non-outcome of the World Trade Organization talks in Hong Kong, held in December 2005, was 'depressing.' Both groups have been furious with each other" (Glennie 2006, 258). Although the MPH coalition is still operating, there are deep divisions and one key member stated that coalition members are "reluctant to work together."[19]

The Power of the Coalition

Power, or more specifically the influence of this type of coalition form, can be helpful in examining why member organizations join coalitions.[20] Some

17. Interview conducted March 25, 2003, Johannesburg.
18. Interview conducted March 25, 2003, Johannesburg.
19. Personal correspondence, May 10, 2007.
20. Both power and influence are relational. Bachrach and Baratz (1971, 30) claim that they differ in that "the exercise of power depends upon potential sanctions, while the exercise of influence does not." The connection between governance and influence becomes more evident when comparing and contrasting the influence of governance to the power of government. Rosenau (1992, 7) distinguishes the two when he states that "governance is associated with occasions when power is exercised independently of the authority of government." Thus,

key questions include: How is J2K and MPH's influence related to their net-worked structure? What are the advantages and disadvantages of the coalition organizational form in achieving certain aims? What can be learned about the role of these actors in international governance?

In looking at the J2K and MPH examples, there are various advantages to their organizational form. Both campaigns were exceptionally skilled at mass mobilization, scaling up their membership base at very little cost, building on the experience of other campaigns, and moving the debate toward justice. Other actors, such as states, corporations, or international organizations, would not be able to achieve the mass public mobilization to the same degree as these coalitions.

The success of the J2K and MPH coalitions is highly debated. On the one hand, they had a great deal of impact in bringing organizations and individuals together around the issues; however, many argue that this has not actually changed the structures that are causing the problems of poverty, and the high levels of debt, the injustice of the international trade system, and insufficient aid are still issues; that we have not made poverty history.

Even though there are different perceptions of the success of the coalitions, it is undeniable that both coalitions were influential. For example, Collins, Gariyo, and Burdon (2001, 138) characterize it as a turning point when British prime minister Tony Blair, during the G7 summit in Birmingham in 1998, "conceded Jubilee 2000's growing political influence when he reversed an earlier decision and met with British campaign leaders immediately after the rally." By April 1999, all G7 governments had devised proposals for debt cancellation, and although debt cancellation campaigns had existed for a few years, they now became part of the mainstream discussion, reaching a mass audience. An employee from the UK's Department for International Development stated that "it would be fair to say that Jubilee 2000 has staked out a position, requiring much more debt relief than the British government is arguing for . . . it's [Jubilee 2000] been extraordinarily successful."[21] Donnelly (2002, 170) argues that it was the NGOs' persistent advocacy efforts, even before the mass J2K campaigns, that helped push debt cancellation forward at the government and World Bank level, particularly "Swedish, Danish, and British verbal commitments to the need for multilateral debt reduction in mid-1994. The networks then collaborated with the Non-Aligned Movement and the G7 which had adopted positions similar to that of the network, in lobbying and conducting media work on the issue."

Throughout 2005, MPH mobilized over half a million people who wrote letters and postcards to Tony Blair and over eight hundred thousand e-mails were sent through the MPH website that were forwarded to the UK govern-

---

the use of influence would be considered governance, whereas governments, particularly in the national domain, may use other forms of power, such as coercion.

21. Interview conducted July 9, 1999, DFID, London.

ment. The G8 meeting at Gleneagles, Scotland, in 2005, promised to increase international development aid by US$50 billion a year by 2010 and the World Bank, the International Monetary Fund (IMF), and African Development Fund pledged to cancel their share of debt for eighteen but possibly up to forty countries. With respect to trade justice, the EU and the United States did not give up their agricultural subsidies, and the WTO negotiations on services and industrial goods have made things worse for poor countries.[22]

It is unlikely that governments would have made these commitments without the pressure of J2K and MPH. Although the UK government appeared sympathetic to the ideas of MPH and Tony Blair and Gordon Brown were using the same language as MPH, they used the same terms in different ways to that of many campaigners. This caused a problem within the MPH coalition as many activists felt uncomfortable with the coziness between some campaign organizers and Blair and Brown. Hodkinson (2005) argues that "on paper at least, MPH's policy demands on the UK government are fairly radical. . . . The problem, however, is that when these policies are relayed to a public audience, they become virtually indistinguishable from those of the UK government." Hodkinson quotes John Hilary, campaigns director of UK development NGO War on Want, who argues that "this was brought home back in March this year [2005] when Blair's Commission for Africa set out its own very different proposals on Africa but under the identical headlines used by MPH 'trade justice', 'drop the debt' and 'more and better aid'. In return, most MPH members, led by Oxfam and the TUC, warmly welcomed the report's recommendations. African activists and many MPH members have a different view" (Hodkinson 2005).[23]

Although J2K and MPH have influenced the priorities of governments through lobbying and campaigning, there have also been problems. Interpretations of frames have been divisive within the coalitions, which cannot but affect their efficacy. Mass mobilization occurred as a result of these two coalitions, but it is questionable how deep this mobilization actually was.[24] Both J2K and MPH have influenced governments, sometimes just through sheer numbers of supporters and public actions; however, there are also clear cases of government co-option of the language of campaigns, as well as G7

22. www.makepovertyhistory.org.uk/verdict.
23. For the operation of the 2005 campaign, see Hodkinson 2005.
24. Supporters of MPH had a number of actions available to them, but of all the actions available, buying or wearing a white wristband was by far the most popular form of involvement. In a study conducted in early 2006, when MPH supporters were asked "How have you been involved in the MPH campaigns?" 61 percent of respondents said that they wore the MPH wristband. Another 29 percent said they were involved by watching the Live8 concerts on television, 15 percent registered on the MPH website, 13 percent sent an e-mail to a politician, 10 percent participated in an MPH event, 8 percent sent a postcard to a politician, and 2 percent joined the MPH rally in Edinburgh. The preliminary findings of this study imply that many supporters see involvement in MPH as increasingly being equated to wearing a wristband, and little else (Darton 2006, 2). An astounding 29 percent of those who did feel that they had been involved with MPH felt this connection through watching the Live8 concerts.

promises of debt cancellation that have not materialized. It is undeniable, though, that these groups are playing a role in international governance.

The Jubilee 2000 and Make Poverty History coalitions have illustrated how the scaled-up network-of-networks structure can have advantages over other forms of organization in mobilizing publics around international justice-based issues. These coalitions have shown that frames are powerful, that scaling up can be effective but that it is not problem free, and that these coalitions as an organizational form are increasingly prevalent. These two coalitions have shown that influence comes from a vast and diverse membership base. Examining such networks will become increasingly important, particularly in light of initiatives such as the Global Justice Movement, which are becoming more prominent in international politics.

5

Turning to the "Dark Side"

COORDINATION, EXCHANGE, AND LEARNING IN CRIMINAL NETWORKS

Michael Kenney

Much of what we think we know about networks is based on research about legally sanctioned interactions and institutions. Until recently, the teeming body of scholarship on social and organizational networks has largely overlooked the work of researchers that study criminal associations. Perhaps understandably, mainstream scholars have preferred to focus on more accessible networks of affiliation. But in doing so, they have missed an important insight: illicit entrepreneurs exploit network forms of organization to engage in criminal activity, while avoiding government efforts to destroy them. No less than their lawful counterparts, criminals have found networks to be useful for coordinating behavior, sharing information, and building relationships among conspirators. And no less than their conventional colleagues, but with a lot less fanfare, scholars of organized crime have used network analysis to enhance their understanding of these enterprises, illustrating how criminal networks promote collective action in hostile environments.

Today, illicit networks' marginalization in ivory towers and power corridors appears to be eroding. In yet another indication of how 9/11 changed the way we view the world, scholars and policymakers now proclaim that network forms of governance, with their embedded social ties and structural malleability, can be found in legal and illegal enterprises. But if the study of criminal networks is edging toward the academic and policy mainstream, our understanding of these phenomena, victimized by the secrecy of illegal exchange and the politicization of law enforcement and counterterrorism, remains inadequate.

Beyond the methodological difficulties in studying organized crime, scholars have contributed to the problem by creating discrete bodies of literature that, intentionally or not, hinder cross-pollination. Although students of illicit networks have long observed the ways in which criminals exploit networks to engage in collective action, and the collusive relationship that exists between political power and organized crime, international relations scholars and organization theorists have largely ignored these insights. Meanwhile, in spite of a large body of literature on organizational learning, criminal network scholars have not mined this research to deepen their understanding of how lawbreakers acquire information and how they adapt their operations in response to feedback. In dynamic, hostile environments, where criminals and terrorists (see Kahler, chapter 6) face intense pressure from law enforcers, the evolution of illicit networks is a relevant, if understudied, concern.

This book provides an opportunity to explore, and bridge, these fissures. Like other contributors, I study networks to comprehend social phenomena of direct relevance to world politics. In this chapter, I exploit insights from network scholarship to analyze one case ripe for such treatment: Colombian drug trafficking enterprises. In doing so, I aim to validate the analytical value that network theory holds for international relations. Networks matter, both as objects of reality that influence world politics—and as subjects of inquiry that deepen our understanding of that reality.

Why "Colombian" traffickers?[1] Few conflicts more dramatically signal the importance of clandestine transnational actors to American foreign policy than Colombia's decades-old war on drugs. During this protracted struggle, substate criminals have persistently challenged states' ability to prevent their citizens from consuming psychoactive drugs they have declared illegal and stop traffickers from operating, indeed flourishing, within their sovereign shell. Along the way, illicit "economic" networks have emerged as important political actors in world politics, undermining the legitimacy and authority not only of weak states like Colombia but hegemons such as the United States. As the drug epidemic in the United States worsened in the 1980s, fueled by the widespread availability of crack cocaine, politicians and policymakers effectively securitized the issue, insisting that the United States was at war with the criminal networks coordinating the cocaine trade and channeling greater resources toward this effort. Yet the growing involvement of military and intelligence agencies in what was conventionally a public health and law enforcement matter did not prevent criminals in Colombia from smuggling more than enough cocaine to satisfy American consumers.

The evolution of the Colombian drug industry in the face of escalating law enforcement underscores the resilience of network forms of organization in competitive environments. Over the past several decades, Colombian traffickers have evolved from being relatively minor players in the international

---

1. These transnational criminal networks are "Colombian" in the sense that core nodes and network leaders are based in Colombia. However, peripheral nodes are located in numerous countries and network participants represent a variety of nationalities. In this chapter, I use the modifier "Colombian" as shorthand to refer to illicit networks that are often multinational enterprises.

drug trade to becoming major suppliers of cocaine and heroin to world markets. These changes were driven by the rise and fall of organizational networks that responded to environmental pressures while producing, transporting, and distributing illegal drugs. Networks that failed to adapt to local conditions were often removed from the trafficking system by government authorities—or their illicit competitors. Along the way, the structure of the system coevolved with the criminal networks and law enforcement bureaucracies that sustained it. When U.S. and Colombian law enforcers cracked down on the largest, most successful smuggling enterprises in the 1990s, Colombia's industry decentralized as smaller, organizationally flatter "chain" networks arose on the institutional residues of the relatively centralized "wheels" targeted by the state. If chain networks were not as efficient or as powerful as the wheel networks they replaced, they still maintained Colombia's prominent position in the international trade, even in the face of increasingly hostile law enforcement. The power of criminal networks to adapt to ecological stresses by recombining into new organizational forms helps explain the resilience of Colombia's drug industry—and the limitations of state power over these enterprises.

In this chapter I examine the "dark side" of political networks: transnational criminal syndicates that defy government authority. In writing about such a secretive, methodologically challenging subject, I have chosen to focus on the criminals I know best, from having studied them over the past decade. Between 1997 and 2003 I conducted extensive fieldwork in Colombia and the United States, interviewing dozens of law enforcement officials from both countries and a small sample of former traffickers, all of whom were convicted of drug-related offenses and openly discussed their involvement in criminal activity.[2] In a tentative effort to generalize beyond this sole, if surprisingly rich, case I also consider other illicit networks, drawing on insights provided by contributors to the relevant, if traditionally marginalized, literature on this topic.[3]

Corresponding to the interlocking themes of network structure, power,

2. Like all research on criminal networks, my data should be interpreted with caution. Although I have sought to minimize problems with data reliability and informant deception by cross-checking information from my respondents, I do not claim to have eliminated all potential sources of measurement error. Miles Kahler's observation about selection bias among successful terrorist networks is relevant here (chapter 6, this volume). My sample privileges criminal enterprises that were successful enough, at least initially, to receive the attention and opprobrium of state authorities. However, the fact that I interviewed former traffickers in jail, where they were serving lengthy sentences for drug-related crimes, suggests that they made critical mistakes, contributing to their eventual apprehension by law enforcers. In other words, my sample likely underrepresents both the failed criminal groups that never got off the ground *and* the most successful ones that left the business before the authorities caught them.

3. However, readers should not disabuse themselves of the inductive nature of my approach. I make inferences to general theory by "unpacking" one case and drawing reference to others. The generality of my findings will have to be established through systematic comparisons to parallel cases (Padgett 2001, 213).

and evolution that guide this book, my analysis unfolds in three sections. First, I examine secrecy as the driving force behind network structure, highlighting how criminal entrepreneurs exploit strong ties and "structural holes" to manage the concealment-coordination dilemma. Second, I stress the value of political power for illicit enterprises, illustrating how traffickers seek to reduce their exposure to risk and uncertainty by forming social connections with government officials. The ability of criminals to survive hostile law enforcement often depends on their access to political power, what I call the power principle. Finally, I explore how traffickers exploit "weak ties" and flat decision-making hierarchies to share information and adapt to external pressure, demonstrating the power of illicit networks to resist law enforcement crackdowns, while shaping the evolutionary trajectory of the Colombian drug trade.

Secrecy and Network Structure

Whether they exchange drugs, weapons, antiquities, or any number of commodities that command robust demand in black markets, illicit entrepreneurs confront a dilemma based on their competing needs for concealment and coordination (Baker and Faulkner 1993). To protect their operations from exposure by law enforcers and competitors, they must conduct their activities in secret. The need for concealment encourages criminals to minimize personal contact and limit information sharing on a need-to-know basis. Yet, to make decisions, perform tasks, and acquire new ideas criminals must communicate with each other and coordinate their activities. The need for collective action encourages criminals to communicate with colleagues and share sensitive information that could undermine, even destroy, their operations, if it falls into the wrong hands.

Even a cursory review of the literature suggests that criminals specializing in a variety of vices exploit network forms of organization to help them manage the concealment-coordination dilemma. In their study of Chinese human smuggling networks, Sheldon Zhang and Ko-Lin Chin argue that secrecy is paramount, leading some smugglers to segment their workers into ad hoc, task-specific working groups and to restrict information sharing among participants to a need-to-know basis (Zhang and Chin 2002, 757). Jean Marie McGloin shows how loosely coupled street gangs in New Jersey use "cut-outs," or intermediaries, to link individuals and groups within otherwise disconnected networks (McGloin 2005, 622). Similarly, Carlo Morselli demonstrates how one transnational trader opportunistically filled structural holes between nonredundant contacts in the marijuana industry by brokering deals between exporters and importers (Morselli 2001, 205). And numerous scholars have shown how Italian mafiosi and Italian American mobsters rely on strong ties within close-knit family networks to coordinate their activities, while protecting themselves, if not always successfully, from police informants (Albini 1971; Arlacchi 1986; Blok 1974; and Ianni 1972).

Like other organized criminals, Colombian traffickers have found network forms of organization to be useful for facilitating illicit transactions among different groups. Traffickers exploit networks to share information, coordinate activity, and resolve disputes between interdependent groups that perform different services, including processing raw materials into refined drugs, transporting them to consumer countries, distributing them to wholesalers, and laundering profits from drug sales. These networks contain numerous mechanisms to protect participants from unwanted interlopers, reflecting entrepreneurs' concern with operational security. Rather than forming a single corporate hierarchy, participants work in different groups, with their own leaders and decision rules. Within and across these nodes information sharing may be restricted, with workers told only what they need to know to perform their activities. To prevent infiltration by law enforcers and other adversaries, and to limit the damage of penetration when it does occur, entrepreneurs limit contacts between nodes, creating structural holes in the network topology. Entrepreneurs exploit these holes to control the flow of information and resources across nodes and to buffer themselves from direct complicity in criminal activity. They turn to trusted intermediaries and independent brokers to span these holes by connecting different nodes, including exportation and transportation groups or distribution rings and wholesalers, and arranging transactions between them (Burt 1992, 2001; Williams 2001, 78).

Entrepreneurs also rely on social networks, embedded within and across organizational networks, to manage relationships among conspirators. In drug trafficking and other forms of organized crime, where participants lack access to the state's dispute resolution mechanisms, mutual trust is essential (Arlacchi 1986, 198–201). Consequently, traffickers in Colombia and elsewhere often entrust sensitive tasks to those with whom they enjoy "strong," emotionally salient ties—family members and close friends—to protect their operations from theft and police penetration (Granovetter 1973; Centola and Macy 2007). Similarly, network entrepreneurs exploit their participants' strong ties to build social capital, and check misbehavior, among participants. Strong ties allow leaders to recruit people "of confidence" they can depend on to perform illegal activities without harming the enterprise, while increasing the costs of errant behavior by holding loved ones accountable for the actions of wayward employees. Strong ties are a critical resource in Colombian trafficking networks, helping entrepreneurs manage their exposure to risk and uncertainty.

As these examples suggest, the need to maintain secrecy in hostile environments exerts a compelling influence on Colombian trafficking networks, shaping how entrepreneurs exploit strong ties and structural holes to recruit participants, build trust, and share information among conspirators. These network theory concepts, often missing in discussions of international security, help us understand how traffickers engage in collective action in secret settings—and their resilience in the face of state efforts to destroy them.

Wheel and Chain Networks

Viewed from an organizational level of analysis, the Colombian drug trade contains two types of networks, which exhibit distinct coordination patterns and authority relations. The first type, wheel networks, resemble scale-free networks. Both contain relatively few hubs linked to many peripheral nodes, which are themselves poorly connected (Barabási 2002; Watts 2003). However, unlike scale-free networks, wheel networks in the Colombian drug trade are not scalable, for reasons I will describe below.

Wheel networks are built around a hub or core node that coordinates the overall network and peripheral nodes that perform specific tasks, sometimes for different core groups. Core nodes are multitask enterprises. They organize transactions among different nodes; they supply money, equipment, and other resources; they arrange financing for large drug shipments; they resolve disputes among participants; they suborn police, prosecutors, politicians, and military personnel; they gather intelligence about law enforcement activities and criminal competitors. In sum, core nodes serve as the steering mechanism for wheel networks, channeling communication and coordinating relations among nodes. If something goes wrong with a transaction, the core node's ability to monopolize force throughout the network ensures that participating nodes will answer to the core, protecting leaders and investors from theft and other uncertainties (see figure 5.1).

In wheel networks, capabilities are not evenly distributed: core groups, as Phil Williams observes, enjoy a preponderance of "power, influence, and status within the network" (Williams 2001, 72). Not surprisingly, core groups and the entrepreneurs that lead them also enjoy a preponderance of the profits when they crown, or successfully complete, drug shipments. Core group leaders use their resources not only to enrich themselves but to resolve disputes that inevitably arise in illicit transactions and to build redundancy in their operations. Dispute resolution is a persistent challenge for trafficking networks. As clandestine enterprises that operate outside the rule of law, criminal networks cannot rely on written contracts and courts to settle conflicts between disputants (Reuter 1983). Instead, core groups resolve disputes by threatening to exclude participants from future transactions and monopolizing force throughout the network. When peripheral nodes cannot settle a conflict among themselves, core node leaders will be called upon to mediate. The decision of core group leaders is binding on the disputants, and enforced by the threat and, if necessary, use of force by armed actors on their payroll.

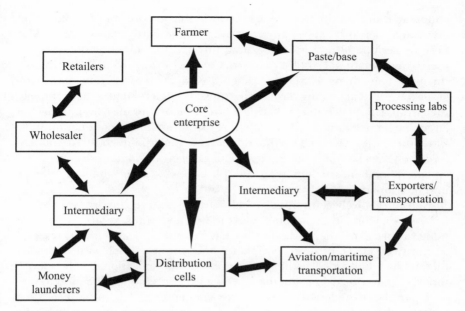

Figure 5.1. Drug trafficking "wheel" network
Source: Kenney 2007.

Core enterprises build redundancy into their operations by exploiting the services of multiple peripheral nodes that perform the same task. Typically, core enterprises based in Colombia transact with different processing labs, transportation rings, distribution groups, and money launderers to avoid concentrating their resources in a single set of service providers. Such redundancy builds network resilience by preventing law enforcers from immobilizing the entire enterprise by dismantling a single transportation route, distribution system, or money laundering scheme. It also increases the power of core groups by allowing them to avoid peripheral nodes that have not accepted entrepreneurs' dispute resolution decisions or honored their commitments from previous transactions.

The core node's power, however, is not absolute. Like the core, many peripheral nodes build redundancy into their operations by transacting with multiple partners. Drug processors, transporters, distributors, and money launderers often provide their services to different, even competing wheel networks, belying the popular notion that a monolithic association, such as the Medellín "cartel," ever controlled Colombian, much less international, cocaine production. Peripheral nodes that transact with different core groups increase their power by maintaining viable delinking or exit options. If a transportation ring or money launderer is unsatisfied with one core node, it may choose to transact with other wheel networks that provide more reliable, and rewarding, network externalities. Although some core groups may seek to prevent peripheral nodes from exiting through the threat or use of force, there is a reputational cost for doing so. Contrary to stereotypes of the bloodthirsty kingpin, many core group leaders are reluctant to use violence too liberally for fear of alienating business partners. Peripheral nodes that complete their transactions without pilfering entrepreneurs' money or putting the larger wheel network at risk often enjoy the autonomy to conduct business with other enterprises. Those that do increase their ability to survive law enforcement crackdowns that target specific core groups. For both core nodes and peripheral ones, maintaining multiple business partners builds resilience into their operations.

Even in relatively centralized wheel networks, where core groups seek to hold service providers accountable for botched transactions, peripheral nodes are largely independent. They have their own leaders, workers, and authority relations. In short, peripheral nodes contain their own corporate hierarchies, embedded within the larger interorganizational network. Although some core groups use the threat of violence and intimidation to prevent peripheral nodes from stealing or cooperating with the police, such coercion shapes relations between *different* organizations, some of which have more capabilities than others. Consistent with Podolny and Page's definition of networks, wheels resemble fluid sets of interdependent groups that "pursue repeated, enduring exchange relations with one another" rather than following a monolithic command structure (Podolny and Page 1998, 59).

However, given core groups' ability to "arbitrate and resolve disputes," wheels ultimately diverge from Podolny and Page's view of networks (ibid., 59). In fact, wheels do not fit the ideal type of networks or hierarchies. Instead, like the terrorist networks examined by Miles Kahler in the next chapter, wheels represent an organizational hybrid, mixing elements of both. Not only do they count hierarchical "organizations" among their nodes, but some nodes, in particular core groups, enjoy the authority to settle disputes that arise during transactions. In secret societies, and in collective action more generally, boundaries between organizations, networks, and markets are often ambiguous. Consequently, we should resist the temptation to reify the three ideal types into "essentialist" categories. In practice organizational networks "combine some of the incentive structures of markets with the monitoring capabilities and administrative oversight associated with hierarchies" (Powell and Grodal 2005, 60). Even as the ideal types prove difficult to apply, the trichotomy remains useful, if only as a heuristic device, because it provides distinct models for thinking about how human beings coordinate their behavior and engage in social relations.

Chain networks, which lack the steering and dispute resolution mechanisms provided by core groups, more closely resemble organizational networks, as understood by Podolny and Page and others (Powell 1990; Keck and

Sikkink 1998). In chain networks autonomous nodes exchange directly with other nodes, sans the mediation and oversight provided by the core. While both wheel and chain networks are organizationally "flat," containing two to four management levels, chains are more diffuse and self organizing than wheels. In chain networks, drug shipments proceed through a series of transactions among independent nodes that coordinate their activities, largely on an ad hoc basis. Over time and repeated interaction, participants from different groups build trust and reciprocity, distinguishing social relations in chains from markets.

Like wheel networks, however, even chains contain hierarchy, both within nodes and throughout the intergroup network. Individual nodes contain a division of labor among participants, with workers that perform tasks on behalf of leaders, whose authority stems from informal, yet collectively agreed on, norms. Nodes may be quite small, with a single boss that directs the group, and one or more workers that carry out his or her orders. But within the group, decisions flow downward and accountability flows upward. In addition, the leader has the authority to resolve disputes among workers. When disagreements arise between separate nodes, chain networks rely on horizontal, if not necessarily peaceful, relations of accountability among relatively coequal nodes. Nodes may seek to solve their differences through negotiation, and some nodes may use coercion to influence others. However, unlike wheel networks, there is no core group that monopolizes violence within the network, exploiting this capability to resolve disputes.

Power is more evenly distributed in chain networks than within wheels. But even in chains some nodes are more equal than others. Without a core group to coordinate transactions between nodes, independent brokerage becomes even more decisive in chain networks. With their ability to bridge structural holes by linking previously unconnected individuals and groups, including transportation specialists and distribution cells, or money launderers and investors, brokers create network externalities. They also enjoy a measure of influence over other nodes. But in chains the power of brokers depends more on their ability to facilitate exchange than to resolve disputes. The most influential brokers maintain the most nonredundant contacts, allowing them to span structural holes and to create entrepreneurial opportunities that other brokers cannot (Burt 2001). The willingness of brokers rich in nonredundant contacts to generate transactions can spell the difference between fantastic profits and financial ruin. Such brokers are rewarded handsomely for their efforts. Conversely, brokers that enjoy fewer nonredundant contacts provide smaller externalities and, by extension, enjoy less influence and affluence within their networks.

The Power Principle

Organized criminals possess an intensely ambivalent relationship with political authorities (Blok 1974, 6). On the one hand, they often ignore the law and seek to avoid or harm government officials intent on disrupting their activities. On the other hand, as illegal actors that operate in hostile environments, they understand the value of political connections and seek to co-opt police officials and politicians willing to protect them. Illicit entrepreneurs may operate outside the rule of law, but they exist within the realm of power. Their ability to remain beyond the purview of law enforcers often depends on their access to resources only authorities can supply. This is the power principle of criminal networks: illicit entrepreneurs' ability to survive hostile environments correlates with their own accumulation of power. Access to political power is essential to illegal networks. Without it they cannot long survive social systems where state security agencies and other competitors seek to weaken them and disturb their operations.

The need for power encourages illicit entrepreneurs to build mutually supportive relationships with state authorities. Entrepreneurs must convince upper-world partners they can fulfill some essential, usually material, need. If there's no reason for officials to cooperate, they will be reluctant to accept the costs that accompany illicit partnerships, even if the risk of detection is low. But criminals do not enter into these relationships empty-handed. In exchange for access to political power, they provide their partners with a range of resources, including money, votes, property, and other enticements. In this manner, underworld criminals establish symbiotic relationships with upperworld authorities. These exchange relationships distinguish organized crime from common delinquency, banditry, even some forms of substate terrorism, where illicit actors' power clashes directly with government authority (Blok 1974, 6). In drug trafficking and other forms of organized crime, entrepreneurs seek to co-opt public officials, exploiting state power to create an alternative political space that tolerates, even supports and legitimizes, their activities.

Criminal network scholars have long privileged the role of power and political connections in their research. In his classic study of organized crime in western Sicily, Anton Blok defines mafiosi as "power brokers" that mediate patron-client networks between national-level politicians and rural peasants. Mafiosi managed the estates of absentee landlords, selling land to local peasants in exchange for electoral support for legislative representatives, who often happened to be the owners of the estates run by the mafiosi. In recognition of the valuable service they provided, urban patrons protected mafiosi "against the demands of the law" (Blok 1974, 177). In his research on organized crime in New York City, Alan Block suggests that the "pursuit of power in one guise or another was the cement holding together under- and upperworlds" (Block 1980, 239). Politicians, labor leaders, and criminals formed opportunistic "alliance networks," allowing them to penetrate local industries, including the garment, restaurant, and waterfront trades, and to neutralize the criminal justice system (ibid., 240). Similarly, William Chambliss shows how a "coalition of businessmen, politicians, law enforcers, and racketeers" ran a prosperous crime network in Seattle that dominated local vices for years, including gambling, prostitution, loan-sharking, and drug distribution (Chambliss 1988, 73). The enterprise was broken, as the power principle would suggest, only after rival politicians gained control of key government positions, such as the county prosecutor's office, and began investigations culminating in the indictment of more than fifty government officials (ibid., 146). So effectively had the illicit network manipulated political resources to its advantage, undermining the authority of city and state institutions, that it took a fundamental change in the distribution of political power to destroy the coalition.

Knowingly or not, drug traffickers in different countries and time periods also follow the power principle of criminal networks. Illicit entrepreneurs establish mutually supportive relationships with public officials so they can pursue their trade with minimal interference from honest authorities, enhancing their ability to survive otherwise hostile settings. In Imperial China, personal connections to state officials were essential for opium traffickers, particularly after the government formally banned the drug trade early in the twentieth century. Although the shift to opium prohibition did not create vice markets in China, it did generate a new business climate in which "illicit entrepreneurs and criminal gangs" gradually replaced traditional businessmen, according to Kathryn Meyer and Terry Parssinen. Essential to success in the new environment was traffickers' ability to "reach accommodations with men in power" (Meyer and Parssinen 1998, 4–5). Over time, entrepreneurs with strong political connections came to dominate the opium trade by providing money, weapons, and information to their patrons in exchange for political protection and assistance with sundry "business difficulties." Similarly, drug traffickers in San Diego before World War II built webs of influence with "corrupt politicians, law enforcement agents, customs brokers, civil servants, and businessmen, not to mention other professional criminals," observes Jeffrey Scott McIllwain. Smugglers lacking such connections were more vulnerable to police crackdowns and illicit competitors that enjoyed "the proper protection of upperworld allies" (McIllwain 1998, 47–48). To operate effectively in this environment, criminals required access to political power.

Drug traffickers in Colombia have also established relationships with men in power to reduce their exposure to risk and uncertainty. Over the years, many traffickers have cultivated connections with Colombian politicians and state officials to help them avoid or co-opt those intent on disrupting their activities. Although drug prohibition did not create organized crime in Colombia, police pressure did encourage traffickers, like opium smugglers in China, to form ties with officials who were willing to protect their interests or at least tacitly condone their activities. Ironically, the power states wield over illicit networks, exemplified in the spirited efforts of U.S. and Colombian police in the "war on drugs," provides criminals with the need, and the opportunity, to increase the power of their networks by building collusive relationships with upper-world authorities. In this sense, prohibition and counter-drug law enforcement helped transform economic networks into political-economic ones that manipulate state authority for pecuniary gain.[4]

Drug prohibition also generates resources that facilitate networking among lawmakers and lawbreakers by artificially inflating the price of, and the profits from, illegal drugs. Many smugglers have adroitly exploited these resources to form mutually beneficial ties with a range of Colombian officials. In exchange for money, gifts, votes, and lucrative investment opportunities, politicians provide traffickers with social acceptance, political protection, and influence on certain questions of public policy; judges and prosecutors subvert criminal justice proceedings against prominent smugglers; and police and military officials selectively enforce the law and share intelligence about counter-drug efforts with their putative adversaries (Krauthausen and Sarmiento 1991; Betancourt and García 1994).

These exchanges are mediated not through markets or hierarchies but through social networks based on bonds of friendship and norms of reciprocity. Over time and repeat exchange, traffickers and their upper-world partners trade "favors" and build social capital, transforming transient exchanges into enduring relationships, at the expense of larger societal interests that authorities are supposed to serve. Critical to these social networks are the ubiquitous brokers who, for a cut of the action, span structural holes between both worlds (Williams 2001). Brokers include well-connected lawyers and journalists that link traffickers to sympathetic decision makers in the government, influential politicians that connect traffickers to other members of the ruling class and support their interests in the Colombian Congress, and former police and military officials that tie traffickers to old colleagues who are willing to share information about law enforcement operations.

Once intermediaries establish the essential link to upper-world figures, entrepreneurs may rely on *plata* (money) and personal rapport to fortify the connection. However, they willingly resort to the threat—and use—of *plomo* (lead—as from a bullet) to compel their "friends" to provide the necessary favors. In this manner, relationships entered into voluntarily, or even rejected initially, may become coercive if they fail to satisfy traffickers' expectations

---

4. Even in select areas of the Colombian countryside, where until recently the national government ceded its monopoly on force to armed substate actors, drug traffickers followed the power principle of criminal networks, forming alliances with right-wing paramilitaries or left-wing guerrillas that protected their operations from hostile interlopers. In this chapter, my focus is on Colombia's more "governable" urban spaces, where national authorities exert their authority, more or less effectively. However, for discussion of Colombia's larger "war system," see Richani 2002.

of reciprocity. For government officials, and intermediaries themselves, involvement in these social networks is often a hazardous undertaking, replete with lucrative payoffs when things go right, and tragic consequences when they do not.

And things do not always go right in these relationships. In spite of their best efforts, many traffickers have discovered that there are significant limitations to the amount of influence that *plata,* or even *plomo,* can buy in Colombia. Indeed, the country's status as an alleged "narco-democracy" is profoundly misleading. Although many politicians and public officials have willingly lined their pockets with largesse from drug traffickers, they are quick to turn against their allies when their own interests are threatened by the association. After Pablo Escobar was elected as an alternate member of the Colombian Congress in 1982, he was publicly attacked by members of his own party and forced to resign his seat in disgrace. Despite contributing more than $6 million to Ernesto Samper's 1994 presidential campaign, several prominent Cali traffickers were targeted in a police crackdown once their generosity was exposed, creating a sweeping political scandal and subjecting the Samper administration to intense diplomatic pressure from the United States.[5] While Samper struggled to save his presidency, the Colombian police and military, in close cooperation with the U.S. Drug Enforcement Administration, hunted down his erstwhile benefactors. These examples, as Francisco Gutiérrez Sanín suggests, "do not convey the image of a 'narco-state,' but rather a torn and precarious, but no less real, pluralism—different state agencies responding on the basis of varying motivations, to different pressures and interests" (Gutiérrez Sanín 2000, 78).

Flexible Operations, Learning Networks

One of the major themes in the sociological literature on networks is that they facilitate learning. Organizations learn when their participants acquire, analyze, and act on information and experience, changing existing practices or creating new ones (Argyris and Schön 1996; Levitt and March 1988). Learning requires information: if there is no knowledge for participants to acquire and share among their colleagues, learning will not occur. Networks provide access to new information through "weak ties"; they facilitate information sharing through structural holes and flat decision-making hierarchies (Gra-

5. Ironically, around the same time that the Clinton administration, under pressure from congressional Republicans, reacted to the drug money scandal by decertifying the Colombian government in the "war on drugs" and denying President Samper a U.S. travel visa, prominent Democrats and Republicans were allegedly committing their own campaign finance abuses, leading one scholar to suggest that they were implicated in separate political-criminal networks based on extensive patron-client ties among "legitimate" businessmen, fund-raisers, party officials, and politicians. See Liddick 2001.

novetter 1973; Centola and Macy 2007; Burt 2001). This is important in competitive environments where the demand for fast, reliable information is high, as in many of today's legal—and extralegal—business environments.

Although criminals operate in competitive settings that demand rapid information and swift action, the learning abilities of illicit networks have been largely ignored. One possible reason for this is that, unlike the legal business networks studied by Powell and others, criminals do not learn. After all, to protect their operations from law enforcers and competitors, many entrepreneurs compartment their operations, organizing workers in semi-isolated cells and restricting communication within and between them. Given the segmented, clandestine nature of drug trafficking, where information sharing is restricted, there are compelling reasons to believe that smugglers do not learn and are condemned to commit the same mistakes repeatedly.

What students of criminal networks do emphasize is the fluid nature of illegal transactions, where entrepreneurs and organizations interact according to market opportunities and regulatory constraints. In volatile black markets, supply sources and distribution venues change regularly, encouraging the formation of "flexible, adaptive networks that readily expand and contract to deal with the uncertainties of the criminal enterprise" (Mastrofski and Potter 1987, 275). Hence, cocaine trafficking in Progressive Era New York, according to Alan Block, was coordinated by different networks of "criminal entrepreneurs who formed, re-formed, split, and came together again as opportunity arose and when they were able" (Block 1979, 94). Likewise, organized crime in Seattle during the 1960s was dominated by flexible networks of criminals that adapted in response to the city's shifting political currents. When rival politicians and honest officials dismantled the original crime network, another one soon appeared in its place, "more subtle than the older one, less open . . . but in most important respects different from the older one only in the faces that ran the enterprises and shared the profits" (Chambliss 1988, 149). When Chinese authorities outlawed the opium trade in the early twentieth century, smugglers responded by creating clandestine delivery systems, developing new sources of supply, and co-opting politicians that provided protection and resolved disputes (Meyer and Parssinen 1998, 4–5). More recently, immigrant smugglers in Germany, Mexico, and China have adapted to law enforcement pressure by changing their routes, professionalizing their services, and suborning government officials (Heckmann 2004; Andreas 2000; Zhang and Chin 2002). Some scholars assume that police pressure inevitably weeds out inefficient or incompetent criminal enterprises, leaving more capable groups in their wake. Although this may be true in select cases, we should avoid elevating it to a general principle, lest we ascribe teleology where there is none.

Whether such "flexible, adaptive" enterprises foster learning along the lines suggested above has received scant attention. Scholars that have addressed the question have been content to equate behavioral change in criminal networks with "learning," implying that this necessary condition is also a sufficient one. However, there are many sources of change in organizations that have little to do with knowledge sharing and application. These include leadership turnover, group and coalition dynamics, and pressure from powerful external actors (Tetlock 1991, 22–23). Just because an organization has changed a practice does not mean it has learned, in a cognitive or behavioral sense.

In spite of these challenges, my own research on Colombian drug traffickers suggests that some illicit networks do indeed learn. Like other organizations, trafficking groups learn when their participants learn for them: collecting information about their activities, interpreting this knowledge with their colleagues, and enacting these interpretations in practices that produce satisfactory, if not necessarily optimal, results. Traffickers gather information about drug smuggling and counter-drug law enforcement from different sources, including fellow smugglers, the news media, transcripts of criminal trials, and police reports. They interpret information in meetings, social gatherings, and everyday interactions through which participants share past adventures, discuss ongoing challenges, and brainstorm potential solutions. And they change their practices in response to interpretation and experience at virtually every stage of the production, transportation, and distribution of illicit drugs. Processing labs develop better methods for refining cocaine and learn how to recycle acetone and other scarce inputs. Smuggling rings move their transportation routes and switch among different ships, planes, and automobiles to counter government interdiction efforts. Financial consultants develop new schemes for laundering drug profits, exploiting developments in electronic commerce to transfer currency through complex webs of international finance.[6]

Network forms of organization facilitate learning among Colombian drug traffickers. Social networks aid learning by providing entrepreneurs with access to new ideas and innovations, often through weak ties that connect socially distant nodes in the network topology (Granovetter 1973; Centola and Macy 2007, 704). Although strong ties based on kinship and friendship are important for building trust and facilitating high-risk activity, like drug trafficking and terrorism, they are not optimal for diffusing new information among participants. Strong ties tend to contain redundant sources of information, inhibiting the spread of innovations. If close friends "all know the same things," explain Centola and Macy, this "will not help them learn about opportunities, developments, or new ideas in socially distant settings" (2007, 704). This weakness of strong ties applies to drug trafficking, where access to new ideas is complicated by entrepreneurs' need to manage the concealment-coordination dilemma. To protect their activities from unwanted expo-

6. For additional discussion and examples of the trafficker learning process, see Kenney 2007, especially chapter 2.

sure, entrepreneurs prefer to rely on trusted confidants for information. However, entrepreneurs already know most of what their family members and closest friends know about their business. They have little to learn from their strongest ties.

To learn quickly about novel business opportunities, smuggling innovations, and counter-drug law enforcement entrepreneurs need information from people who move in different circles and have access to different information. Weak ties among acquaintances that share few network "neighbors" offer shortcuts to such knowledge (Centola and Macy 2007). Traffickers leverage their own and their participants' weak ties to fellow criminals, corrupt officials, and consultants that "beat a path to their door with new ideas, technologies, techniques, and investment opportunities" (Lupsha 1996, 34). Through such ties entrepreneurs learn about new maritime and aviation smuggling routes, innovations in transportation and communications technologies, such as the use of semisubmersible vessels to transport cocaine in the Caribbean, and ongoing criminal investigations targeting network leaders. This information is vital, providing entrepreneurs with opportunities to improve existing operations and avoid government efforts to disrupt them. The search for such knowledge may be intentional, as when traffickers seek to resolve specific problems, or merely fortuitous, as when they gain useful information through everyday conversations not directed toward criminal ends (Van Calster 2006). What matters in both cases is the strength of traffickers' weak ties, which connects them to nonredundant sources of knowledge and increases the rate at which information spreads in the network (Centola and Macy 2007, 704).

If social networks foster learning through weak ties, organizational networks promote it through flat decision-making hierarchies. This is true of both wheel and chain networks, irrespective of their different coordination patterns and mutual tendency toward compartmentation. In wheel and chain networks, unlike government hierarchies, information flows through relatively few layers of management. Flat decision-making hierarchies limit the number of administrative bottlenecks that can slow information sharing. Flat decision-making hierarchies also limit opportunities for information distortion or suppression because there are fewer managers that, whether due to self-interest or human fallibility, manipulate, misplace, or withhold information from others.

Wheel networks combine the flatness advantage with another: network centralization. In wheels, core groups channel communication between nodes, acting as a central conduit that quickens knowledge diffusion and fosters learning. Peripheral nodes learn from other nodes when core groups propagate information, often through intermediaries that bridge structural holes. However, in wheel networks entrepreneurs exploit brokers to control the flow of information and protect themselves from direct complicity in criminal activity. Core group leaders may not always wish to encourage information sharing, particularly if this increases their exposure to risk and uncertainty. If they decide to restrict information sharing, entrepreneurs will limit the ability of compartmented nodes to obtain new information that could improve their operations. This imposes a significant opportunity cost on enterprises that rely on their adaptability to survive hostile environments. On the other hand, if entrepreneurs allow robust information sharing, they can mitigate the effects of compartmentation by directing intermediaries to span structural holes between nodes, increasing participants' access to new ideas and innovations. In this manner, entrepreneurs' competing needs for concealment and coordination shape learning in wheel networks. Entrepreneurs can influence whether learning remains localized in nodes with direct access to the innovation or experience, or whether these ideas and lessons will diffuse to other nodes in the network.

In chain networks, there is no "kingpin" to steer the flow of information through the enterprise. Communication between nodes occurs laterally, without mediation from a core group. In these networks, the influence of independent brokers is decisive. Brokers that are skilled in spanning structural holes are a primary source of information diffusion—and learning. In connecting socially distant nodes, brokers provide shortcuts in network topology, allowing new ideas to spread faster than would otherwise be possible in chain networks. Similar to core group leaders, they alleviate the impact of compartmentation on information sharing by increasing information flows between otherwise disconnected nodes. Brokers' value as facilitators of learning increases with the number of structural holes they bridge, and the number of transactional opportunities they provide. Brokers rich in nonredundant contacts will have access to more diverse sources of knowledge and exchange and be able to transmit these opportunities faster than less well-connected intermediaries (Burt 2001).

To be sure, brokers and kingpins are not the only sources of nonredundant contacts in chain and wheel networks, and we should not overemphasize their significance as facilitators of learning. Core group leaders and brokers influence, but do not determine, learning in trafficking enterprises. Managers and workers also possess weak ties from their own professional and social circles, including connections to people that work in different nodes or for separate enterprises. By design or happenstance, these people occasionally meet, in social venues or when conducting transactions, where they share information about their activities and local smuggling conditions. In doing so they effectively bridge structural holes, creating opportunities for improving their operations. Arturo, a U.S. distribution manager for a Colombian trafficking network, describes how his group adopted the idea of a "suicide" car (for crashing into police cars conducting surveillance on drug traffickers) by interacting with members of another criminal enterprise: "The suicide car, we learned that . . . from Pablo [Escobar]'s organization. We would share information. We would not share information as to exactly how we did things, but we would share information like, for example, the cars you use."[7] Significantly, Arturo's group was independent from and, in some respects, a competitor to Escobar's enterprise. Yet, contacts between workers from both groups allowed them to share knowledge, with or without the consent of their respective leaders.

The Evolution of Trafficking Networks: From Chains to Wheels and Back Again

If drug traffickers learn, does their ability to modify practices in response to experience account for larger, macrolevel changes in the Colombian drug industry? In evolutionary terms, what explains the development of Colombia's illicit trade and the organizational forms that sustain it: adaptations to local conditions or variation among existing populations generated by environmental selection? After all, the structure of the Colombian drug trade did not crystallize overnight or in a vacuum, devoid of social relations and historical context. Rather, it emerged over time, through interactions among real-world actors that shared ideas and practices. Change has been a persistent feature in Colombia's decades-old drug trade. The industry, and the illicit networks that coordinate it, have coevolved through different periods of activity and organization.

In the 1950s and 1960s, drug trafficking was a minor industry in Colombia.[8] Most of the country's professional smugglers worked in more prosaic black market commodities: coffee, cigarettes, emeralds, whiskey, and domestic appliances. Those that did dabble in drugs took advantage of Colombia's long tradition in export contraband and its geographic location between drug-producing areas and consumer markets to serve as redundant suppliers and transporters of marijuana, cocaine, and heroin for organized crime networks directed in other countries. To perform these services, Colombian entrepreneurs formed small, hierarchical groups based on strong family and friendship ties. These enterprises represented peripheral nodes in transnational wheel networks coordinated by U.S., Cuban, and Chilean "gangsters." Due to their superfluous status, Colombian traffickers enjoyed minimal affluence and power in these operations.

In the late 1960s and early 1970s, a handful of Colombian entrepreneurs began transporting marijuana and cocaine directly to the United States, where it was distributed by family members and friends. Although the amount

7. Author interview with "Arturo" [pseudonym], former drug trafficker, Atlanta, Georgia, August 29, 2000.
8. My evolutionary analysis of the Colombian drug trade draws on historical work by several scholars, including Arango and Child (1984), Betancourt and García (1994), Castillo (1987), Cervantes (1980), Krauthausen and Sarmiento (1991), Roldán (1999), Salazar and Jaramillo (1996), and Thoumi (1995).

of cocaine smuggled by these enterprises was small, often four kilograms or less, their forward integration in the international trade represented a critical juncture in the evolution of Colombia's industry. For the first time, Colombian traffickers developed their own distribution networks in New York, Miami, and other cities, exploiting their social ties to the Colombian diaspora in the United States. In doing so, these entrepreneurs surpassed their traditional role as suppliers for Cuban and U.S. criminals. Colombian traffickers now received a greater proportion of the profits from smuggling ventures, whetting their appetite for additional transactions. They also established ties with local wholesalers, who shared their desire for bigger shipments and better cocaine to satisfy the growing American demand.

These developments laid the institutional foundation for the emergence of Colombia's infamous wheel networks a decade later, during the 1980s. However, like the wheels that would later dominate Colombia's cocaine trade, these enterprises were not new organizational forms, but variations on preexisting ones. Experienced smugglers, sensing lucrative opportunities driven by rising drug consumption in the United States and Europe, diversified their criminal repertoires, expanding first into marijuana trafficking and then into cocaine. In doing so, they drew on the contacts, knowledge, and experience they gained from exchanging other contraband. Enterprising *contrabandistas* discovered that smuggling practices for coffee, emeralds, and later marijuana transferred well to cocaine. The "new" class of cocaine traffickers also developed their own innovations, packing small amounts of the drug in condoms for human couriers to swallow and carry, and hiding cocaine in everything from false-bottomed wine bottles and picture frames to customized bras and girdles. Corruption of public authorities, as in contraband smuggling more generally, was often necessary and therefore common. But given the small size of their operations, traffickers paid off local politicians and police officials with jurisdiction in their area of operations. Different groups contained their own decision-making hierarchies, and relations between groups resembled chain networks. Small-scale traffickers based in Colombia typically purchased several kilograms of cocaine from independent suppliers in Colombia, Ecuador, and Peru and transported them to the United States through human couriers. In the United States, the cocaine was sold to loosely affiliated, but essentially autonomous, distribution groups. Missing from these arrangements were core groups to steer the overall enterprise and fix disputes between different nodes.

This began to change as entrepreneurs secured the contacts and capital to produce, transport, and distribute first dozens, then hundreds, and finally thousands of kilograms of cocaine to the United States. The resources required for such large transactions developed gradually, as traffickers crowned profitable shipments that grew in volume over time. By the early 1980s a number of Colombian entrepreneurs were organizing multi-ton cocaine shipments from South America to the United States and Europe. As the size of their shipments grew, so did their information processing needs and coordination challenges. To manage these increasingly complex transactions, while protecting their investments, entrepreneurs centralized their operations, similar to price-fixing conspiracies in the heavy electrical equipment industry (Baker and Faulkner 1993) and al Qaeda following its decision to target the "far enemy" (Kahler, chapter 6). In the Colombian drug industry, entrepreneurs used their buying power and ability to bridge structural holes to increase their leverage over service nodes, including processing labs, transportation rings, distribution groups, and money launderers. In some cases, entrepreneurs established their own processing labs in Colombia and distribution cells in the United States; in others, they transacted with formally independent groups over which they enjoyed considerable influence. What was common to the emerging wheel networks was their leaders' ability to monopolize violence throughout the enterprise. Entrepreneurs hired former soldiers, policemen, even gang members to do their violent bidding, both to resolve disputes between nodes and to eliminate nettlesome competitors and government officials.

Entrepreneurs also weaved webs of influence with corrupt officials. Predictably, as the size of their criminal operations expanded, so did their economic —and political—interests. Leaders of the most successful wheel networks increasingly found it necessary to suborn not just local authorities but regional and national-level figures to protect their growing operations and to shape public policies of interest, such as outlawing the extradition of Colombian nationals to the United States. A number of entrepreneurs went beyond interest group politics to become political patrons in their own right, financing public works and social welfare programs to win acceptance from their communities and votes for politicians that supported their interests.

Although wheel networks with substantial weak ties attracted people with new ideas, practices, and skills, network scalability was constrained by entrepreneurs' desire to protect their illicit operations. In spite of their best efforts to purchase social acceptance and political protection, core group leaders realized that every new node added to their enterprise increased the chance that honest officials could damage their operations. Although economically desirable, the rapid expansion of network ties was potentially hazardous. Weak ties might provide entrepreneurs access to new information and business opportunities, but strong ties were safer. Savvy entrepreneurs managed the liabilities of largeness by privileging, to the extent that they could, strong ties with dependable family, friendship, and professional connections. While the need for coordination (and information) compelled wheel networks to expand through weak ties, the need for concealment prevented many potential weak ties from linking with well-connected hubs, irrespective of their "preferential attachment" to do so (Barabási 2002). Unlike scale-free networks, the wheel networks that emerged in Colombia were not scalable, at least not to an infinite degree. Scale-free networks may be as prevalent among movie stars, Internet websites, and airline transportation systems as some scholars suggest, but their applicability to clandestine networks that operate in hostile environments, where the need for secrecy often trumps the desire for efficiency, remains uncertain.

Drug trafficking wheel networks may not have been scale free, but they were successful. For much of the 1980s and 1990s, Colombia's drug trade was led by several wheel networks, including the infamous, and misnamed, cocaine "cartels" based in Medellín and Cali, that evolved from earlier contraband smuggling operations. With their ability to coordinate large drug shipments, manipulate state power, and minimize their exposure to risk and uncertainty, wheel networks flourished. Eventually, however, they paid the price for their success, as U.S. and Colombian authorities became increasingly alarmed about their political influence and violent tactics. Following a rash of bombings, kidnappings, and assassinations by the Medellín network in the late 1980s and early 1990s, and Cali traffickers' ill-fated attempt to purchase a Colombian president several years later, the alternative political space entrepreneurs built to protect their operations collapsed, providing earnest law enforcers the opportunity to apprehend their adversaries. Unable to avoid challenging Colombia's political elites or to shield their activities from the pealing bells of public scandal, traffickers destroyed the symbiotic relationship they enjoyed with upper-world allies that supported their activities. In failing to follow the power principle of criminal networks, these entrepreneurs sowed the seeds of their own demise.

In close cooperation with U.S. agencies, Colombian police and military units initiated a series of crackdowns against the Medellín and Cali enterprises. These operations, part of a broader effort that American officials dubbed the "kingpin strategy," exploited wheel networks' centralized structure by attacking their hubs: core group leaders and their closest associates. The strategy produced results. Law enforcers arrested hundreds of suspected traffickers, destroyed dozens of drug processing labs, and seized hundreds of kilograms of cocaine. Most significantly, between 1989 and 1996 law enforcers apprehended or killed virtually all of the Medellín and Cali "kingpins," and degraded their illegal operations.

Rather than destroying the Colombian drug industry, however, the kingpin strategy decentralized it, as dozens of chain networks emerged in the wake of the few wheels targeted by the state. These enterprises were smaller, flatter, and less hierarchical than the wheels they replaced. Individual nodes transacted through ad hoc support networks, sans the mediation and oversight provided by the core. Some chains arose from the institutional residues of the former wheels, while others had been quietly coordinating drug shipments for years without attracting the attention of U.S. and Colombian law enforcers. As Miles Kahler illustrates in the next chapter, al Qaeda underwent a similar metamorphosis in response to the U.S.-led war on terrorism. In both cases, relatively centralized wheel networks responded to increasingly hostile environments by decentralizing their operations, becoming more amorphous—and resilient—than before.

To answer the evolutionary questions raised earlier, the reemergence of chains in Colombia's drug trade was due to organizational adaptation, as surviving criminals adjusted to law enforcement crackdowns by changing their operations, and to environmental selection, as numerous enterprises were removed from the system by police pressure, only to leave smaller, low-profile enterprises behind. A number of chains were led by former wheel network managers that avoided capture. These entrepreneurs drew on their contacts and experience to reengineer their activities. Some apparently learned from the mistakes of their old bosses and downsized their operations to avoid unwanted attention. They reduced the size of their loads, and developed new smuggling routes, communications practices, and money laundering schemes in response to police pressure. Some traffickers formed close ties with different paramilitary organizations and guerrilla fronts that increased their participation in the trade, while others pursued alliances with "new" armed actors that themselves evolved from older paramilitary groups that demobilized in response to government pressure. Like their predecessors, these next generation paramilitaries supplied drugs or protection in their area of operations (International Crisis Group 2007). Corruption remained prevalent, but entrepreneurs directed their bribes toward local authorities, rather than to national politicians and administrators (Bagley 2004). Meanwhile, millions of Americans continued to enjoy ample access to their drugs of choice thanks to the adaptability of Colombian production, transportation, and distribution networks.

Colombian drug traffickers exploit network forms of organization to further their activities in multiple ways, each of which speaks to a different "face" of network power explored in this book. Traffickers use organizational networks to facilitate economic transactions prohibited by national governments, undermining the normative and material power that states enjoy *over* them. They use networks to govern relations, share information, and mediate disputes between nodes, exercising power *within* networks. And they use social networks to span structural holes and learn from fellow conspirators and public officials, increasing the power *of* networks that build trust, reciprocity, and honor among thieves.

At a time when scholars trumpet the virtues of transnational networks in spreading human rights norms, protecting the environment, and promoting international trade, the evolution of the Colombian drug trade provides a sobering reminder that not all networks are engaged in benevolent pursuits. The ability of criminal networks to manage the concealment-coordination dilemma, access political resources, and learn from knowledge and experience helps explain the resilience of Colombia's decades-old trade—and states' limited ability to defeat it.

Change has been a persistent feature in the "recombinatorial history" of this illicit industry (Padgett 2001, 213), which has evolved through different periods of development. The dominant organizational form during each period, to the extent that there was one, reflected the aspirations and capabilities of different social actors operating within environmental constraints and opportunities. During the 1970s, a few smugglers exploited their family and friendship ties to develop their own distribution networks in the United States. Several years and numerous transactions later, some entrepreneurs leveraged their brokerage position and capacity for violence to build large, relatively centralized wheel networks. By the late 1990s, many of these so-called cartels were selected out of the system, only to be replaced by an apparent evolutionary throwback: smaller, flatter enterprises that more closely resembled the chain networks of the 1970s than the wheels they succeeded.

Revealingly, each phase was marked less by "speciation," the birth of completely new organizational forms, than by "sedimentation," the emergence of recombined forms arising "on the shoulders of older historical 'residues'" (Padgett 2001, 215–16). The chain networks of the 1970s emerged from the peripheral nodes of the 1960s, the wheels of the 1980s emerged from the chains of the decade before, the chains of today emerged from the wheels of yesterday. During each period, at least some traffickers learned from those that went before them, drawing on their predecessors' practices, experiences, and mistakes. At the heart of these path-dependent processes stood organic social networks that formed, grew, and folded into larger organizational networks, providing entrepreneurs with contacts, capital, and know-how.

Expressed sequentially, this narrative evokes a sense of progress, and we might be tempted to view the history of the Colombian drug trade in teleological terms, with each new phase characterized by the ascendancy of superior adaptive forms. In fact, however, the evolution of Colombia's trade is marked by the unpredictable process of historical contingency rather than the steady drumbeat of progress (Gould 1989, 283). Wheel networks arose from chains' experiential sediment, but they were not necessarily superior to them. Indeed, wheels contained a critical vulnerability, core node centralization, which allowed U.S. and Colombian officials to attack them successfully, once they mustered the political will to do so.

Chain networks have proven more impervious to head-hunting drug control strategies, fulfilling an ecological niche that makes them well fitted to hostile law enforcement systems. But chains, which contain their own vulnerabilities, do not represent the pinnacle of adaptive superiority, any more than the wheels did before them. Lacking a central node to steer communications and resources, chains often fail to coordinate action and share information efficiently. And without core groups to monopolize violence, they are susceptible to internal theft and other shenanigans. In short, survival in the Colombian drug trade does not demonstrate optimality, neither in form nor function. Many traffickers survive environmental pressures not because they are inherently "smarter" than their predecessors, or because their network forms of organization are superior to markets or bureaucracies. They survive because their adaptations, simple as they often are, are sufficient to keep them out of harm's way, or because bounded police agencies focus limited resources on targets they have already identified, or because (notions of evolutionary progress be damned) they are simply lucky.

Today, organizational networks, buttressed by their participants' social networks, remain a basic feature of the Colombian drug trade. Although some wheels continue to function, chains appear ascendant. These enterprises are frequently less efficient—and less powerful—than the wheel networks they replaced, a striking rejection of the evolutionary ladder of progress, and a victory of sorts for the United States and Colombia in the war on drugs. However, before proclaiming the superiority of law enforcement hierarchies, we should remember that even as the government of Colombia captures more drugs, destroys more drug crops, and extradites more traffickers to the United States than ever before, chain networks stubbornly maintain the country's prominent position in the global drug trade. Nor is there any reason to believe that wheels, or some other network variation, won't (re)emerge as a dominant organizational form in the future. For now at least, criminals' persistent ability to learn ensures that Colombia's illicit industry remains a productive, if not necessarily a progressive, one.

6

Collective Action and Clandestine Networks

THE CASE OF AL QAEDA

Miles Kahler

The organization of sustained, transnational collaboration for political ends is difficult. Many transnational activist networks have been identified, in some cases dating to the nineteenth century. The contribution of their network form to success or failure at sustained collective action is more difficult to assess. Networks are often designated the "most informal configuration of non-state actors," distinguished from other transnational social movements by their lower level of coordination and collective action.[1] Measuring the ability of networks to set international agendas, forge common goals, and coordinate the action of disparate actors in different jurisdictions is an essential first step in estimating the value of network organization in promoting collective action across national borders.[2]

Even before the attacks on New York and Washington, D.C., on September 11, 2001, dark networks—clandestine transnational actors that use violent or potentially violent tactics—had emerged as a neglected and malign face of globalization. In the wake of the 9/11 attacks, claims were advanced for the superiority of networked organizations, particularly when compared to the lumbering, hierarchical bureaucracies of nation-states. Like the international human rights network described by Lake and Wong (chapter 7) or the International Campaign to Ban Landmines, the Colombian drug cartels described by Michael Kenney (chapter 5) and al Qaeda's terrorist network were alleged

1. In a recent survey of transnational social movements, networks are contrasted with coalitions, which are able to coordinate "shared strategies or sets of tactics," and with transnational social movements, which involve "coordinated and sustained social mobilization" across national boundaries. (Khagram, Riker, and Sikkink 2002, 7–8). See also Levi and Murphy 2006 and Tarrow 2005.
2. On the importance of agenda setting in networks, see Lake and Wong, chapter 7, this book.

to be better equipped for the new international environment than conventional governments (Arquilla and Ronfeldt 2001). Observers who praised or condemned the actions of these new networks-as-actors, however, seldom specified how and under what conditions their network characteristics promoted successful collective action.

Investigating Clandestine Cross-Border Networks: The Case of al Qaeda

Transnational terrorist networks are particularly useful objects for an investigation of the sources of successful collective action. Unlike criminal networks, whose collective purposes are obscure, terrorist networks are political in their aims. Because their actions are, by definition, violent and illicit in the eyes of at least some governments, their actions must also be clandestine. These networks-as-actors encapsulate questions posed in the introduction regarding definition, agency, structure, and power:

- Can these transnational actors be defined precisely as networks (in other than the most inclusive sense of network as structure)?
- Under what conditions will networks emerge rather than hierarchies? (The answer to this question is related to the relative success of networks in promoting collective action.)
- What characteristics of transnational networks are most likely to produce successful collective action (defined as establishing common goals and coordinating action to achieve those goals)?
- How does the clandestine nature of these networks affect their structure and strategies?

In providing initial and tentative answers to these questions, one violent and clandestine cross-border actor will be examined in detail: al Qaeda, the entity responsible for the terrorist attacks on New York and Washington, D.C., on September 11, 2001. The analysis and evaluation in this chapter centers on al Qaeda's character and performance as a *network of groups and organizations,* rather than a network of individuals.[3] Al Qaeda and its ability to forge structures of cross-border collective action in pursuit of violent ends have intrinsic importance: the U.S. government and other governments have defined it as a major security threat since the late 1990s. It serves as an exemplar of dark networks that have received increased attention in the new century. Its campaign of terrorist acts in multiple political jurisdictions and its ability to attack the world's dominant military power have also produced claims that

---

3. Using social network analysis, Marc Sagemen (2004) has produced an pathbreaking description of al Qaeda as a network of individuals.

violent transnational networks have become and are likely to remain formidable competitors of states.

Al Qaeda is one representative of cross-border organizations engaged in illicit activities, a class that also includes the criminal networks described by Michael Kenney (chapter 5). Although it may not be typical in every respect, al Qaeda's notoriety has produced more data on its internal operations than can be found for most other clandestine international networks. Unfortunately, that data must be used with great care for two reasons. First, much of the available information derives from unreliable or questionable sources. Given the covert nature of measures taken against al Qaeda and other terrorist groups, available public information is often based on official sources promoting their own agendas and counterterrorist strategies (of which information manipulation may be a part). Even relatively reliable and well-researched sources, such as the *9/11 Commission Report,* contain portraits of al Qaeda that may be based on coercion or torture.[4] Second, given the clandestine nature of al Qaeda and similar networks, an inevitable selection bias results in evaluations of successful collective action: violent attacks against prominent targets are widely reported (even if their authorship is disputed); failures are seldom revealed, unless they result from counterterrorist actions by governments (whose own accounts may be less than reliable). As a result, successful collective action by these networks may be systematically overestimated.

Despite these obstacles and caveats, an assessment of al Qaeda can be undertaken through careful comparison of existing sources. Many of the accounts of al Qaeda are similar in their details; the shortcomings of analysis to date are owed more to a failure to extend network analysis rather than substantial disagreement over sources. Examined as a single case, however, al Qaeda can at best offer a means of hypothesis formation rather than definitive hypothesis testing.

Defining al Qaeda: Network, Hierarchy, and Hybrid

The definition of network offered by Podolny and Page (1998) provides a means for distinguishing among networks, markets, and hierarchies, although boundaries among the three will not always be sharply defined. The level of analysis must be specified clearly. Networks are found at different levels of aggregation: for example, hierarchies of individuals may be networked

4. Hamilton-Hart (2005) provides a particularly scathing review of reports on al Qaeda in Southeast Asia. Gerges (2005) notes that the *9/11 Commission Report* is heavily dependent on the point of view of Khalid Sheikh Mohammed, one of the highest ranking al Qaeda operatives captured by the United States. Since he was likely subject to torture or coercion, his account probably elevates the role of Osama bin Laden and the al Qaeda leadership (and diminishes his own autonomous role in the 9/11 attacks).

to one another. A single entity can therefore combine networks, hierarchies, and markets in a hybrid formation. Hybrid has two different meanings in this context: networks that include hierarchies among their nodes or networks with nodes that wield power within the network through centrality or other structural characteristics. A network with relatively few well-connected nodes (hubs) may introduce hierarchy into the "flatness" and apparent egalitarianism of networked spaces.[5]

Even before the attacks of September 11, 2001, al Qaeda was characterized as a new form of global terrorist organization, distinct from the more hierarchical and spatially confined terrorist organizations that had preceded it in the Middle East. Network was used so loosely to describe this new and threatening entity, however, that some questioned whether al Qaeda—apart from individual terrorists—really existed. As Jonathan Raban complained, "the name al-Qaeda means something different practically every time it's used" (Raban 2005, 23).[6] Even among expert investigators of al Qaeda, portraits of the terrorist organization are often dissimilar. Jason Burke claims that Osama bin Laden and his partners "never created a coherent terrorist network in the way commonly conceived," instead adopting a model that was much more like a "venture capital firm" (Burke 2004, 18). Olivier Roy tags it as "an organization and a trademark" (Roy 2004, 294). Marc Sageman portrays al Qaeda as part of a "global Salafi jihad," which is "not a specific organization, but a social movement, consisting of a set of more or less formal organizations, linked in patterns of interaction from the fairly centralized . . . to the more decentralized" (Sageman 2004, 137). Rohan Gunaratna has an expansive view of the boundaries of al Qaeda's network, but also includes a "vertical leadership structure that provides strategic direction and tactical support to its horizontal network" (Gunaratna 2002, 54). Much of the disagreement among these observers originates in different understandings of networks as applied to al Qaeda.

Al Qaeda's Organizational Life Cycle

The structure of al Qaeda evolved over time in tandem with changes in its strategy and the expansion of its operations. Four distinct periods can be identified. After the Soviet Union announced its withdrawal from Afghanistan in 1989, Osama bin Laden, scion of a well-known and wealthy Saudi family, began organizing a group (then called the Islamic Army) that would become al Qaeda (Benjamin and Simon 2003, 103; Sageman 2004, 37–38). He also began his search for a new target for jihad. In 1990 the organization transferred to the Sudan, which was ruled by an Islamist government. In this sec-

---

5. This is a principal theme of Barabási 2002.
6. Raban also describes a three-part British television series that portrays al Qaeda as a product of the fevered imaginations of neoconservatives and intelligence operatives.

ond period (1990–96), al Qaeda became a formal organization with a small central staff. It promoted a global terrorist network through coalition building and the provision of small-scale seed money and training. Al Qaeda established links to regional terrorist hubs and was able to draw on the skills and resources of a wider network of jihadist groups. Al Qaeda then began a fateful shift in its targets from the "near enemy" (Middle Eastern regimes that were viewed as anti-Islam) and conflicts on the Muslim periphery (such as Bosnia) to the United States, the "far enemy" that had established bases in Saudi Arabia during the Gulf War and then intervened in Somalia. Al Qaeda cultivated its local Sudanese host, but its growing visibility and terrorist activity led to successful pressure on the Sudanese government to expel Osama bin Laden and his organization.[7]

Al Qaeda returned to Afghanistan in a weakened financial state, where it aligned itself with the Taliban regime, offering military support in its conflict with the Northern Alliance. The third period (1996–2001) marked a decisive shift in strategy toward targeting the United States and the West, confirmed in the fatwa of February 23, 1998 that declared jihad against Jews and Crusaders on behalf of a World Islamic Front. This "apogee of the global Salafi jihad" was also the period of al Qaeda's most active and deadly terrorist attacks, against the U.S. embassies in Nairobi and Dar es Salaam (August 1998), the USS *Cole* (October 2000), and New York and Washington on September 11, 2001. The fourth and final, post-9/11 period was marked by U.S. intervention against al Qaeda and its Taliban sponsor; the dispersal, imprisonment, or elimination of much of al Qaeda's leadership; the elimination of its Afghanistan training camps; and severe pressure on its finances and communications. At the same time, terrorist attacks in Indonesia, Europe, and Iraq were associated with "al Qaeda-linked" groups, although the content of those links was often uncertain.

Mapping al Qaeda

Valdis Krebs deployed network analysis to analyze al Qaeda shortly after the 9/11 attacks (Krebs 2002). Using the tools of social network analysis, Marc Sageman has diagrammed the structure of al Qaeda in the 1990s (figure 6.1).[8] Sageman's version of al Qaeda's structure is based on links among individuals. The clusters that he identifies in the al Qaeda network, particularly the Maghreb Arabs and the Southeast Asians, map the organizational and group nodes described by other analysts. Two key structural questions have important implications for the success or failure of al Qaeda and similar illicit, cross-border organizations: the relations of its central organization (what Sageman labels the Central Staff) with the regional hubs in the network and the rela-

---

7. Benjamin and Simon 2003, 123; 9/11 Commission 2004, 60–61; Sageman 2004, 39–41.
8. Sageman 2004, 138.

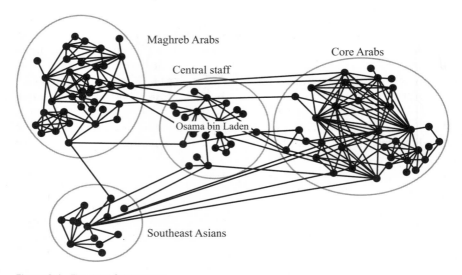

Figure 6.1. The global Salafi network
Source: Sageman 2004, Fig. 2, p. 138. Reprinted with permission of the University of Pennsylvania Press.

tionship of the al Qaeda network to governments and to a wider constituency
of Islamic organizations on its periphery. The first of these questions reflects
on the networked or hierarchical structure of al Qaeda, the second on its
boundaries. Osama bin Laden assembled a core al Qaeda leadership that was
highly capable; many held professional and technical degrees. The core organization was multinational in composition, although members of Egyptian
terrorist organizations, particularly the Egyptian Islamic Jihad (EIJ) of Ayman
al-Zawahiri, played a dominant role.[9] In formal organizational terms, the core
of al Qaeda (Central Staff in Sageman's diagram) was clearly a hierarchy, with
Osama bin Laden as emir, supported by a *shura majlis* (consultative council).[10]
Together the shura and bin Laden set the evolving strategies of al Qaeda. This
leadership oversaw what appeared to be a tidy organization of committees
with different responsibilities that reported to the shura and bin Laden, "a hierarchical, top-down group with defined positions, tasks, and salaries" (9/11
Commission 2004, 67). Hierarchy and the position of Osama bin Laden were
reinforced by sworn oaths of personal fealty (*bayat*) to bin Laden on the part
of some, but not all, of the operational staff.[11] As Sageman points out, however, even the formal organizational core was a "self-organizing group of

9. This Egyptian core formed another network that had known each other and collaborated before the Afghanistan resistance of the 1980s. On the Egyptians and their conflicts, see
Gunaratna 2002, 25–27; Benjamin and Simon 2003, 69–78; Sageman 2004, 25–34.
10. Benjamin and Simon 2003, 104–8; Gunaratna 2002; 89. Burke 2003, 13, labels this
group the hard core of about one hundred individuals from throughout the Islamic world;
many had sworn an oath of allegiance to bin Laden.
11. Coll 2004, 403; see also Gerges 2005, 36–37.

friends and acquaintances" as well as a hierarchy (Sageman 2004, 171). The role of Osama bin Laden himself within the leadership appears to have strengthened over time, but as late as the weeks before the September 11 attacks, he faced resistance from those who felt that the attacks were a mistake (9/11 Commission 2004, 250–52). Gerges, for example, argues that the inner group was a "network riven by ethnic, regional, and ideological rivalries" including "intense struggles between the 'hawks' and 'doves'" (Gerges 2005, 19).

Relations between the central organization of al Qaeda and other regional terrorist organizations—the other clusters in Sageman's diagram—were more clearly networked. Whatever authority Osama bin Laden and the core leadership exercised over the Central Staff, their writ did not extend to the operations of regional groups, particularly those that had a base of support in the local population. Roy labels these (Indonesia, Saudi Arabia, and Pakistan in particular) as subcontractors, who joined with al Qaeda against certain enemies but maintained substantial autonomy (Roy 2004, 321). (Little is known about al Qaeda's links to Saudi jihadist groups.) For these groups—and Central Asian terrorist groups could also be included here—local political dynamics often weighed more heavily than global jihad. For example, Jemaah Islamiyah (JI), al Qaeda's principal Southeast Asian affiliate, was more hierarchical than networked in its internal organization. JI received some financial support from the network as well as important access to al Qaeda training camps in Afghanistan. It retained control of local operations, however, which continued to focus on Indonesia (ICG 2003; 9/11 Commission 2004, 151).

Al Qaeda's organizational form was a hybrid of network and hierarchy in the first sense described earlier—a network that included hierarchical nodes. The inner core or Central Staff was hierarchical in organization, although the charismatic head of the hierarchy did not enjoy unchallenged authority. A network of personal ties also sustained hierarchy at the core. When defined to include its regional affiliates, al Qaeda assumed a clear network form: al Qaeda did not exercise authority over these affiliates and did not claim to resolve disputes among or within them. Its network position was a negotiated one, based on a combination of underlying personal ties, links of funding and training, and strategic network positioning. These were also the sources of al Qaeda's successful collective action.

Al Qaeda and Transnational Collective Action: Explaining Success and Failure

Three features of a network-as-actor explain successful collective action. First, *social networks and embeddedness*. As Sageman's mapping of al Qaeda suggests, networked individuals—linked by ties of friendship, family, or other affinities—provide a crucial support for collective action by social movements. An organization such as al Qaeda may also be embedded in a larger network of related organizations with which it maintains weaker ties, whether the wider community of Islamist or jihadi groups or sympathetic governments. Whether al Qaeda is embedded in a wider Islamic insurgency directed at the United States or is a more narrowly circumscribed, if effective, network is a point of controversy, one that has important implications for its resilience and for counterterrrorist strategies.[12]

Preexisting social networks (and the networked organization itself) may also strengthen collective action through a reinforcement of common identity. The ability of networks to socialize and to create identities is a theme of research in social movements. If behavior follows from identity, according to a logic of appropriateness, then reshaping identity serves to promote collective action. Doug McAdam connects informational network links to identity in a two-stage process of collective action: information alone will not stimulate coordinated action without an "attribution of similarity," in which groups or individuals come to identify with one another, "producing new identities more durable than the incidents that gave rise to them." Based on that shared identity, linked individuals or groups move toward joint action through emulation (McAdam 2003, 294–96).

Second, successful collective action may be based on the *links* within an interorganizational network, links that represent the flow of resources or information. Borgatti and Foster describe two approaches to network ties and their functions, contrasting "a structural, topological approach that tends to neglect the content of the ties and focuses on the patterns of interconnection" with a "connectionist" approach that emphasizes "the resources that flow through social ties" (Borgatti and Foster 2003, 1002). Network effects in the latter case incorporate the material flows that constitute network links. The provision of scarce resources through networks is often a major element in strategies of persuasion or leverage aimed at collective action. Valued resources may also be nonmaterial: firms, for example, may obtain legitimacy or higher status from participation in a network and that resource may have positive, material consequences such as higher stock valuation (Podolny and Page 1998, 64–65).

Information is another constituent of links that has value for collective action, as well as providing networked organizations an advantage over hierarchies or markets. Network forms of organization and governance may influence collective action through the quality of information, information-processing capabilities within networks, and the diffusion of information that illuminates behavioral interdependence. Powell claims that "networks are particularly apt for circumstances in which there is a need for efficient, reliable

---

12. Anonymous (2002, 2004) offers the strongest claims for al Qaeda's position in a wider insurgency; see also Sageman 2004.

information" (Powell 1990, 304). In the case of transnational activist networks Keck and Sikkink have echoed Powell's assertion that networks supply more credible and useful information (Keck and Sikkink 1998, 18–22). A second claim concerns information-processing capabilities: a decentralized (distributed) form of network governance is likely to be more efficient than centralized or hierarchical organizations in information-processing tasks that involve more uncertainty or complexity (Baker and Faulkner 1993, 844). Finally, networks spur collective action through the diffusion of information.[13] Lohmann has modified threshold models of collective action by incorporating a signaling approach in which the revelation of private information may initiate an information cascade and thereby promote collective action (Lohmann 1994). Although Lohmann does not explicitly incorporate networks into her analysis, network links could facilitate information diffusion and cascades more rapidly than the broadcast model of information incorporated in Lohmann's model.

Third, network *structure* also explains successful collective action in cross-border networks. The configuration of network ties between groups and organizations may advance or hinder collective action. Michael Kenney's account of Colombian drug traffickers (chapter 5) presents two different network structures—wheel and chain—that alternate over time, affecting the behavior of network actors and the distribution of power in the network. In the same way, network structure presented strategic choices or dilemmas for al Qaeda that affected the success of networked collaboration. The first is the relative value of weak and strong ties. Strong ties among network members may produce cliques, nodes that display dense links to each other, but few, if any, ties to those outside the clique. This pattern of network formation may appear among groups with "strong ideological and/or cultural affinities" coupled with emotional resonance.[14] Clique formation may promote effective collective action by the clique, but it poses barriers to the widening of action. Nodes with weak ties outside the clique networks may play a critical role in extending cooperation and collective action; those with weak ties may play a disproportionately influential role within the wider network as a result.

Mario Diani (2003a) proposes two strategic alternatives that flow from different network structures. Network leadership or external representation has been related to centrality, defined as the number of ties to other members of the network.[15] Equally important may be brokerage, a less public role (and strategy) of developing linkages with segments of a social movement or wider network that do not have direct communications with one another. McAdam notes that brokerage is more costly in terms of time and entrepreneurial in-

13. On diffusion models of collective action within networks, see McAdam 2003 and Oliver and Myers 2003.

14. On cliques, see Diani 2003b, 307–8; Marwell and Oliver 1993, 123–26.

15. Definitions of the different types of centrality—degree, closeness, and betweenness—are given in Gulati, Dialdin, and Wang 2002.

vestment, but that its effects on collective action, by bringing together previously disconnected groups, will often be much more significant (McAdam 2003, 296). The strategy of brokerage is key in reducing network segmentation, reduction in communication between nodes or actors because of a barrier (Diani 2003a). Segmentation is a particular problem for cross-border networks, whether illicit or legitimate. Although the literature on transnational actors sometimes suggests that border effects have been radically reduced or have disappeared within cross-border networks, such actors must adopt strategies for collective action that attempt to overcome national or ethnic segmentation.

Finally, certain network structures can disguise effective hierarchy. Networks are distinguished from hierarchies by the absence of a "clearly recognized, legitimate authority . . . to resolve disputes among actors" (Podolny and Page 1998, 59). In a highly centralized network with a few hubs that are linked to most of the other nodes, authority may inhere to position, without formal recognition. Authority may also be asserted by means of the leverage created by centrality, particularly betweenness centrality, the "extent to which a [node] lies between other [nodes] in the network" (Gulati, Dialdin, and Wang 2002, 289). As Lake and Wong describe in the case of Amnesty International and the human rights network (chapter 7), nodes (actors) may actively develop and exploit their structural position in the network in order to increase their network power and advance their goals.

Al Qaeda and Collective Action: Setting the Network Agenda

As a prerequisite to collective action by its network, al Qaeda had first to set goals that were accepted by members of the network, goals that those members would act on. The definition of al Qaeda as a purposive or rational actor whose strategy relates means to ends is itself a point of controversy, particularly as its goals took an increasingly expansive, anti-American, and violent turn. The role of U.S. policy in those shifts is contested. Robert Pape (2005), for example, views al Qaeda's strategic evolution as a reaction to U.S. policy, particularly the stationing of U.S. troops in Saudi Arabia and U.S. and United Nations intervention in Somalia.[16] Al Qaeda produced a strategy with "intelligible goals and methods."[17] Roy, on the other hand, contends that "al Qaeda has no strategic vision," and that its anti-Americanism long predates American actions in the Gulf War and Somalia (Roy 2004, 293–94). Others find in its escalation of violence and expansion of goals an apocalyptic vision, one that cannot be placated or appeased by any plausible American action.[18]

Whatever the source of al Qaeda's strategic shifts, they had significant consequences for its network. Its means of exerting influence over the network's

16. "American military policy in the Persian Gulf was most likely the pivotal factor leading to September 11" (Pape 2005, 104).

17. Benjamin and Simon 2003, 119, 156–57; compare to Gunaratna 2002, 45.

18. See Benjamin and Simon 2003, 158; Byman 2003, 147.

agenda ran counter to the approach of legal nongovernmental organizations that mobilized for political influence. For the campaign networks described by Yanacopulos (chapter 4), scalability—the ability of political networks to grow rapidly at relatively low cost without altering the fundamental form of the organization—were central to their political power. For a clandestine and ideologically driven organization such as al Qaeda, rapid increases in network size were undesirable. Over the course of the 1990s, al Qaeda set a new agenda by *segmenting* the existing jihadi network. Rather than expanding the network, the new strategic direction reduced its scale in the short run.

Debates over strategy within the network were not empty discussions. At each step, dissent was apparently voiced and internal consensus had to be built. As the Afghan resistance to the Soviet Union wound down, the first strategic adjustment occurred in a contest between bin Laden's mentor, Sheikh Abdallah Azzam, and the Egyptians who would dominate the new organization. Azzam argued for a global jihad that would move from Afghanistan to defend other Muslim lands that were under attack and eventually to reclaim lost Muslim lands. He rejected violence against Muslim governments (the "near enemy").

At the time of the Gulf War and the U.S. intervention in Somalia, Osama bin Laden redefined this defensive jihad strategy to focus on the "far enemy," the United States. The corrupt rulers of the Muslim lands would be undermined by attacks on their source of support. The shift became definitive in the August 23, 1996, declaration of war against American troops in Saudi Arabia. Although more clearly directed against the United States, this statement retained the priority of expelling foreigners from Muslim lands. The final strategic adjustment came with the February 1998 fatwa against the "Crusader-Zionist alliance," a "manifesto of the full-fledged global Salafi jihad" and an endorsement of the killing of Americans wherever they might be.[19]

Bin Laden's steady escalation of violent ends and his redirection of al Qaeda's energies away from Muslim governments and toward the United States produced conflict within the network. Most of the violent jihadi movement was dedicated to the overthrow of local regimes.[20] When the 1998 declaration abandoned attacks against the "near enemy" of Muslim governments in favor of an intensified global jihad against the United States, members of the EIJ rebelled against al-Zawahiri, who had supported bin Laden's strategic turn. Many ultimately left the EIJ. A parallel revolt occurred within the rival Egyptian Islamic Group (EIG), which had declared a cease-fire with the Egyptian government. Its leader was replaced, even though he retracted his support for the declaration (Sageman 2004, 47).

Evolution in al Qaeda's strategy may have been a rational adjustment to

19. The shifts in the goals of al Qaeda are documented by Benjamin and Simon 2003, 117–18, 140; Sageman 2004, 18–19.
20. This is a major theme of Gerges 2005.

changes in organizational requirements and the international environment. By emphasizing the "far enemy" of the United States and a global jihad, al Qaeda, a relatively small organization without a mass base, was able to distinguish itself from other jihadist organizations. The new emphasis on attacking the United States was also testimony to the failure of attacks on authoritarian Arab states such as Egypt, which crushed its violent Islamist groups in the 1990s. Although the shift in strategy may have been designed to unite a demoralized radical Islamist movement in the face of local defeats, many jihadis opted out of bin Laden's globalized struggle against the United States (Burke 2003, 150; Gerges 2005, 24). Given a lack of hierarchy within the broader interorganizational network, scaling down network size, rather than scaling up, was the optimal means for Osama bin Laden and his associates to retain control of the network agenda.

Social Networks and al Qaeda

Preexisting social networks are often sources of recruitment and commitment to social movements. Al Qaeda benefited from such networks, which formed the core of its leadership and a source of new recruits. One critical early source of personnel were the networks that resulted from a specific historical event: Afghan resistance to the Soviet invasion during the 1980s and the support that it attracted from other Muslim countries. Experience of the Afghan resistance provided solid personal links—a network of militarily trained and politicized individuals—that recalled right-wing nationalist organizations in Europe after World War I. That earlier conflict had produced an even larger group of rootless and restless young men, prone to violence, in search of a cause. Combat experience also produced high levels of trust conducive to network formation.[21]

The Afghan conflict also facilitated the network-in-formation in three other ways. Its veterans possessed military skills that would be essential resources in attracting other groups to the network. The experience of the Afghan conflict also produced "a concrete internationalization" based once again on personal ties that may have been essential for the cross-border network to succeed.[22] This ingrained internationalism at the core provided individuals who could readily serve the brokering function that would be required as al Qaeda linked to other nodes in the evolving network.[23] Finally, the core of veterans provided a link to many of the second generation of al Qaeda recruits. As Olivier Roy describes, the second generation that arrived

21. As testimony to those levels of trust, the CIA reported its inability to recruit a single agent inside the al Qaeda core (Coll 2004, 492).

22. Roy 2004, 300; Zahab and Roy, 49. Afghanistan was a key link among operatives in several terrorist attacks, such as the bombing of U.S. embassies in East Africa (Coll 2004, 403).

23. For example, all of the top leadership of Jemaah Islamiyah trained in Afghanistan during the late 1980s and early 1990s. In those camps, they "developed jihadist fervor, international contacts, and deadly skills" (ICG 2003, i). Afghan "alumni" in JI are given in ICG 2003, 7–10.

in the 1990s and filtered through the camps that Osama bin Laden had established in Afghanistan were not veterans of the anti-Soviet resistance. They rarely came directly from the Middle East; they were "part of the deterritorialised, supranational Islamic networks that operate specifically in the West and at the periphery of the Middle East," members of a *"jihadi* jet set" (Roy 2004, 302–3; Zahab and Roy 2004, 71). Often their first point of contact with the jihadi movement and al Qaeda was one of the Afghan veterans who had returned to his country of origin. Even among these recruits, however, personal ties played an important role: those who joined the jihad tended to join as part of a network of friends or family members (Sageman 2004, 108).

The emerging structure of al Qaeda eliminated the need for large-scale active recruitment. Control over the Afghanistan training camps in the late 1990s allowed al Qaeda to pick and choose among those who wished to join, enabling it to retain its tight web of personal links at the core. The training camps in certain respects re-created the experience of combat in Afghanistan at least for those undergoing "elite" training, building group identity and solidarity (Burke 2003, 154). Al Qaeda's identity as an elite, ideologically motivated vanguard organization was also secured in this way. Its network ties to other clusters of jihadis committed to terrorist action meant that direct recruitment was often a less efficient means of expansion than brokering coalitions or alliances.

Embeddedness and Network Boundaries

Boundaries present a dilemma, particularly for a clandestine network. Scalability may not offer the same political benefits that it provides to licit, nonviolent organizations, but a network linked to other community organizations may provide valuable resources and new members. Networking into state bureaucracies and militaries undermines the network's principal adversary. The risks of penetration and repression by the forces of legal political authority must be set against these potential gains. As in the case of agenda setting, a wider network also brings more conflict over goals and strategy and greater costs of collective action. When calculating the addition of a node to the network, the networked organization must carefully balance the marginal benefit of new resources and recruits against the risk of exposure and less effective collective action. Selecting ideologically motivated individuals and organizations for the network may lower, but does not eliminate, this trade-off.

The boundaries of the al Qaeda network, like many networked organizations, are blurred. Links between al Qaeda and wider Muslim networks, particularly those individuals and groups advocating militant, if nonviolent, Islamist politics, are a controversial boundary issue.[24] For some, al Qaeda's

---

24. U.S. intelligence in the late 1990s, for example, saw the organization as concentric circles with "softer circles of financial, recruiting, and political support" in the outer rings (Coll 2004, 471).

networks are "intertwined in the socio-economic, political and religious fabric of Muslims living in at least eighty countries" (Gunaratna 2002, 10). Other observers who examine the network dynamics of the organization describe an organization of cliques with weak ties to these larger Muslim constituencies.[25] Individuals may have found an initial contact with al Qaeda at a mosque or another community gathering place, but entry into the al Qaeda network meant a progressive loss of bonds to the larger Muslim community. In effect, dense network ties based on identity weakened and erased links to the world outside al Qaeda. The contrast between EIJ (al-Zawahiri's group), which became fully incorporated into al Qaeda, and the EIG, which declared a truce with the Egyptian government in the late 1990s, is telling. The EIG had discovered that local terrorism was fatal to its support within Egypt; the EIJ had become "globalized": neither its target nor its network ties were Egyptian any longer (Sageman 2004, 147–49; Roy 2004, 307–9).

Possible links between al Qaeda's network and governments have also been controversial. Even with its principal hosts—the Sudanese regime of Hassan al Turabi and the Taliban in Afghanistan—al Qaeda's relations were often uneasy.[26] Both of these states were desperately poor, which allowed a network to win favor among their elites using modest financial resources. Al Qaeda also performed a valuable service for the Taliban by taking charge of the "Arab" fighters in Afghanistan, who were widely unpopular among the local population. By late 2001, al Qaeda could ignore the wishes of the Taliban: when Mullah Omar, the Taliban leader, opposed an attack on the United States at that time, his preferences were simply overridden. The Taliban were dependent on al Qaeda for military support against the Northern Alliance and for the planned assassination of its commander, Ahmed Shah Massoud.[27]

Al Qaeda's relations with other governments, particularly Iraq and Iran, were nonexistent or fleeting.[28] Al Qaeda required no state sponsor for its activities. What al Qaeda needed was the absence of a state, at least in its internal manifestations. It required a territorial base from which it could carry out certain organizational functions, particularly training and indoctrination, without restraint. A shell of sovereignty to ward off external intervention made a failed state such as the Taliban's Afghanistan a feasible, though hardly ideal, headquarters. Overall, however, the organization's networked structure

25. Gerges (2005) argues that, in contrast to groups such as the Muslim Brotherhood or Hamas, al Qaeda, "a skeleton of an organization," had "no parallel supporting social, political, or educational institutions" (40).

26. When Osama bin Laden returned to Afghanistan in 1996, for example, he did not enter through territory controlled by the Taliban (Coll 2004, 327). Burke (2003, 164–67) points to doctrinal divisions with the Taliban and a reported plan by the Taliban to turn bin Laden over to the Saudi government in April 1998. (The agreement was overturned after the U.S. missile strikes on Afghanistan in April 1998.)

27. Osama bin Laden apparently claimed that Mullah Omar had no authority to stop al Qaeda's conduct of jihad outside Afghanistan (9/11 Commission 2004, 252).

28. U.S. intelligence believed in the late 1990s that bin Laden maintained links to Pakistani intelligence in order to "coordinate access to training camps for volunteer fighters headed for Kashmir" (Coll 2004, 439).

did not seem to mesh well with governments. Even in the case of weak or failed states such as Sudan and Afghanistan, traditional instruments of corruption appeared more useful than an ongoing and deeper networked relationship. Al Qaeda's network appeared to stop at the boundaries of governments. On this dimension, al Qaeda's behavior contrasted with systematic efforts by drug and criminal cartels to penetrate and corrupt government authority (Kenney, chapter 5). In the trade-off between an embedded network with larger scale and resources, on the one hand, and successful clandestine collective action, on the other, al Qaeda once again tilted toward the advantages of sharper boundaries and smaller scale.

Network Links and Collective Action

The content of network links provides an alternative explanation for the ability of al Qaeda to sustain collective action within its organizational network. Links were primarily resource driven: al Qaeda provided financial and logistical support for terrorist operations as well as training in camps that it established and controlled.[29] Although its financial support has received more attention, access to training camps was the scarce resource that provided al Qaeda its most significant link to network partners, from the Sudan years through terrorist actions planned just before the 9/11 attacks.[30] The use of training camp access as a means to build network ties was later imitated by JI in its Mindanao camps (ICG 2003).

During the years in the Sudan (1990–96), al Qaeda's financing was directed particularly to North African Islamist groups; it was described as the "Ford Foundation of Sunni Islamic terrorism, a grant-giving source of cash for violent operations" (Coll 2004, 269). The level and sources of al Qaeda's financial support were long controversial, but it now appears that two alleged sources—Osama bin Laden's personal wealth and the profits of al Qaeda's Sudanese enterprises—were not significant sources of network resource flows. During the Sudanese years, al Qaeda provided only small-scale finance in any case. Financial resources became even more problematic in Afghanistan: profit-making enterprises could not succeed in that impoverished environment. The major sources of al Qaeda funding became Islamic charities, a target of al Qaeda infiltration, and private donors in Saudi Arabia and the Gulf states. While based in Afghanistan, al Qaeda may have been a subcontractor for Pakistani military intelligence in Kashmir, but there is no evidence that it profited from the drug trade (in contrast to its Taliban allies).[31]

In addition to these links of finance and training to its outer network,

29. Burke (2003, 12) describes the provision of "training, expertise, money, munitions and a safe haven" as the al Qaeda contribution; also Abuza 2002 on al Qaeda's links to JI.
30. Bin Laden authorized the terrorist actions in Istanbul that killed fifty-eight people in November 2003. The leadership of the group that executed those bombings was trained at the Afghanistan camps during the 1990s (Vick 2007).
31. Benjamin and Simon 2003, 143–46; Gunaratna 2002, 62–65, 68.

al Qaeda also provided a "brand," one that was strengthened in the late 1990s by its propaganda and its terrorist acts. Khalid Sheikh Mohammed, principal planner for the 9/11 attacks, was reluctant to engage with al Qaeda until the 1998 embassy bombings convinced him that Osama bin Laden was serious about attacking the United States (9/11 Commission, 149). Osama bin Laden used network strengthening (more operatives, greater financial and logistical support) as a justification for escalating violent attacks against the United States (9/11 Commission 2004, 251). For groups as well, accepting an al Qaeda franchise could offer status and prestige in local jihadist circles, while at the same time increasing the risks of retaliation from local governments allied with the United States. The al Qaeda franchise would become even more important with the destruction of the Afghanistan infrastructure of al Qaeda in 2001–02.

Network Structure, Strategy, and Collective Action

Network structure and its variation over time provide a third explanation for the trajectory of al Qaeda's collective action. Clique formation—the utilization of dense network ties within al Qaeda—has already been noted as a barrier to widening the network. A second characteristic of al Qaeda's position within the wider jihadi network was a form of brokerage, as described earlier. Al Qaeda became a link among groups that had previously been disconnected. A key element in this network strategy was, once again, al Qaeda's training camps, where localized militants could be both trained and inculcated with a transnational vision of Islamist resistance. Throughout its history, al Qaeda demonstrated a key strength of network organization: adaptability. Whether its successive adaptations were ultimately conducive to more successful collective action and to its own survival remain open to question in the post-9/11 international environment.

During the years when al Qaeda was headquartered in the Sudan (1992–96), its networked operations, supported from the center, appeared to produce results: increased global terrorist activity by its network partners.[32] The demands placed on the network were not great, however. The local interests of network partners limited the coordination of terrorist operations. Despite bin Laden's emerging concentration on the United States as a principal adversary, the regional networks continued their efforts at fighting secular Muslim regimes and defending Muslim lands in Bosnia and elsewhere.[33] The degree of formal or centralized structure at the core of al Qaeda was not clear in this period (Gerges 2005, 55). Although large numbers of Islamist militants were reported to train in the Sudan, al Qaeda may not have controlled all of

---

32. As the 9/11 Report makes clear, the al Qaeda role in some of these attacks, including the 1993 World Trade Center bombing, remains unclear.

33. Sageman 2004, 40–41; Burke (2003, 16) notes that the local members of the network were often "deeply parochial."

the training camps (Burke 2003, 133). Reported links between al Qaeda and attacks on U.S. forces in Somalia are open to question: other terrorist groups, such as Egyptian Islamic Jihad, may have been more engaged (Burke 2003, 136). Even the analogy to a foundation in its funding of network terrorist operations suggests that al Qaeda exercised little hierarchical authority over other parts of the network; its brokerage role within the network structure also appeared to award it little leverage over other members. Alliances did not always succeed: the Groupe Islamique Armée, an Algerian terrorist group, reportedly declined al Qaeda's assistance in 1994 because of the degree of operational and ideological control demanded (Burke 2003, 185).

As the United States became al Qaeda's principal target, the organization of network activity changed. The bombing of the Kenyan and Tanzanian embassies was the first terrorist operation that al Qaeda planned and carried out on its own, under the direct supervision of bin Laden and the core leadership.[34] The network form of organization that al Qaeda had developed allowed it a high degree of flexibility, however. Burke notes a continuum in the terrorist actions planned and executed during the late 1990s: from tightly run operations that were conceived by the al Qaeda leadership (1998 embassy bombings) to those operations in which local groups took the initiative on the basis of shared aims but limited links to the network. In other cases, a senior member of the al Qaeda core would organize local operatives for an action (Burke 2003, 179, 194). Burke's analogies to the "Holy War Foundation," a television production company, or a commissioning editor at a publishing house suggest that the degree of direct operational authority (hierarchy) could vary according to circumstances (Burke 2003, 208). For example, the Turkish cell that carried out the deadly 2003 bombings in Istanbul approached al Qaeda in Afghanistan and obtained both financial support and technical advice from the network, even though they declined to pledge allegiance to the organization (Vick 2007).

Despite the flexible and networked strategy in al Qaeda's promotion of collective action, a second pattern also emerged: al Qaeda shifted toward more intensive use of its hierarchical core when its target was the United States. The 1998 terrorist attacks on U.S. embassies in Kenya and Tanzania were directed by the top al Qaeda leadership, as was the attack on the USS *Cole* (9/11 Commission 2004, 67, 190). The 9/11 attacks against New York and Washington, D.C., also involved close supervision and intervention by al Qaeda's leadership, including personal selection of the plane hijackers by bin Laden (9/11 Commission 2004, 235). The September 11 attacks also represented the same mix of human resources, drawing on different parts of the network: senior aides and veterans of other campaigns; the Hamburg cell (three of four pilots), which was similar to other networked but independent groups allied to

---

34. 9/11 Commission 2004, 48; Burke (2003) notes that al Qaeda was unable to co-opt local groups as collaborators in this case.

al Qaeda for access to resources; and finally the young Saudi volunteers who had been least engaged with the network (Burke 2003, 219).

If the leadership of al Qaeda hoped to strike a devastating blow against the United States in September 2001 and maintain their sanctuary in Afghanistan, they made a major strategic miscalculation. What is striking about the planning for 9/11 is the apparent absence of efforts to comprehend or undermine the likely U.S. response: apart from escaping from Afghanistan, the leadership does not appear to have made substantial efforts to disperse key assets such as their training camps. These shortcomings may point to weaknesses in the structure of al Qaeda that produced a near-term failure, even though it had succeeded in carrying out a series of increasingly devastating attacks against American targets in the years before 2001. One of those failures may have been informational: its relatively closed network did not provide it with useful information about the motivations and likely actions of its principal adversary.

Following U.S. intervention in Afghanistan in 2001 and initiation of a global campaign against al Qaeda and its allies, structural decentralization was imposed on the al Qaeda network. The Central Staff was dispersed and in hiding, its key sanctuary and training facilities were lost, and those financial resources that could be reached were increasingly frozen. Most observers saw little chance that al Qaeda could carry out large-scale operations. Terrorist actions linked to jihadist groups since 9/11 have nearly all been aimed at soft (undefended, civilian) targets, and nearly all, including the deadly Madrid bombings of March 2004 and the London bombings of July 2005, appear to have been initiated by local networks (Sageman 2004, 52–54; Burke 2004, 18; Felter et al. 2006, 9).

In many respects, the current segmentation of the network under external pressure resembles the early 1990s, when unaffiliated individuals were able to organize actions (such as the 1993 World Trade Center bombing), with little or no link to a larger group or network (Burke 2003, 94). Al Qaeda may have been reduced to "desperate local affiliates and cells," and what remains of the core is "an ideological label, a state of mind and a mobilizational outreach program to incite attacks worldwide" (Gerges 2005, 40). Using the Internet and other media, al Qaeda has undertaken a broadcast strategy and a franchising of affiliates whose actual network links to al Qaeda are difficult to discern.[35] Al Qaeda in Mesopotamia, which was led by Abu Musab al-Zarqawi, is a prominent case in point: a sometime rival of Osama bin Laden, al-Zarqawi submitted to bin Laden's authority in 2004.[36] What remained was Osama bin

---

35. For the post-9/11 structure of al Qaeda, see the authors in Greenberg 2005.

36. A revived faction of the Egyptian group, Gamaa Islamiyah, was also claimed for al Qaeda in August 2006 ("Egyptian Militant Group Joins al Qaeda," http://online.wsj.com/article/SB115480925496527975.html). In January 2007, the Salafist Group for Preaching and Combat changed its name to al Qaeda in the Maghreb, claiming that Osama bin Laden had ordered the change.

Laden's propaganda appeal to a larger insurgent movement and the threat that the unique organizational structure of al Qaeda could be rebuilt or imitated, a threat that resides both in failed or fragile states, where terrorist training can be resumed (in particular, Iraq and Pakistan), and in the dispersed communities of globalized Islam, the source of most localized post-9/11 terrorist acts.

Al Qaeda as a Clandestine Network

If transnational collective action is difficult for open political networks, it is even more challenging for clandestine networks. The clandestine character of cross-border networks shapes both structure and strategy. As described earlier, the risk of exposure to legitimate political authority circumscribes the extent of the network, reduces its embeddedness in more extensive networks, and raises the bar for establishing trust among its members. The transfer of resources through network links is also taxed by countermeasures of scrutiny and repression by governments.

Clandestinity also imposes a choice between avoiding disclosure and the complexity of tasks undertaken by the network. In their classic study of clandestine price-fixing networks, Wayne E. Baker and Robert R. Faulkner posit a tension between the efficient accomplishment of tasks and the demands of secrecy. Concealment of illicit activities usually points toward "sparse and decentralized networks" that permit the evasion of scrutiny by law enforcement. Efficient planning and execution of "difficult, complex, and ambiguous tasks" in secret requires centralization, however.[37] This prediction is matched by al Qaeda's embrace of greater centralization and hierarchy in tandem with its strategic turn toward its "far enemy," the United States. Such operational requirements carry with them much greater risk for those at the center of the network, as bin Laden and the core leadership would discover after September 11, 2001.

Al Qaeda demonstrated a crucial distinction between terrorist networks and other clandestine networks, particularly the criminal networks described by Michael Kenney in chapter 5: criminal networks, like price-fixing conspiracies, thrive on complete secrecy. In contrast to criminal networks, terrorist networks confront a steep trade-off between the need for political communication and publicity on the one hand and their requirements of secrecy and concealment on the other. Secrecy is essential for some terrorist activities, but terrorist networks require publicity for political success. A completely clandestine terrorist network would fail. The al Qaeda network had never been a master of covert activity, often acting in ways that reflected personal network

37. Baker and Faulkner 1993, 854–56. This finding runs counter to original predictions based on research on secret societies and small-group/organizational theory.

ties rather than the ethos of a professional underground organization (Roy 2004, 322). Bin Laden's overt propagandizing of the Western and Arab media was hardly a classic strategy for a truly clandestine organization. The central tension between the network's need for a public communication and branding strategy directed toward local militant groups and its need for a minimal public profile in carrying out illegal and violent activities only increased with the network's segmentation after 9/11. The Internet, which enables network communication with lower risk that the source of the communication will be revealed, has proven an essential asset to the remains of the network in its latest phase of operations.

The Dilemmas of Networked Collective Action

Al Qaeda's history as a clandestine, transnational network allows a reexamination of both the trichotomy of market, network, and hierarchy and the conditions under which networks successfully promote collective action. Without obscuring distinctions among these forms of governance, al Qaeda demonstrates that a single organization may combine different forms. In the case of al Qaeda, a hierarchical core based on personal networks forged in the Afghan conflict became linked over time in both enduring and transient organizational networks with other terrorist organizations.

The advantages of this hybrid organization were several. Al Qaeda could support a growing level of terrorist activity against a wide range of targets during the 1990s without a large expenditure of resources or trained personnel. The informational advantages were also considerable: al Qaeda, acting as a "Holy War Foundation," could rely on ideas that were provided by those on the periphery of the network, ensuring ownership and effective implementation if those projects were supported. It was this willingness to trade hierarchical control for cost-effective implementation that distinguishes al Qaeda from other contemporary clandestine political organizations. Finally, although its targeting of the United States ultimately increased hierarchy and direct involvement in terrorist action, the network form of its organization did provide some measure of resilience when massive American retaliation finally arrived in late 2001.

Al Qaeda's hybrid organization did not eliminate the organizational dilemmas associated with its network structure. Although the boundaries of its network were blurred, the density and strength of the personal networks that facilitated its collective action also served to limit the degree to which it was embedded in surrounding societies by similar network ties. Claims that al Qaeda is the pinnacle of a global Muslim insurgency overlook both its own distance from Muslim societies (many of its second-generation members "originated" in the Middle East only via Europe) and the likelihood that a more deeply embedded organization would lose some of its facility at collective action. Al Qaeda also found it difficult to infiltrate and incorporate state bureaucracies into its network. Perhaps this demonstrated homophily—the tendency to network with similar partners—but other illicit and licit non-governmental networks have certainly been able to forge such links with governments, as the corrupting strategies of drug traffickers demonstrate.

Al Qaeda's primary network links to other terrorist organizations were financial resources and services, particularly training and logistical support. One resource in particular was critical to the success of its network: access to its training camps. The provision of training at al Qaeda-linked camps reinforced the social networks among individual members, provided a valued resource to other organizations in the network, and contributed to al Qaeda's role as a broker within its network.

The links among individuals in al Qaeda's core network were identity based: al Qaeda only accepted individuals and groups that shared the same ideology and were willing to support terrorist operations (Sageman 2004, 63–64). Many in the core leadership were part of social networks based in the Afghan resistance. Al Qaeda's training camps provided a continuing substitute for the experience of the Afghan resistance and its creation of social networks that spanned national borders. The services provided by the camps were also a scarce and valuable resource that linked al Qaeda to its network affiliates. The role of al Qaeda's core as a broker, linking disconnected nodes in the wider terrorist network, was also reinforced by the availability of the camps. Elimination of al Qaeda's training camps in Afghanistan removed one of its most valuable instruments for network construction. Only two alternatives have emerged in the medium term: the de facto terrorist training for a new jihadi generation provided by U.S. intervention in Iraq and the continuing sanctuary for terrorist training provided by Pakistan. The rebuilding of al Qaeda's infrastructure of training camps in Pakistan's Federally Administered Tribal Areas has tempered earlier claims that the network had been effectively disrupted.[38]

The destruction of al Qaeda's bases in Afghanistan, the scattering and elimination of much of its leadership, and the heightened counterterrorism efforts of the United States and its allies points to limits to the success of networked organizations, particularly clandestine, illicit networks that directly confront states. The evolution of al Qaeda in the late 1990s suggests three hypotheses regarding network structure, clandestinity, and collective action. First, in line with the findings of Baker and Faulkner, a more centralized network structure may emerge when increasing task complexity is coupled with the requirement of clandestine operations. Second, if a networked organization engages in competition with a hierarchical organization (in this case, a state), network centralization will become more pronounced or the hierarchical constituents in the networked organization will become more in-

---

38. One American government official declared in early 2007 that al Qaeda's "chain of command has been re-established" (Mark Mazzetti and David Rohde, "Al Qaeda Chiefs Are Seen to Regain Power," *New York Times*, February 19, 2007. Available at http://www.nytimes.com/2007/02/19/world/asia/19intel.html).

fluential. In other words, the network is likely to become a hybrid in one or both of the meanings defined earlier. Finally, the tension between clandestine requirements and the political need for publicity raises the risks of increasing hybridity for a terrorist network. Rather than a series of comparable network nodes that could be difficult to map and eliminate, hierarchical elements in al Qaeda became prominent targets for retaliation by the United States and its allies. The hierarchy that is implicit or explicit in many networks runs counter to the network triumphalism that emerged after 9/11.[39] As Podolny and Page (1998) ask, if networks possess persistent advantages over markets and hierarchies, why do these other modes of governance persist? Network failure and its causes must also be considered.

Al Qaeda was able to extend its reach globally through a relatively decentralized network structure, brokering relationships with allied organizations, severing ties with others. The network facilitated collective action but, at least in the first half of the 1990s, the goals pursued by its networked organization were often those set locally, directed at national regimes or at encroachment on Muslim lands. Decision rules were relatively simple and modest contributions of resources could provide low-cost links to local and regional networks. That relatively undemanding form of collective action was no longer adequate when al Qaeda directed its jihad at the United States. Its short-term success in plotting and implementing complex plans of attack in the late 1990s was overwhelmed by the devastating response launched by the United States and its allies after 2001. Its hierarchical core was weakened, if not eliminated; its network has become radically segmented and decentralized.

Contemporary al Qaeda returns us to the question of network definition. Was al Qaeda's post-9/11 configuration—in which a hidden central leadership broadcast its messages to a diffuse audience through videotapes and the Internet—a network? Al Qaeda continued to inspire many violent actions against soft targets, but, with the important exception of its affiliate in Iraq, it seemed to have little remaining ability to plan and execute more complex attacks. For Marc Sageman (2008) and other observers, the radically decentralized network had become leaderless; any trace of hierarchy had disappeared. As it has rebuilt its organizational core and infrastructure of training camps in Pakistan, however, the risk increases that a new-old al Qaeda network could reemerge (Mazzetti 2007). A revived leadership node or group of nodes would again be able to use the network to plan and direct more complex and deadly terrorist actions against the United States and its allies.[40] The adaptability of network organization could permit a much higher level of transnational collective action, even in the decidedly harsher post-9/11 environment.

39. For example, "Networks—supple, malleable, invisible—have the advantage over hierarchical organizations, like law-enforcement and intelligence agencies" (Benjamin and Simon 2003, 170).

40. For a debate concerning the risk of a rebuilt al Qaeda, see Hoffman (2008a and b) and Sageman (2008b).

PART III

Power and Accountability in Networks

7

The Politics of Networks

INTERESTS, POWER, AND HUMAN RIGHTS NORMS

David A. Lake and Wendy H. Wong

Network theory has recently gained importance as an interdisciplinary approach for understanding complex systems. Network theory has roots in the physical sciences and sociology, and scholars have identified common features of networks in diverse physical and social settings (Barabási 2003; Watts 1999, 2003). Despite considerable interest in political networks, especially transnational advocacy networks (TANs), political scientists have imported few insights from network theory into their studies.[1] Nor have political scientists apparently exported their insights and knowledge of political processes to network theory.[2] This essay aims to begin an exchange between network theorists and political scientists by addressing two related questions: How can network theory inform the study of international relations, particularly in the examination of TANs? Conversely, what problems arise in political phenomena that can enrich network theory?

We make two general arguments focusing on the process of norm emergence in networks based on the history of the global human rights movement and the formation of Amnesty International (AI). First, political power can be an emergent property of networks, found most likely in scale-free structures. That is, central (or more connected) nodes can influence a network directly or indirectly and thereby shape the ends toward which the nodes

---

1. The prize-winning study of Keck and Sikkink (1998) was, admittedly, published before the recent explosion in network theory. Nonetheless, they do not directly cite the earlier work by sociologists like Stanley Milgram (1967) and Mark Granovetter (1973). This is not a criticism of these political scientists; our point is simply that the literatures have developed independently and with little apparent interaction. An exception is Hafner-Burton and Montgomery 2006.

2. Network theory has developed in apparent ignorance of the work on networks in political science as well (an exception is Watts 2003, 253–89).

collectively move. Power, in turn, is efficient and perhaps even necessary for overcoming conflicts of interest within networks. Incorporating distributional conflicts into network theory highlights a new and broader role for political power than now recognized. Our conception of networks considers the differences between nodes, taking into account specific characteristics that may privilege their likelihood of gaining links to other nodes and, therefore, of increasing their power in the network. Although TANs are sometimes celebrated as spontaneously organized, horizontal, and egalitarian alternatives to states, power may be crucial in the early stages of advocacy network development, as we demonstrate in the case of AI.

Second, norms are also emergent properties of networks. In the earliest stages of change, many ideas compete for acceptance and many *potential* networks built on different ideas or combinations of ideas exist but are not yet activated. In the case of human rights norms we argue that the network that eventually emerges is not a function of the inherent "goodness" of one set of ideas over another, since the quality of any norm is difficult to judge prior to its manifestation in a network of shared adherents. Nor is it the result of fortuitous "percolating clusters" of early adopters in a developed network. Rather, at least in the case of human rights, the crystallization of the observed network from the range of possible alternatives preceded the widespread acceptance of the norm and occurred as a result of a central node that exercised agenda-setting power by controlling the flow of information in the network. Although we do not argue that the characteristics of the ideas competing for attention at the moment of creation were irrelevant, we nonetheless find that, in this instance at least, the network created the norm rather than vice versa.

This chapter is not a test of propositions derived from network theory or added to that theory. Rather, it is more a framing essay or, perhaps, a hypothesis-generating study based on political scientists reading and drawing inspiration from network theory. We first survey, analyze, and extend network theory from the point of view of political science. We then examine the case of the global human rights network by analyzing AI's role in creating the modern human rights regime based on Western, liberal conceptions of political freedom.

Networks and Politics

Network theory has its origins in the random graph theory of Paul Erdos and the early experimental work in sociology of Stanley Milgram (Barabási 2003, 13–30; Watts 2003, 37–47).[3] With the rise of the Internet as a real world phe-

---

3. There is an abundant literature concerning networks in sociology (Powell 1990; Podolny and Page 1998). These analyses tend to focus on what differentiates networks from hierarchies and markets, in effect, creating networks as a category.

nomenon and "chaos" or nonlinear theories in the sciences, networks have gained new prominence. Unfortunately, network theory has largely ignored the politics of networks.

Network Theory

In network theory, networks are typically treated as varying along three related dimensions: (1) the number of nodes; (2) the density of the network or the frequency of interactions between nodes; and (3) the structure of the network, defined as the pattern of connections between nodes. In turn, these dimensions, and especially structure, have been used to analyze and explain the efficiency and robustness of different networks. Efficiency is the ability to transmit information across the network "quickly," with speed defined as the number of links between nodes through which a message must travel before reaching its target. Robustness, by contrast, is the ability of the network to function (i.e., transmit information) after the "failure" of a node or its removal from the network (Barabási 2003, 111–22). Networks, then, are defined as a set of interconnections between nodes, differentiated by the quality and quantity of connections.

Each network is likely to possess a unique pattern of connections that, as dynamic systems, constantly change and evolve. Nonetheless, three "generic" structures are commonly identified: distributed, small world, and scale free.[4] We focus on scale-free networks, which are characterized by a small number of nodes that are connected to a large number of other nodes that are not themselves highly connected. The connections in such networks follow a power-law distribution (Barabási 2003). Although we do not analyze degree distributions in this chapter, we find the conditions necessary for the creation of a scale-free network in the case of AI. We therefore apply the insights of network theory, acknowledging that scale free in this case may be more metaphorical than actual. Nonetheless, the insights that emerge from scale-free network dynamics are applicable in our analysis of political networks.

Scale-free networks are often characterized as hub-and-spoke systems; an archetypal example is the national airline system, which operates through hub cities (Barabási 2003). Barabási and Albert (1999) demonstrated that any network that (1) grows in the number of nodes and (2) follows the rule of "preferential attachment," a tendency for new nodes to link to already well-connected nodes (the "rich get richer" rule), will be scale free. Scale-free networks are highly efficient and relatively robust, as the random failure of any

4. See Barabási (2003, 41–78) and Watts (2003, 43–100). In a distributed network, the links between nodes are normally distributed; that is, most nodes possess the same number of links and nodes with many or few links are rare. Such networks are exemplified by a lattice with each node connected to its neighbors. Small world networks are defined by clusters of nodes intensely connected to each other with few links to other clusters. The long-range links between clusters allow information to nonetheless move efficiently through the entire network.

node will have little effect on the system because it is far more likely to be poorly connected than well connected (Barabási 2003, 113). Yet, scale-free networks are vulnerable to the failure of their "central" nodes or hubs, with potentially catastrophic results.

A Political Perspective

Although relevant to many important topics, network theory, as it has developed to date, does not address issues directly related to politics. Implicit in that theory are several assumptions that, perhaps unwittingly, rule out politics within networks. More positively, a political approach to networks is necessary when (1) nodes are cognizant actors able to formulate and make utility-improving choices; (2) alternative outcomes have distributional implications for nodes, favoring some over others; and (3) nodes vary in the power or influence they possess. When all three conditions hold, nodes will attempt to manipulate others in the network to produce desired outcomes, requiring a more political approach.

Choice. In network theory, nodes are often treated as passive transmitters rather than strategic actors.[5] This is particularly true in models of disease transmission, where nodes infect one another without requiring any agency on their part. In social networks, on the other hand, nodes as people or organizations choose to pursue more or less clearly defined ends—one does not accidentally join networks, and one usually can leave networks voluntarily. This implies first that nodes must worry about whether other nodes have incentives to perform in the way required for the network to succeed.

Nodes also choose whether to participate in networks at all. Networks are voluntary, with entry and exit determined by the nodes themselves rather than mandated by any "higher" authority. This implies, secondly, that nodes must reap a return from the network that is greater than or equal to what they can achieve in their next best alternative. Thus, networks must create benefits—network externalities—that cannot be created in an alternative. Put succinctly, the network must be greater than the sum of its parts. This benefit holds networks together, making the network more attractive than its alternatives. This very important point is seldom made explicit in network theory, and it plays a substantial role in our analysis.

The voluntary nature of social networks, moreover, also implies limits to the ability of central nodes to abuse the power they may acquire. Central nodes can manipulate the network to their advantage, but only up to the point where the members become indifferent between continuing to participate in

---

5. Emirbayer and Goodwin (1994) criticize sociological network analysis for neglecting the role of agency. Their concern, however, is the role of culture rather than power. Not surprisingly, economists are the exception to this rule. See Jackson (2005).

the network and exiting in favor of their next best alternative. The greater the range or the more attractive the alternatives to members of a particular network, the less the central node will be able to exploit others.

Interests. Network theory assumes that all nodes possess identical or at least highly similar interests. The problem to be solved, in most cases, is transmitting information efficiently. Despite some references to mixed motives such as the "diner's dilemma" (Watts 2003, 201–3), conflicting interests and nodes acting strategically in their own interests do not figure prominently in network theory.[6] In political settings, actors always possess conflicting interests. Sometimes these interests are zero-sum, but more often there are mutual gains from cooperation but varying preferences over the exact outcome selected (see Krasner 1991). Importantly, stalemate over the division of the gains can thwart cooperation entirely (Fearon 1998). In any network in which the nodes have conflicting interests, the problem is not only one of transmitting information but of managing and overcoming these conflicting preferences. As a result, actors can be expected to try to manipulate the flow of information and even the structure of the network itself to their advantage. In the case of human rights networks, examined here, many alternative rights exist. Even as most member states have signed the United Nations human rights covenants—covering variously racial discrimination, political and civil rights, economic, social, and cultural rights, and genocide—different countries and certainly different human rights advocates emphasize some rights over others (e.g., "Asian values").

Power and Influence. A final assumption implicit in network theory is that all nodes are equally powerful[7] or influential.[8] As we shall see below, this tacit restriction does not follow from the theory. Rather, the assumption is revealed only by the "silences" in the theory. Nonetheless, from a political perspective this is a grave oversight. Perhaps if all nodes are engaged in the same harmonious enterprise, differences in capabilities can be safely ignored. But if interests are not shared, and nodes struggle over competing interests, differences in capabilities become important.

The same structural characteristics that make a network more or less robust also generate an endogenous potential for power.[9] To put this point somewhat differently, power is an emergent property of networks themselves. Critical nodes that would significantly degrade the network if eliminated possess

6. See discussion by Watts (2003, 254–60) of Toyota's supply system for an example.
7. Hafner-Burton and Montgomery (2006) refer to power as "prestige," but otherwise overlap with our discussion.
8. A notable exception is Padgett and Ansell (1993), which demonstrates that the Medici rose to power through their positions in, and their leveraging of, the social and economic networks in Renaissance Florence.
9. Nodes within a network can differ in power for many reasons, including some unrelated to their position in the network. Here, we focus on *endogenous* sources of power within networks.

the potential to influence others. By threatening to exit, they can force other nodes to comply with their wishes up to the point where the latter are indifferent between remaining in the network and leaving themselves. The more essential a node is to the functions of a network, and the larger the benefits of the network to its members, the greater the potential power of that node. Alternatively, all nodes have power up to the marginal value they add to the network. In this way, varying patterns of connections in networks create different potentials for power and, in turn, empower different nodes.

We conceptualize power here in two ways, following conceptions of the "faces" of power (Bachrach and Baratz 1962; Lukes 1977; James and Lake 1989).[10] In the first face, power is directly coercive. Central nodes can threaten to sever network links to a particular node to alter its actions. AI's leadership can sanction rogue members, for example, through suspension or expulsion. In the second face, power is used to structure an actor's incentives by manipulating the terms of debate. Most important, central nodes can set conditions on participation in the network and exercise discretion in whether or not to pass messages throughout the network, in effect limiting the "acceptable" types of information. By defining what it means to be a node in a particular network or influencing the form and content of participation, central nodes are exercising power over members of that network and raising the likelihood that their preferences rather than the preferences of others will be translated into outcomes. As we explain below, this is how the London-based International Secretariat (IS) for AI exercises its agenda-setting power within the organization. This second face of power may be both far more relevant and less obvious in networks than the first, more directly coercive face.

Both distributed and small-world networks possess little potential for power differentials, given the redundancy of connections and the equitable distribution of links in both types of structures. Highly connected nodes in scale-free networks, on the other hand, are likely to be the most powerful. Because of their critical role and the likely dissolution of the network should they be eliminated, central nodes can exploit the value created by the network to gain influence over other members. When distributional conflicts arise, these hubs are more likely to be able to impose their preferences on others. More directly, they will be able to move the network in directions they prefer and extract a relatively greater share of the network's value.

The differential power of nodes emerges from the pattern of interconnections within the network. Central nodes can also capitalize on that "structural" power by making the network more efficient and valuable to its members, further enhancing the power of the central node. The emergence of power within networks is a dynamic and self-reinforcing process.

---

10. The third face of power is typically described as influencing the preferences of others so that they "want what you want them to want" (Lukes 1977). This parallels our notion of norms emergence developed in the section on diffusion below.

First, the central node can reduce the transaction costs of interacting within the network by setting standards of behavior and enforcing these standards. Similarly to international regimes, central nodes facilitate cooperation (Keohane 1984). Second, because central nodes determine the norms for the network, they can adjudicate disputes between members of the network by setting standards that not only promote network efficiency but also protect its power. Third, a central node can act on behalf of others to "grow" the network by recruiting new members. Given preferential attachment and the benefits it receives from a large number of links, the central node receives these private benefits (the rich get richer) while the network benefits from the additional nodes. In these ways, central nodes enhance the value of their networks and simultaneously increase their own power over other members by making the network more valuable to all.

Power may be weakest and, paradoxically, most important in the earliest stages of network formation. In embryonic form, all networks are extremely fragile. With few members, the network produces few externalities that bind members to the group. The whole is not yet very much greater than its parts. Appropriate behaviors are not well defined and information on members is scarce. There are few ties of reciprocity and only weakly developed reputations that might otherwise allow for self-enforcement mechanisms to prosper. With small benefits from cooperation in the network, and high levels of uncertainty, it seems unlikely that any social network could take off in the absence of some central node wielding a modicum of influence.

Once they succeed, however, networks that produce larger benefits for their members, more readily available information, or better developed standards of behavior may allow networks to grow further and prosper even in less centralized forms. Given the large individual and collective gains for all members, a mature network appears to function through self-enforcement. There is, we suspect, an important life cycle in networks, missed by those who study only well-developed or already successful networks. Self-enforcing networks based on reciprocity may well reflect earlier, more power-based structures and, in crisis, may manifest the power that remains latent in central nodes.

Pointing to the multiple faces and emergence of power in networks illustrates how the different preferences and capabilities of participants force analysts to reconsider the conventional wisdom on networks as relatively "flat" and "powerless" entities. Nonetheless, the voluntary nature of social networks constrains the exercise of power by the central nodes. To retain members—the basis of their power—central nodes must use their power to make the network sufficiently valuable to members so that they will join or not exit for their next best opportunity. Members may accept the power wielded by others over them voluntarily, and that power may leave them better off than they would be without the network, but this does not make the use of that power any less manipulative.

A Political Model of Diffusion in Networks

Having outlined a more political approach to networks, we now apply this framework to the process of network and norm diffusion. Due to their connections, networks are often characterized by criticality, a condition in which small perturbations diffuse throughout the network in a "global cascade." This has been a topic of considerable interest among network theorists and, of course, among political scientists working on norm diffusion (Sunstein 1996; Finnemore and Sikkink 1998; Keck and Sikkink 1998).

In a nonpolitical approach to networks, Watts (2003, 162–94, 220–52) poses a model of social diffusion based on percolation theory. Assuming that nodes are influenced by and conform to the beliefs of those to whom they are linked, Watts shows that innovations that arise in vulnerable (receptive) clusters of "early adopters" can gain a foothold and then possibly diffuse throughout the network. These "percolating vulnerable clusters" must be (a) tightly connected with their member nodes, so that the initial innovation is reinforced by "internal" peer acceptance, (b) loosely connected to the remainder of the network, such that early adoption is not counteracted by "external" peer disapproval, and (c) yet still sufficiently well connected to the network that the innovation can eventually spread beyond the initial cluster. The conditions required for diffusion are a form of Goldilocks's problem: there can be neither too many nor too few links from the vulnerable cluster to the rest of the network. For this reason, diffusion may be perfectly explicable ex post, but it is near impossible to anticipate ex ante (Watts 2003, 243–44, 250).

A key problem with this approach, however, is that it assumes a preexisting network. Nodes are already interacting, and what is explained is how innovations take root and spread throughout the network. This may be appropriate in some cases, but it cannot explain diffusion when a network does not yet exist. In the case of human rights that we consider, a global network was not already present; it had to be created. A small group of activists existed, but the rest of the network had to be constructed node by node. Nodes had to be recruited to the human rights movement and, as we shall see, to a particular conception of human rights. Importantly, the norms could not spread of their own accord, as envisioned in Watts's model, because the network itself did not yet exist. Models of network diffusion are less relevant here than models of network creation, which appear to be far less developed.

A second problem is that the model ignores the implications of power differentials between nodes. The content of the innovation and how it is evaluated by nodes does not matter in the process of diffusion. All that is necessary for the innovation to diffuse is that nodes want to "be like" those nodes to which they are connected and that an innovation arises fortuitously in a cluster that is neither too well nor too poorly connected to the larger network. Watts's model may well be sufficient for explaining fads and other social innovations that do not impose differential costs on nodes, and to which he limits his analysis. But it appears ill-suited to explain how innovations that have substantial differential effects—such as human rights—can take hold and diffuse broadly.

Our discussion suggests a second, more political model of both network creation and diffusion. Unlike previous efforts, such as Finnemore and Sikkink's (1998) idea of norm life cycles and norm entrepreneurs, we emphasize the effect of network structure on the creation and spread of norms, rather than the characteristics of the norm itself. We focus on the widespread activation of a particular set of beliefs with differential costs and benefits from within a larger universe of existing beliefs that, in turn, creates a network where none previously existed. The physical analogy is nucleation, the random formation of "seeds" that attract additional molecules and eventually form crystals from supersaturated liquids. In essence, diffusion is the crystallization of a particular network from the range of many possible networks, and it is a function of the structure rather than the content of the network.

The process of "political crystallization" unfolds in three major steps. At the beginning, before the network arises, there is a heterogeneous population with varying preferences over outcomes, in our case below different preferences over alternative sets of human rights. Within this primordial soup of varying preferences, there is no "natural" focal institution. Indeed, given that a norm becomes a norm only when it has a sufficiently large number of adherents, it is hard to say that one set of preferences is somewhat "better" or more "preferable" than others. At this stage, ideas compete against one another, but none triumphs.

In the second period, a small cluster or "seed" arises. In our example, a small number of individuals who adhere to and give priority to a particular conception of human rights come into contact with one another. As in Watts's model, these contacts can occur randomly, as a by-product of other interactions, or consciously in response to events in the world. This is a critical turning point for the eventual network. If the mass of newly connected nodes is too small, the potential cluster dissolves back into the larger "liquid" of society. If the cluster is large enough, it coheres and begins to work together to create value in a network. The collective voice of the members is louder in external circles than their individual voices. The information they share enhances their effectiveness. By creating value, the nascent network creates incentives for its members to stay in contact and work together.

In the third period, the network begins to attract new adherents. As the network gains value, others who prefer closely related sets of norms "convert" or, at least, espouse support for the cluster's norms in order to gain access to the network and its benefits. In this way, the original seed becomes a central node and, in turn, begins to exercise power indirectly over other nodes by defining who participates in the network according to which normative beliefs. As the network grows and its value expands with each subsequent iteration, it draws in the next most closely related set of adherents. Like seeds, then, clusters that become large enough attract yet more members (molecules) and thus create an ordered, rigid structure (crystal) from a disordered society (liquid); in this third period, the system undergoes a phase transition from one state to another. From the initial cluster, a larger network forms, centered on the beliefs of that cluster. The larger the value created by the network, the greater the pull of participation and the power exercised by the center. In this way, the initial success of the seed builds upon itself: the greater the value created by the network, the more additional nodes are willing to compromise on their preferences in order to reap the benefits of membership in the network. And the greater the value created by the network, the greater the power of the central node to direct the network as a whole toward its preferred ends.

As above, power is both necessary to and an emergent property of this process of diffusion. If the center exploits others and seizes a disproportionate share of the benefits created by the network, other nodes will exit. Exploitative centers create less value for others in the network, making further growth of the network unlikely. If the center restrains its demands and provides information and dispute resolution procedures, it not only gains power but builds a larger and more valuable network that, ultimately, diffuses its preferences more broadly. Success breeds further success.

In this model of network formation, it is not that innovations diffuse outward from the percolating cluster to an existing network, but rather that a network literally grows from the cluster or "seed." Similarly, it is not that one set of ideas is more "normative" than others, but a particular set of ideas gets taken up by a seed and then attracts additional adherents because of the value the network itself creates. By attracting new members who benefit from their participation, one particular network is created from the larger universe of possible networks. In our case, one particular set of ideas about what constitutes human rights gets embodied in a network and, in the end, privileged over other possible sets of ideas that all had roughly equal standing at time zero. Substantively, the "seed" sets the agenda for the network. In the next section, we explore the seed of the human rights network, AI, and how this NGO's particular conception of human rights came to dominate, and indeed become, the norm of the human rights network.

Over time, the power of the central node may appear to recede. Once the innovation has diffused broadly, and a network is created around selected principles, the network appears to become self-sustaining. As the network matures, the original innovation is "normalized" such that nodes within the network can barely imagine that it could have been otherwise. Nonetheless, even though it is seldom made manifest, the power of the central node still resides in the background and, indeed, grows ever stronger with the success of the network.

Summary

With an eye toward the case of the international human rights network discussed below, we can summarize our attempt to inject politics into network theory in four broad conjectures. First, in political networks, the problem to be solved is not only facilitating cooperation between nodes but also resolving distributional struggles that arise from differences between nodes. Second, in scale-free networks, central nodes acquire power that privileges certain interests at the expense of others. Third, this agenda-setting power is particularly crucial—and, in fact, most clearly evident—at the network formation stage and may become less overt subsequently as it attains the status of a norm within a stable network. Fourth, both power and norms are emergent properties of networks. They are not given by external forces, but arise from the self-interest and practice of the members of the networks themselves. We now apply these insights to the case of AI and the international human rights network.

Networks and Human Rights

The thirty articles of the Universal Declaration of Human Rights (UDHR) enumerate a long list of rights, including the right to life and liberty (Art. 3), to an adequate standard of living (Art. 25), and to education (Art. 26). At the time the Declaration was written, all rights were strictly ideals toward which countries promised to strive in their own way and at their own time. Yet, by the beginning of the 1980s an international human rights regime had emerged that focused almost entirely on civil and political rights, especially those associated with the treatment of political dissidents. Countries were willing to sanction one another for detaining or mistreating political prisoners, but not for the full range of human rights embodied in the UDHR.

The story of the human rights regime is long and complicated and we do not attempt to treat all of its facets here, but we do highlight a previously neglected dimension brought into relief by network theory and the case of AI's emergence in the 1960s. Where others have emphasized how networks diffuse norms, we attempt to demonstrate how AI's network helped define human rights norms in the mid-twentieth century. We make two claims in this section, one about the establishment and functioning of the AI network in the 1960s, and one about how the structure of AI campaigns affected its advocacy.

First, our case study shows that networks, even if they become egalitarian and flat, do not necessarily arise from such origins. AI's early success comes from its organizational structure and the center's ability to leverage a volunteer-based network. AI has struggled as an organizational paradox—hierarchical and heavily bureaucratic, but at the same time aspiring toward democratic ideals and volunteerism (Winston 2001). Whatever its organizational pathologies (see Hart 2001), AI pioneered its own method in grassroots human rights advocacy that not only separated it from predecessors like the International Committee of the Red Cross but also contributed to the human rights TAN. We argue that this combination of hierarchical structure and grassroots mobilization actually helped propel the organization to prominence. Although we lack data on the precise connections between nodes, AI appears to have approximated a scale-free network in its early days, with the IS in London acting as the central hub. This staff-based office continues to possess broad authority to set the agenda for the network as a whole. At the same time, the voluntary nature of the network and the growing strength (particularly financial) of national sections has strengthened the hands of the lower-level nodes, leading to a loosening of London's hold on the organization. In this chapter, we focus on AI's letter-writing campaign, which relies on a network structure to be effective.

Second, AI was the seed around which the postwar human rights network crystallized. At the time AI formed, a network of human rights activists did not exist in the sense that we understand TANs now. AI galvanized activists in Europe and beyond, attracting those who had previously believed in human rights but had no venue or terminology with which to express their beliefs. It has not addressed or promoted all of the rights enumerated in the UDHR, narrowing the number of rights investigated in favor of covering more countries (Welch 2001), but its campaigns, particularly in the 1970s against countries in Latin America, had the effect of privileging a particular set of human rights that persisted largely unchallenged until the end of the cold war. In the end, the regime adopted those rights propounded by AI and not other rights that had equal standing in the UDHR.[11] Network theory helps us to understand this particular conception of norms as an emergent property of social interaction.

Thus, our approach differs from previous efforts in political science by focusing on the politics *of* human rights, rather than politics *and* human rights. Using network theory, we show the implications of network structure (i.e., the quantity and quality of connections) on the emergence of human rights norms; given a different initial seed, other norms might have emerged as "human rights."

Amnesty International: A Primer

When British lawyer Peter Benenson penned the now-famous 1961 London *Observer* editorial that highlighted the stories of eight "forgotten prisoners,"

11. Although it might be argued that civil and political rights were more normatively important than other kinds of rights because of the nature of the nonderogable rights outlined in the International Covenant on Civil and Political Rights (1966), we point to the aspirational UDHR as evidence that *normatively* different kinds of rights had equal standing, even if *legally* some were given more importance than others. Laws are not necessarily norms, and the converse is also true.

human rights had received broad acclaim but little real support in international politics. Benenson's essay had the effect of mobilizing hundreds, rather than tens, of nonspecialized, "regular" people in a grassroots movement. Following the publication of "The Forgotten Prisoners," public support began pouring in: letters, donations, and information about other individuals who formed what eventually became known as "prisoners of conscience" (POCs). Benenson and two colleagues then began what was to become AI, the first grassroots, nonprofessional human rights organization. Holding to a narrow focus on POCs, they emphasized the reasons for which the dissidents had been incarcerated and the conditions inside the prisons. Prisoner adoption groups were set up to follow the cases of these prisoners through letters written to prisoners and offending government officials. In December 1961, the first country section outside of the United Kingdom was established in West Germany. The next year, other national sections began in Australia, Belgium, France, Greece, Ireland, the Netherlands, Norway, Sweden, Switzerland, and the United States, and Amnesty added "International" to its name. Two years after Benenson's piece, the Amnesty network had grown from small groups that mainly exploited extant community organizations to the foundation of the international network that forms the NGO today. Since its founding, AI notably won the Nobel Peace Prize in 1977 for its investigation of Argentina's "dirty war." It was also instrumental in the attainment of the UN Convention Against Torture, which was drafted in December 1984 and went into effect in June 1987 (Clark 2001). These accomplishments, subsequent international human rights efforts, and its network structure have resulted in AI's prominent position among other human rights NGOs.

Today, Amnesty's mission is "to undertake research and action focused on preventing and ending grave abuses of the rights to physical and mental integrity, freedom of conscience and expression, and freedom from discrimination, within the context of its work to promote all human rights."[12] As stated in its governing Statute, AI (1) addresses all political actors, state and nonstate; (2) provides information on human rights abuses quickly, publicly, and accurately; and (3) provides education on human rights. It not only continues the tradition of adopting prisoners but has expanded its activities beyond letters to more generalized regional and issue-centric campaigns, as well as cultivating influence at the UN and international organization level. It campaigns internationally against human rights abuses, facilitates networks of professionals and activists, raises funds, provides input to policymakers (especially the UN), and organizes letter-writing campaigns for those it feels are wrongfully imprisoned. As a self-proclaimed "international movement,"[13] AI

12. Taken from "AI—Statute of AI" http://web.amnesty.org/pages/aboutai-statute-eng (accessed February 6, 2005). The Statute may be amended by supermajority at the biennial meetings of the International Council.

13. AI refers to itself as such in its Statute, which can be found at http://web.amnesty.org/web/web.nsf/print/aboutai-statute-eng (accessed February 6, 2005).

engages in multiple functions—lobbying, direct advocacy, and research in the field.

Power and Structure. The IS in London has more than 410 staff members and 120 volunteers from fifty countries.[14] The IS, itself a hierarchical organization, is the central node in the AI network. It has agenda-setting power as a result of both the structure of AI and its adherence to a self-imposed mandate that limits the scope of cases that fall within its reach. Nonetheless, the power of the center is constrained by the voluntary quality of the network and the dependence of the center on cooperation and financial support from the lower-level nodes. Moreover, AI demonstrates network qualities because nodal relations are reciprocal and participating as part of AI produces greater benefits than any one node working alone. In fact, given the letter-writing advocacy of Urgent Action campaigns, we argue that AI's networked structure is what generates the NGO's efficacy.

The tension within the NGO between its hierarchical center and extended grassroots network structure is precisely what makes it a good case to look at from a network perspective. On the one hand, it has 1.8 million activists claiming membership. On the other hand, it has historically been fiercely protective of what it produces, especially the research generated out of the London office, its reputation of impartiality and professionalism, and its self-imposed limits on what it can do, reflected in its mandate (Korey 1968, 21). The balance between these two priorities results in a network of professionalized country sections and volunteer groups that are composed of local and campus units. Individual members who pay their dues are also part of the Amnesty universe. The structure AI has adopted makes sense for its goal of achieving both its unified purpose and diverse representation.

At the international level, daily operations are overseen by the IS in London, led by the secretary general. Every two years or so the International Council, composed of elected representatives from AI's sections, meets and discusses changes to the Statute, as well as any other concerns the collected members might have (Winston 2001). The International Council also elects the nine-member International Executive Committee, which oversees the organization's priorities and policies according to what is decided at these meetings. The International Executive Committee appoints the secretary general.

A primary task of the IS in London is to research individual cases of prisoner abuse. To ensure the integrity of its research, as well as its accuracy and impartiality, nearly all research is conducted in-house at the IS and the information is disseminated to national offices and then on to the membership in a top-down fashion. The large number of potential cases for AI to investigate and declare POCs gives London considerable influence and the ability to set

---

14. Taken from "Amnesty International—Facts and Figures" http://web.amnesty.org/web/web.nsf/print/aboutai-facts-eng (accessed February 6, 2005).

the agenda for the organization. Members, national offices, and others may bring cases to the attention of the London office, but only the central node can declare a country in violation of the rights of particular prisoners. This is the filter through which all accusations of human rights abuses must pass.

Despite this centralized structure, the national sections have considerable flexibility in implementing the priorities and distributing responsibility for the campaigns to support individual POCs. Country sections mirror the institutions at the international level, with an executive director who is appointed by the membership-elected Board of Directors. He or she is in charge of the administrative staff in the country section. The staff helps coordinate the membership's activities. Sections also conduct Annual General Meetings, at which members come together to learn more about what is going on in their sections. Although AI has been seen as centralized because of the importance of the IS and the London staff in day-to-day operations, country sections maintain a great deal of leeway in executing the mandate.

AI is also "networked" through the center's dependence on finances provided by the national sections. Every year, national sections send funds to the IS as part of their voluntary contribution for being part of the network. Many of the concessions the IS has made in terms of allowing national sections to pursue their own advocacy campaigns have been a result of large sections such as Amnesty International USA (AIUSA) leveraging their economic contributions; after all, AIUSA contributes more than other national sections to the IS coffers and has demanded a degree of choice in conducting its affairs.[15]

Seeds of Change: The Early Years of the Human Rights Network

If there is anything that Amnesty can rightfully claim credit for in the human rights network, it is in using the concept of the POC to define human rights.[16] Within AI, the POC is a concept that many have remained loyal to, seeing POC cases as the lifeblood of the NGO. As a consequence, this focus pushed AI toward an emphasis on civil and political rights, reflecting a liberal democratic position.[17] More important, the concept has had an impact outside of the NGO. AI's focus on individual claims to universal political and civil rights, we argue, was important in setting the human rights agenda and constituting the human rights network as it has developed over time. AI's focus on the unjustly imprisoned and its successful advocacy opened up a channel for other like-minded NGOs and activists to follow, giving activists a shared language (Kaufman 1991) and a common injustice against which to agitate.

15. Correspondence with AIUSA Director, Individual Giving, Louis Lo Ré, February 15, 2005.
16. The early history of AI is compiled from a number of sources: Amnesty's own websites (www.amnesty.org and www.amnestyusa.org); Larsen 1978; Power 1981; Korey 1998; Clark 2001; Welch 2001; Winston 2001.
17. See Howard and Donnelly (1986) and Sikkink (1998) for discussion of the relationship between human rights and liberal states.

AI does not cover the gamut of rights enumerated in the UDHR; rather, it selected several rights from the beginning to focus on in its campaigns. As the organization grew, more issues were added to the original concerns about imprisonment based on one's beliefs. However, this core notion of the POC is indicative both of Amnesty's approach to human rights and how the organization narrowed the scope of what qualified as "human rights." It is critical to think about the narrowness of AI's initial mandate as political, practical, and strategic with implications for internal organizational dynamics and the human rights TAN.

Setting the Principles. A "prisoner of conscience" was defined by Benenson as "any person who is physically restrained (by imprisonment or otherwise) from expressing (in any form of words or symbols) any opinion which he honestly holds and which does not advocate or condone personal violence" (as quoted in Clark 2001, 12). The violence clause came under scrutiny in the case of Nelson Mandela. Adopted as a POC in 1962 because of his history of organizing African strikes in protest of apartheid, Mandela was convicted on the charge of sabotage in 1964. The definition of POC has been debated and revised repeatedly in AI's history, as groups have been included or excluded under the label, but the Mandela case was the first major dilemma members faced, with both his prominence as the antiapartheid leader and his advocacy of violent techniques.[18] In the end, the NGO chose to take away Mandela's designation as a POC, but still advocated his release from life imprisonment.

The Mandela debate shows several things about the NGO. For one, AI resisted his imprisonment on the basis of its terms, without coming out against apartheid. Amnesty as an organization has sought to defend the rights of all political prisoners regardless of their beliefs. Secondly, the Mandela debate shows the importance of definitions for AI in determining whether an individual falls under the AI rubric. AI dropped Mandela's POC status because of his involvement in violence despite wide international sympathy for his cause.

At times, AI's limited mandate and impartiality have been controversial. Because it viewed apartheid as ideological and therefore beyond its mandate, AI tried to maintain an impartial political stance on state policy, while advocating a change in practice on the individual level. It also refused to advocate economic sanctions against South Africa. These two policy positions led to AI "falling off the boat" on the worldwide movement against South Africa's racial practices. But in not taking a stance on apartheid, Amnesty maintained its position against passing judgments on ideology, choosing impartiality. This is an example of how "Amnesty activists would not 'use' human rights as a tool for advancing other agendas" (Hart 2001, 139).

The concept of POCs has endured through the forty-odd years that the

---

18. However, as Winston (2001, 33) notes, Amnesty never took an official stance on apartheid, citing it as an "ideological"—and therefore non-Amnesty—issue.

NGO has been in existence. An important part of the seed set at AI's origins, POCs have become embedded in the discourse of those working on human rights (Kaufman 1991) and have provided AI's international audiences with enduring symbols of individuals imprisoned for their beliefs (Winston 2001). Because of the success of POCs as a concept, those organizations that followed Amnesty in international human rights advocacy have had to reckon with the prominence and effect of focusing on individuals in specific cases of political abuse. One way in which the idea of POCs was propagated was through the success of AI's Urgent Action campaigns (UAs) in the 1970s, which employed the structure of AI on a large-scale basis.

Urgent Action and the Network Nature of AI. Though London sets the agenda for the organization, the implementation of decisions from the center by the national offices and membership is quite flexible. This is seen most clearly in AI's UA campaigns, which extended the original group-based writing campaigns for which AI is famous. UAs are not only one of the easier and more common ways for people to get involved with Amnesty projects, but they are also the primary way in which AI publicizes individual cases of abuse.

UA campaigns began in 1973 and were initially part of Amnesty's Campaign Against Torture. They have gradually come to include all POCs. Urgent Action is what it sounds like: a quick and large campaign designed to last only four to six weeks, mounted on behalf of a prisoner. The UA campaigns employ the tactic of immediate inundation: letters, faxes, e-mails, and telegrams are sent to relevant personnel in countries where a prisoner's rights are violated. In part, this flood of communications is a written warning that human rights abuses will not go unnoticed, but the letter campaigns also demonstrate that these prisoners are not forgotten internationally, even in their imprisonment. This was true in the first UA case of Brazilian Luiz Basilio Rossi, whose government captors found the support he received significant enough to let him go.[19]

The process of UA case compilation is intricate, and yet done quickly— speed is one of the key ingredients in eliciting government response. Country experts at the international headquarters in London gather information firsthand, and verify the details with local networks and domestic NGOs. Even though they can be tipped off by other NGOs and individuals regarding potential POCs, cases are selected by the researchers at AI's headquarters. Amnesty's efforts in recent years have expanded its relationships with domestic NGOs. Instead of relying heavily on its own resources, AI has formed tight relationships with trusted domestic sources. After the researchers in London confirm the information on a prisoner and set the urgency level and the primary objective of the case, a bulletin is distributed to country-level

---

19. Anecdote from AI publication "The Thirtieth Anniversary of the Urgent Action Network."

chapters. Worldwide, there are close to fifty thousand members in the UA network.

For example, bulletins from the IS in London are dispersed to AIUSA UA, located in Washington, D.C. These bulletins, which contain information on the individual being imprisoned, including the reason for imprisonment, are then distributed to the rest of the national network. These chapters in turn distribute UA bulletins to their respective networks of letter writers. The number of people contacted to write letters per UA depends on (1) the volunteer's level of commitment and (2) the strategy that the national UA office decides to adopt in terms of the volume of letters.

Although there are no formal rules preventing local groups from contacting AI officials at the international level, the likelihood of them doing so is lower than contacting the nearest staff in their respective country sections. The lower levels of the organization are less well connected than those higher up. Additionally, although there are methods to facilitate membership input, leaders within the sections tend to make the key decisions. Information is distributed more or less downward, with a high concentration of it in the hands of the staff in London. This is especially evident in the case of UA. Individuals are selected by researchers based at headquarters after careful consideration of the facts and appropriateness of the case for AI, and the information is filtered down to the country-level UA office, where the national director decides how and when to distribute the work for each campaign. Members receive information and shoot letters off as quickly as possible according to the guidelines provided on that particular case.

However, UA is not a story about a simple hierarchical relationship. Unlike a system of coercion where A uses threats and punishments to B to produce an outcome desirable for A, the relationship between members and staff, national and international, is voluntary and mutually beneficial. Members who participate in UA gain from contributing to the global human rights movement. Letter writers rely on the reports that researchers provide, accept AI's information as factually correct, and spend time and money sending correspondence via fax, mail, and e-mail. This reduces their costs of participation in the movement. In turn, the pressure that any individual can bring to bear on a foreign government is multiplied many times by being part of a network of activists. Because they are likely to be more effective in improving human rights practices—even if this is not easily measured or acknowledged—individuals prefer to work within AI rather than outside it. This is the benefit of being part of the network that is Amnesty. There is no sanctioning or monitoring process that ensures people write the letters they promise to write, but letters continue to be written on behalf of prisoners and individuals. By one estimation, three thousand letters go out per UA, with three to four hundred from the United States alone.[20]

---

20. Telephone interview with AIUSA UA director Scott Harrison, January 31, 2004.

Without these thousands of volunteers, in turn, UA would be less effective, and a large part of AI's public image and effectiveness would be lost. AI has incentives to listen to its membership and must find ways to entice new and current members into its grassroots projects. Because it does not limit itself to writing reports and lobbying international organizations and leaders, AI must contend with the benefits and drawbacks of having members all over the world who want different things from their affiliation with Amnesty. In this way, the center is constrained from exploiting its power and must work with rather than simply command the other members of its network.

Nonetheless, the center possesses an important measure of power. In accepting guidance from London on who should be targeted in the letter campaigns, members de facto implement the priorities of the center. By following the directives from the center, they put into practice the particular conception of human rights favored by London. But conversely, the center has continued to have a large and growing audience to which it issues priorities. Volunteers contribute the bulk of the labor in UA campaigns, and carry out the work on their own time. The nodes in the network reinforce the power of the center.

The Politics of Principles: Why Some Rights and Not Others. Given the case of the UA network and POCs, we argue that networks matter for propagating ideas about human rights, and by extension, norms. The countervailing argument by Keck and Sikkink (1998, 26–27) points to several characteristics of issues that lend themselves to TANs. First, the issue should point to a clear choice between right and wrong, which "arouse[s] strong feelings, allow[ing] networks to recruit . . . and infuse meaning into these volunteer activities." Moreover, issues that involve bodily harm and legal equality of opportunity seem to be best suited for effective TAN activity. Finally, issues should provide a causal story—stopping one activity should lead to righting a wrong. As a prominent NGO, we might expect Amnesty to have followed this formula, and to have pushed issues for these reasons. However, given its conservative history, we argue that in fact issues are chosen not for their prima facie fit along these lines. Rather, issues are chosen because they fit the conception of human rights that Amnesty laid out early on in its existence. In this way, issues do not make the network; the network makes the issues. Though this is consistent with Watts's assertion that the successful diffusion depends less on the characteristics of the issue itself than on the structure of the network (2003, 244), our political approach emphasizes how the focus on prisoners initially crystallized in a network and how it spread into the human rights network in general.

Like other organizations with limited resources, the leadership of AI has to carefully wade through a plethora of information to find the cases and issues that it wants to pursue based on organizational priorities. Indeed, in comparison to an organization such as Human Rights Watch, Amnesty's scope is smaller in terms of reporting on types of human rights violations, but its coverage in terms of countries is larger (Welch 2001).[21] This decision-making process is easily lost when we think of human rights NGOs and other actors in this area as "principled" actors, rather than instrumental actors with a principled purpose.[22]

This, however, it not a story merely about administrating a nonprofit organization. What we claim here is that "principle" is in large part determined by the central nodes in the network, which then disseminate norms of behavior through their decrees and actions. We take Amnesty's historical reluctance to deviate from the POC and civil and political rights rubric as setting a seed in the human rights network and practice. This practice did not receive significant challenges from other human rights organizations until at least the end of the cold war.

Principles are not givens—they are defined and refined by the actors who practice and preach the principles. In other words, to conceptualize human rights NGOs as "principled" misses the basis by which we evaluate them to be such. AI and other organizations are principled not only because they promote human rights but also because they say so. As the forerunner to grassroots, international activism against human rights abuses, AI set the agenda for subsequent practitioners of human rights. As evidence of this precedent, its biggest competitor in recent times, Human Rights Watch, began as an NGO dedicated to protecting the civil and political rights enumerated in the Helsinki Accords, which ensured protection from arbitrary arrest for political dissension among other rights and principles.

AI's early success cannot be simplified to the sensationalism of suffering or legality in terms of equal opportunity. Amnesty focused the human rights agenda on political prisoners, which did not always involve gory stories of physical abuse or make equality claims. Rather, they made claims against states for imprisoning individuals based on beliefs, rather than tangible crimes. As it tackled a greater number of issues, Amnesty tried to limit its mandate to issues consistent with its civil and political rights commitment. And for many years, the human rights TAN stuck to this narrow conception of human rights.[23]

Although Amnesty is understood as being impartial toward any particular government, it has been accused of being partial toward Western conceptions of rights (Mutua 2001). There is an obvious truth to this criticism. Of the thirty articles of the UDHR, AI originally focused on the promotion of only

21. See also http://www.hrw.org/about/whoweare.html and http://web.amnesty.org/pages/aboutai-index-eng (accessed February 17, 2005).

22. For a fuller discussion of "principled" actors, see Keck and Sikkink 1998; Clark 2001.

23. It is also difficult to cull out a causal mechanism on this issue: Amnesty's letter writers protested the ill treatment and unjust imprisonment of individuals, and demanded that states adhere to the UDHR. Letter writers wrote not because they were promised a causal outcome, but because of a wrong being committed and the desire to at least protest its continuance.

those dealing with politically motivated detentions and the treatment of prisoners—neglecting a broad range of other principles articulated in the Declaration. Although it has attempted in many ways to maintain its neutral approach, at the end of the day AI is pushing a largely liberal-democratic notion of human rights (civil and political). This may be its largest and most enduring impact on the international human rights regime. Out of all the rights that the movement could have attempted to promote, AI as the seed of the human rights movement attracted adherents and fellow activists to rally under the banner of prisoners' rights rather than other rights. In this way, AI, as the first and most prominent NGO in the human rights TAN, crystallized the movement in a way that reflected its own priorities.

Amnesty's influence on the conception of human rights, and on the human rights network it spawned more generally, can be seen most clearly perhaps in the pattern of economic sanctions imposed on countries due to their human rights violations. Sanctions indicate what practices are deemed sufficiently reprehensible by others to warrant carrying out punishments that are costly not only for the target but for the "enforcer" as well. Table 7.1 summarizes by decade all sanctions episodes between 1900 and 1990, and the percentage of all sanctions that were enacted for human rights violations. The first human rights sanctions began only in the 1960s, and then expanded dramatically in the 1970s and 1980s to over one-third of all sanctions episodes. This coincides with the period when, we argue, AI and the human rights network first succeeded in establishing a norm of international human rights practices.

More specifically, table 7.2 summarizes all human rights sanctions episodes by the specific rights being violated. The final columns summarize our coding of the cases into those that were enacted over the treatment of POCs, the core of AI's activities, for civil and political rights violations more generally, and for economic, social, and cultural rights violations (codings are not ex-

Table 7.1. Economic sanctions episodes by decade, 1900–1990

Decade	Human rights–based sanctions	Total sanctions	Human rights sanctions as a percentage of total sanctions
1910–1919	0	3	0%
1920–1929	0	2	0%
1930–1939	0	5	0%
1940–1949	0	9	0%
1950–1959	0	13	0%
1960–1969	1	22	4.5%
1970–1979	14	37	37.8%
1980–1989	9	25	36%

Source: Hufbauer, Schott, and Elliott (1990) and Drury (1998). For those cases we code as "human rights" sanctions, see table 7.2.

Table 7.2. Human rights sanctions, 1900–1990: Treatment of POCs, general civil and political rights (CPR), and economic, social, and cultural rights (ESCR)

Case No.	Countries	Year begin	Hufbauer, Schott, and Elliott issue summary	Human rights issue	POCs	CPR	ESCR
62-2	UN v. S. Africa*	1962	Apartheid	apartheid		X	X
72-1	UK and US v. Uganda	1972	Idi Amin	property seizure, disappearances	X	X	
73-1	US v. S. Korea	1973	Human rights	political prisoners	X		
73-3	US v. Chile	1973	Human rights	torture, illegal detention	X		
75-5	US v. Kampuchea*	1975	Aftermath of Vietnam War	forcible evacuation, refugees		X	
76-1	US v. Uruguay	1976	Human rights	torture, political prisoners	X		
76-3	US v. Ethiopia	1976	Expropriation; human rights	property seizure, killings		X	
77-1	US v. Paraguay	1977	Human rights	political prisoners, torture	X		
77-2	US v. Guatemala	1977	Human rights	political killings	X		
77-3	US v. Argentina	1977	Human rights	political prisoners, torture, disappearances	X		
77-5	US v. Nicaragua*	1977	Somoza	dissident suppression	X		
77-6	US v. El Salvador	1977	Human rights	torture, disappearances, political persecution	X		
77-7	US v. Brazil	1977	Human rights	human rights		X	
78-5	US v. USSR*	1978	Dissident trials	political prisoners	X		
79-4	US v. Bolivia	1979	Democracy; human rights; drug traffic	coup, press censorship, human rights	X	X	
81-2	US v. Poland*	1981	(no case study)	free dissidents/Solidarity	X	X	
82-2	Netherlands and US v. Suriname	1982	Human rights/Cuban–Libyan influence	political killings, human rights	X	X	
83-3	US v. Zimbabwe**	1983	Foreign policy; Matabeleland	dissident suppression	X		
83-4	US and OECS v. Grenada	1983	Restore democracy; human rights	suppression of elections			
87-2	US v. Haiti	1987	Elections; human rights; drug smuggling	dissident suppression, human rights	X	X	
88-1	Japan, West Germany, and US v. Burma	1988	Human rights; elections	dissident suppression, political prisoners	X	X	
88-2	US and UK v. Somalia	1988	Human rights; civil war	human rights		X	
89-2	US v. China*	1989	(no case study)	Tiananmen Square Massacre	X	X	
89-3	US v. Sudan	1989	Human rights; civil war	dissident suppression, political rights, food distribution	X	X	X

Source: See table 7.1.
* Not coded as "human rights" in Hufbauer, Schott, and Elliott (1990) or Drury (1998).
** Coded as human rights by Drury (1998) but not Hufbauer, Schott, and Elliott (1990).

clusive, such that any sanctions episode may include multiple categories of rights violations). Consistent with Amnesty's narrow focus on prisoners' rights and related practices, table 7.2 indicates that early sanctions episodes focused on the treatment of political dissidents. The noteworthy exceptions are the decades-long fight against apartheid, economic expropriations, or cold war issues (e.g., Kampuchea). Not until the later 1970s did broader civil and political rights become the targets of sanctions and not until the later 1980s do we find the first case that included economic, social, and civil rights violations. Amnesty and its initial emphasis on political prisoners served not only as the seed of the transnational human rights network but also helped define those practices for which states sanctioned gross violators.

The case of AI has important implications for network theory. Precisely because different rights exist and individuals, societies, and states have different preferences concerning these rights, networks—especially advocacy networks—are inherently political entities requiring a political explanation. Unlike theories that focus on the quality of ideas and the effect of external norm entrepreneurs in creating and spreading norms, our conception of how norms are created and spread relies on an analysis of network structure, which determines the direction of information flows within the network. TANs, which have largely been described as principled, rather than political, actors, can evince wide disparities of power between nodes. These power differentials in turn affect the output—the norms—of the network. The power of the norms advocated by the network depends on how successful the network is at gaining adherents. AI succeeded in setting the norms of human rights as a consequence of two factors: the capability of the central node, the IS, to control the content of the AI human rights agenda and its ability to attract new adherents.

Norms are emergent properties of networks. The structure of advocacy networks affects their ability to create and disseminate norms. Looser networks lack a strong central node, which in turn hobbles the network's ability to coordinate action and control normative content. The relative importance of all nodes in the network means that a uniform set of norms will be harder to create, and in some cases this lack of coordination and hierarchy may be a deliberate strategy. AI's scale-free network, by contrast, firmly ensconces the IS as the central node of the network, giving it control over the membership and normative agenda. The IS can therefore both encourage a certain type of member to join the network and maintain control over which cases become "Amnesty cases," a key factor in maintaining a coherent and, indeed, restricted conception of human rights.

Furthermore, the case of AI illustrates how power is an emergent property of networks. As an early mover with a particular conception of human rights, AI set an agenda that attracted shared adherents. As their collective efforts reinforced one another, the initial agenda attracted more adherents into a "movement." As the concept of a "seed" suggests, success brought more success. But as the organization expanded, not only did it propagate a particular conception of human rights but the power of the central node increased. As AI was successful, the value of belonging to that organization also increased, reinforcing the agenda-setting power of the IS in London. The network created its own inertial effect in terms of attracting new nodes, which in turn increased the central node's power within the AI network, but also more broadly in international politics as it emerged as a political force in the 1970s with its outspokenness about human rights abuses in Latin America. As the political value of AI grew with its reputation, joining its network became more valuable and desirable. This, in turn, gave the IS more influence over many more human rights activists, and increased its power as the normative agenda setter of international human rights.

A particular set of norms focused on prisoners' rights emerged as a result of AI's efforts. Although other human rights existed not only in the UDHR but in subsequent, more binding conventions, a certain subset of them continued to receive attention from NGOs and states—rights upon which AI had concentrated its efforts (and had been successful in pursuing). Network theory's focus on structure advances our understanding of how nonstate actors can affect international politics through the creation of norms. Rather than focusing on the quality of the norm pursued, network theory helps us evaluate the reason why some norms float and others sink by examining the flow of information and power within TANs themselves.

8

The Politics and Power of Networks

THE ACCOUNTABILITY OF HUMANITARIAN ORGANIZATIONS

Janice Gross Stein

Donor agencies and humanitarian organizations delivering emergency assistance decided to form a network, the Active Learning Network for Accountability and Performance (ALNAP), in 1997 to address a basket of issues around accountability. This was a puzzling choice. First, why create a network to address accountability? What advantages did donors and humanitarian organizations see in a network as distinct from other kinds of institutional arrangements? A second question deals with power and networks. Given the resistance to what some humanitarian organizations considered a hegemonic discourse of accountability led by international donor institutions, why was a network initiated by donors acceptable to humanitarian organizations? Does a network have a comparative advantage when asymmetries in the distribution of power are sharp? Does it mask the face of the power? I argue that part of the attractiveness of this network for some members was that it helped to conceal the power of both donor agencies and humanitarian organizations, although in different ways. Finally, I briefly consider the contribution of this kind of network to global governance. To address these issues, I first tell the story of the creation of the network and look at its structure to understand how the network works.

This chapter looks principally at networks as actors. It looks at how the relationships among the members allow them to act collectively in ways that would not likely have been possible if the network didn't exist. Here members coordinate their activity, act collectively, and produce joint outcomes. The sum is greater than its parts and what matters is what the network collectively does. Its membership acts together to authorize activity, produces joint reports, and engages in shared programming. Each member acting alone could not accomplish what the network as a whole achieves. In this chapter, I look first at the structure and organization of the network. What kind of network is this? I then examine the network as political bargain within the broader surrounding controversy to understand the politics and power within this network.

The Creation of a Network: ALNAP

The Active Learning Network for Accountability and Performance (ALNAP) was created in 1997. The context was a heated conversation about the accountability of humanitarian organizations delivering emergency relief in war-torn societies, a conversation I explore in much greater detail when I look at the political purposes the network serves. The immediate catalyst was the Joint Evaluation of Emergency Assistance to Rwanda, a comprehensive assessment of the international response to the genocide and to the management of the refugee camps on the Congolese-Rwandan border. The camps were filled with refugees who had fled Rwanda, including those who had perpetrated the genocide. Humanitarian organizations found themselves feeding and sustaining genocidaires.

In this climate of questioning, uncertainty, and a crisis of both conscience and confidence, humanitarian organizations looked for ways to develop new, broader, and deeper concepts of accountability. Several humanitarian organizations collaborated on the Sphere Project to develop a code of conduct in the field. The International Committee of the Red Cross organized several meetings for its members to develop its Code of Conduct for the International Red Cross and Red Crescent Movement and NGOs in Disaster Relief. Other initiatives—the Humanitarian Ombudsman Project and People in Aid—focused on professional behavior in the field. Oxfam International agreed on common program standards for emergency assistance across its eleven member organizations.

There was a consensus that codes of conduct were a first, partial, and somewhat simplified response to a much larger problem. Nor was there agreement among the large humanitarian organizations that these kinds of code were appropriate. Médecins Sans Frontières (MSF) refused to participate formally in Sphere, although they were helpful in much of the concept development and drafting. MSF objected to the emphasis on professionalism and to the limited discussion of accountability, which left little voice for those who received assistance.[1] There was, in other words, no consensus on the way forward in the discussion of accountability in the wake of the genocide. Finally, donor agencies had a long-standing but quite different set of interests. They wanted better data on performance and the delivery of humanitarian assistance. Who got what, how much went through, and which populations benefited?

---

1. Interview with senior official at MSF International (2006).

In this troubled and contested environment, it was donor organizations that took the lead in creating ALNAP. They wanted better information about the performance of humanitarian organizations and better information sharing and learning to improve performance. They decided to take the initiative in creating what they called a learning network. After the release of the review of performance in Rwanda, European bilateral donor organizations met in May 1996 in Copenhagen. Two months later they convened a larger meeting of representatives of UN agencies, humanitarian organizations, and Red Cross representatives in London. The Department for International Development (DfiD) in London commissioned the Overseas Development Institute (ODI) to write a concept paper on accountability that they circulated to bilateral and multilateral donor organizations, UN agencies, and humanitarian organizations in December 1996.

Out of this larger meeting grew the learning network that became ALNAP. Initially, founding members agreed that they would limit membership to thirty members in five categories: multilateral and bilateral donors, International Red Cross/Red Crescent organizations, the large humanitarian organizations, UN agencies, and independent academic organizations and experts. Unlike those networks that hope to influence agendas through growth and critical mass, ALNAP founders quite self-consciously limited the size of the network. Very quickly, as other members sought to join due to interest in the work of the network, membership grew to fifty and then to sixty full-time members in 2005.[2] Members put no limit on the number of "observer members" who could register with the network, attend occasional meetings, and get ready access to the reports the network prepares and distributes. There are now more than six hundred such observers.

What does ALNAP look like? The network is structured around its full members who are expected to contribute financially to the running of the network. If they cannot make a financial contribution, they are expected to contribute in kind. Twenty-six of the members, a mix of UN agencies, national donor agencies, and humanitarian organizations, do contribute to the funding of the organization. The funds do not seem to come disproportionately from any one of the five sectors. ALNAP has a steering committee with eight representatives, at least one from each of the five sectors, and it has a permanent secretariat, located in the Overseas Development Institute in London, with a very small staff of only four people.

Why was ALNAP created? The network was created to provide a sectorwide

2. The full members of ALNAP represent the powerful and important in the community of practice of humanitarianism and emergency assistance across four broad sectors: the United Nations and its agencies most directly involved in humanitarian assistance; multilateral and bilateral donor agencies; the International Red Cross/Red Crescent Movements; and twenty-three humanitarian NGO and NGO umbrella groups. These groups represent most of the largest humanitarian NGOS delivering emergency assistance as well as several consortia and groups focused on accountability. Independents make up the remaining eight full members.

forum, "owned by all and dominated by none," through which to address learning, accountability, and quality issues of sectorwide concern. The emphasis is clearly on change throughout the sector. The humanitarian sector is itself "a network of international, national, and local organizations that respond collectively to humanitarian needs by providing assistance and protection to save life, reduce suffering, and preserve or re-establish the livelihoods of the affected populations" (ALNAP 2002). Existing mechanisms, the founding members argued, were not sufficiently inclusive to facilitate the change that is required throughout the sector. ALNAP is the only inclusive network that fosters active learning and exchange on good practice. One of its objectives is to disseminate knowledge of best practices throughout the sector.

The network has three kinds of core activities. The first—and most important—are information exchanges through biannual meetings, reports, and an annual review series. The second, program activities, include specially commissioned research on key issues of quality and accountability that are of interest to the whole sector. The third, which ALNAP members term "interest group activities," allows proposals developed within ALNAP to go forward under the leadership and funding of a small group of its members with minimal support from the ALNAP secretariat. Groups of ALNAP members piloted its Learning Support Office during the food crisis in Southern Africa in 2002 and collaborated on a comprehensive study on the participation and consultations of populations affected by humanitarian action between 2002 and 2005.

ALNAP has also developed a set of tools that enable meta-evaluation of the evaluations done of humanitarian programs and activities. It seeks to standardize categories of analysis and presentation within reports so that they are more easily compared across the sector. The network has also created an evaluation reports database that is searchable online. The majority of these reports are available publicly, but a minority is confidential and available to full members only through secure access. ALNAP also participates in joint evaluations with agencies, donors, and humanitarian organizations. Finally, ALNAP has facilitated and supported other networks in conducting joint evaluations.

What does this review of the membership, funding, and activities of ALNAP tell us about the structure of the network? ALNAP is an interesting hybrid; it is not easily categorized. It is not a purely distributed network, since not all of the nodes are directly connected to other nodes. Some of the national donor agencies would normally interact very rarely with each other nor would they be connected to the international federation of the NGOs that are the members of ALNAP. The Canadian International Development Agency (CIDA), for example, would have little direct connection with CARE International, the federated headquarters of the CARE family. Rather, it would normally deal directly with CARE Canada, which is only indirectly represented in ALNAP.

ALNAP looks more like a clustered or small-world network where the nodes are connected to only a few "neighboring" nodes (Watts 2003, 90). In these kinds of networks, there are several "long distance" connections among clusters; at a given moment in time, a snapshot of ALNAP would look like a clustered network with clusters defined by type. But these clusters dissolve and shift rapidly as connections cut across to establish lines between donor agencies and humanitarian organizations, and these in turn connect to UN agencies. The network of connections is too dense and too overlapping to be captured by a small-world network.

ALNAP looks most like a scale-free network, but it also differs from that kind of network in important ways. ALNAP has a small number of nodes that are each connected to large numbers of other nodes that are not themselves highly connected. A second characteristic of a scale-free network is also present: new nodes tend to link to already well-connected nodes as they seek entry into ALNAP. The network is also very vulnerable to a failure of its central node. The steering committee and the secretariat in ALNAP play important roles in enabling network activities, in resourcing and in supporting these activities. Network members go through, not around, the central nodes as they exchange information and collaborate in joint activities.

Where ALNAP diverges from a scale-free network is its deliberate decision to restrict the number of full members. Scale-free networks like Google grow the number of nodes so that they become more and more attractive to the unattached. Amnesty International functions very much like a scale-free network (Lake and Wong, chapter 7). Not so ALNAP. In its formative stage, it deliberately chose to limit the number of nodes and only reluctantly and slowly increased the number of members. Some members explained that the limits on membership were imposed to increase familiarity and ease information exchange. I argue that this self-imposed limitation also reflected the political bargain struck between donor agencies and humanitarian organizations on the contentious issue of accountability. Power and politics are an important part of why donors proposed and humanitarian organizations agreed to limits on membership in the network.

The Accountability of Humanitarian Organizations: A Political Context

It may be surprising to those unfamiliar with humanitarian organizations that a discussion of accountability is so recent and so heated.[3] The modern humanitarian movement began more than 150 years ago, but the discussion of the accountability of humanitarian organizations is only about two decades

---

3. The Code of Conduct for the International Red Cross and Red Crescent Movement and NGOs in Disaster Relief was adopted at the 26th International Conference of the Red Cross and Red Crescent, Geneva, Switzerland, December 3–7, 1995. The Providence Principles, a set of standardized rules for delivering relief, were followed by Sphere, a set of minimal standards in delivery of water, sanitation, nutrition, shelter, site planning, and health (Sphere 2000). These codes of conduct were followed by the Humanitarian Charter, which standardized the rules of humanitarian action (Humanitarian Accountability Project 2001).

old. Accountability comes into the world of humanitarian organizations for several different reasons.

An openness to this kind of "professional" language grows in the first instance out of the rationalization and institutionalization of humanitarian organizations that are now embedded within wider processes of globalization (Barnett 2007; Hopgood 2007). Along with organizations in the private and public sectors, organizations operating in humanitarian space increasingly need specialized training and skills, specialists in human resources, business and finance officers, and all the other attributes of large and complex organizations that deliver services through global supply chains. Paradoxically, it was in part the success of humanitarians on the ground in delivering emergency food, water, and medical care and running refugee camps that increased the scope of humanitarian space and led to increased demand for their services. The growth in the size and complexity of a small number of the largest humanitarian organizations opened the door to professionalization, institutionalization, and measurement.

The growth of humanitarian organizations and the demand for accountability cannot be separated from the withdrawal of states in an era of globalization. Today, emergency assistance is channeled almost exclusively through humanitarian organizations. States have withdrawn from "service delivery" and have become "donors," either directly through national development agencies that fund their "own" nationally headquartered nongovernmental agencies or through their funding of international agencies that, in turn, support humanitarian organizations. From 1990 to 2000, development assistance trebled and humanitarian assistance as a proportion of development aid doubled from approximately 5 to 10 percent (Macrae 2002, 14). As states have retreated, however, and contracted out the delivery of emergency assistance, they have increased their monitoring and regulation of nationally headquartered humanitarian organizations and networks. Even as they became physically absent, they became increasingly present as regulators, interested in "outcomes" and "accountability."

Part of what we now see inside humanitarian space is a principal-agent relationship that looks somewhat like domestic public-private and public-voluntary partnerships as states retreat from program and service delivery. States no longer row; they steer. The disbursement of large amounts of public money by humanitarian organizations increased the tendency for states to steer those who were rowing a boat of significant size (Macrae et al. 2002). In this sense, the new language in the relationship between states and humanitarian organizations reflects structural changes in the way states behave. When the state was present, the degrees of separation between state and humanitarian organizations in "the field" were greater. As the state retreated physically but reemerged as a principal funder, the demand for the professionalization and accountability of networks delivering assistance has deepened. Accountability was embedded within a framework of principal and agent and expressed in a language of technical rationality. The language of accountability reflects the deep risk aversion of the regulatory state in a globalizing economy. From the perspective of humanitarian organizations, however, demands for accountability by states that were not only withdrawing from the field but simultaneously transferring risk were, at best, highly suspect. At worst, humanitarians saw the demand for accountability as a reflection of the hegemonic neoliberal discourse of the most powerful states and international financial institutions.

The emergence of a language of accountability was not wholly externally driven. It is too simple to see funders—states and international financial institutions—driving accountability into the heart of humanitarian organizations with the sharp point of their spear. In the wake of the Rwandan genocide, it became clear to the leaders of many humanitarian organizations that their best and "most professional" efforts in the management of refugee camps were producing unanticipated and, at times, pernicious consequences. Many within the humanitarian community have pointed to the shortcomings of humanitarian assistance, to its damaging consequences, to the disruption of local societies and economies, to its capacity to break the social contract on the ground, to the tendency to concentrate on the highly visible emergencies that will "sell in the humanitarian marketplace," and ignore the less visible, the long lasting, the more difficult to reach (de Waal 1997; Rieff 2002; Terry 2002). Whatever credence attaches to these allegations—all need careful attention in the context of available alternatives—the language of "do no harm" shifted the terrain toward a conversation about accountability for outcomes. In order to identify "harm," humanitarian organizations had to identify the broad set of consequences flowing from their actions.

These "negative externalities," as they are described by analysts steeped in the new public management, were often not the result of technical failures or a lack of professionalism. They were the consequences of operating in a radically changed political context that altered the boundaries of humanitarian space. Groups engaged in violent conflict with one another understood humanitarian space as explicitly political and treated it as a political arena for action. Humanitarian reiteration of the neutrality and impartiality of their space avails little when humanitarian resources are large in relation to local resources and can potentially determine the outcome of a conflict.

How did this political debate play out within ALNAP? Donor agencies exercise a great deal of power. They fund humanitarian organizations, and without that funding organizations cannot operate. The largest organizations can go to a very small group of funders for resources. In this sense, power is sharply asymmetrical as donors exercise power through their capacity to fund. But humanitarian organizations are also powerful because they exercise a monopoly on delivery; donors cannot act except through these organizations. It is true that donors have a larger set of choices than do humanitarian organizations, but each group needs the other.

Humanitarian organizations also exercise power in the field, power they have been traditionally very reluctant to acknowledge. They dispose of proportionally very large resources in the contexts in which they operate, and they shape political, social, and economic processes—subtly or unsubtly—through this disposition of resources. They are, in other words, political actors. The language of power fits very uneasily with the core ethics of service that shape humanitarian culture, with the deep normative commitment to help alleviate the suffering of distant strangers, and with long-standing traditions of impartiality, neutrality, and independence. The self-image of a commitment to impartial service to those in need is jarred by an explicit recognition of the significant power and resources that humanitarians command and control in an environment of acute scarcity and insecurity.

With power comes a politics that shapes both choices and responsibilities. This construction of humanitarian space as essentially political is acknowledged openly by very few humanitarian organizations. Yet it is structural and likely to be ongoing in the face of accelerating retreat by states and prolonged civil wars. The language of accountability also grows out of this ecology of humanitarian space, an ecology that is premised on the explicitly political. There is ongoing tension between the explicitly political surround of humanitarian space and the insistence on neutrality by humanitarian organizations.

Why the Allergy to Accountability?

Why has the discussion about accountability within the community of humanitarian organizations been so difficult? Why the allergy to this question? Although accountability is almost always contested in the public and private sectors, the contest tends to revolve around its particular dimensions, its measures, and its capacity to compensate for political and regulatory deficits. The debate is different within the humanitarian community. It is about the appropriateness of having a discussion of accountability at all. There is almost a sense of moral outrage among some humanitarians when the subject is raised.

Humanitarian organizations approach their work within a historical context of principled action in neutral space. Inheritors of the Dunantist tradition, they are morally committed to provide assistance to all the victims of a conflict and self-governed by principles of impartiality and neutrality.[4] These principles served humanitarians well when combatants followed the rules of war and structured the space between them.

War zones in the last three decades do not look much like space that is structured according to shared norms and rules. As civil wars stretched over decades and states were made, unmade, and remade, it became more and more difficult to maintain a restrictive set of parameters for humanitarian

4. J. Henri Dunant, one of the architects of the International Red Cross and a recipient of the Nobel Peace Prize in 1901, is one of the seminal figures in the development of modern humanitarianism.

work. What assistance should be, where in the chain of transformative logic humanitarian organizations should focus their energies, and how humanitarian assistance should be delivered so that it does not create undesirable political consequences are all now hotly contested.

The conversation about accountability is so difficult in part because the humanitarian community is only reluctantly beginning to grapple seriously with its power and with its political roles and responsibilities. Humanitarians cling to the label of "apolitical," a label that foreclosed a discussion of accountability for outcomes that were politically driven. At most, humanitarians could be held accountable for the processes they used. Impartiality was not only principled, it was functional: on the ground, it helped to facilitate access to all sides in a conflict zone, and it avoided explicit discussion of difficult political choices. That the ground no longer permits impartiality, that humanitarians are now witnesses on behalf of the voiceless, that they intervene in political processes, that their resources are appropriated and misappropriated to shift the terms of the conflict, that humanitarian organizations exercise power—all this changes the terms of the debate.

This discussion of accountability, often tense, speaks directly to the norms and practices of humanitarians. Some leaders within humanitarian organizations interpret a demand for accountability from donors as an implicit allegation of failure or, even worse, as a charge of immorality. It is not surprising, then, that accountability strikes at the identity of humanitarians, at the way they construct who they are and the meaning of what they do. The discussion of accountability is now deeply enmeshed in identity politics.

To Whom Are Humanitarians Accountable? The Language of Obligation

Accountability in the world of humanitarians has contested meanings. I argue that donors proposed and humanitarian organizations agreed to construct a network around accountability in large part to change the conversation and to conceal the dynamics of power that structure the practice of humanitarian assistance. These dynamics work in several ways. Humanitarian organizations exercise power in the space in which they operate, but so too do funding agencies that condition grants and demand accountability as a condition of the funding they give. What meaning is given to accountability matters, not only for the construction of humanitarian identity but also for the practices of humanitarian organizations. The debate about accountability speaks very much to what humanitarian organizations think they are and to what they think they do, to their practices.

Humanitarians struggle with multiple accountabilities. Accountabilities to funders, national and international, are the easiest to trace, in part because donors increasingly make their demands explicit. The capacity of humanitarian organizations, working in a sharply skewed marketplace, to shape the terms of the accountability discussion are often very limited (Cooley 2004). Many humanitarian organizations receive the bulk of their funding from one or two large funders. Functioning as agents, they constantly struggle to enlarge their space for action while their principals seek to narrow their space to ensure that, as agents, they serve their principals' purposes.

Much of the scholarly literature on principal-agent relationships focuses on the distortion of principals' interests by agents. It pays less attention to the quite different analytic problem of the challenge to agents' autonomy when they are dependent on a few powerful principals. Although these principals broadly support the purposes of humanitarian organizations, important differences emerge when principals make their purposes more specific and give them shape and meaning by setting conditions for the funding. Funders exercise power largely by controlling the language of the conversation. It is not by happenchance that the focus of the contemporary conversation is on accountability for outcomes and that this conversation is carried on largely in a language of instrumental rationality.

Humanitarians assert strongly that they are accountable not only to their funders and donors but to the people that they help and that this accountability takes precedence over all others. Here humanitarian organizations are trying to shift the terrain of contestation away from accountability constructed as outcome to accountability construed as process. How an accountability relationship works when it is framed this way is often not obvious, especially when people in war zones are terrorized by militias and lose their "voice" (Slim 2002).

The claims of humanitarian organizations to represent victims matter in three important ways. They matter first because humanitarian organizations derive their legitimacy and their authority in large part from their claims of representation. Their authority derives not from what they do—as in most models of accountability—but rather from whom they represent. Second, what victims want matters, even though it is often very difficult for humanitarian organizations to consult the people who are trapped in the throes of violence and war.

The claim to representation matters in a third, less obvious way. What victims want may sometimes compete with core values of humanitarianism. Traditional elites, for example, may not want to devote scarce resources to rebuilding schools and clinics that serve women. Or they may oppose the fair division of resources among majority and minority elements of a community. Here the strongest claims to working with victims compete directly with other values and create acute dilemmas of accountability. Accountability, in other words, is only one of several values in humanitarian culture and not necessarily the most important.

These kinds of challenges are certainly part of the ecological landscape of humanitarian organizations working in a war-torn society and it is this ecology that shifts the terrain of the debate about accountability to the normative principles that shape humanitarian space. There is a distinct tension between representing the preferences of victims who often have little voice and imputing these preferences from outside expressed through the language of ethics, duties, and responsibilities. The subtext of this conversation is about the identity of humanitarian organizations, about who they are as a function of who they represent, and it is not captured in discussions about measures and benchmarks.

A quite different conversation within the humanitarian community led directly to measures and outcomes. After Rwanda, humanitarians began to worry openly about doing "no harm" (Anderson 1996). Humanitarians are now acutely aware that significant amounts of the resources they deliver to those in need are appropriated by militias and armies to prolong conflicts. Humanitarian organizations became more receptive to a discussion about monitoring what they did, so that they would do no harm. This criterion of "do no harm" is minimalist, yet it involves identifying the consequences of humanitarian action, specifying chains of logic, and monitoring systems so that harmful trends could be tracked. Concern to do no harm begins to shift the logic of humanitarian action away from an exclusive emphasis on needs and rights. Here there was some common language with donors.

The change in humanitarian language went beyond the inclusion of a logic of consequence in their templates of practice. Rwanda, Bosnia, Kosovo, Sudan, and Darfur made clear that humanitarians could save people who were at risk, but as the conflict continued over time, these same people would find themselves at risk again. As Médecins Sans Frontières famously put it, there are no humanitarian solutions to humanitarian problems. Some organizations now began explicitly to try to change the structural conditions that made people vulnerable. Any attempt to change structural conditions is, of course, an inescapably and deeply political exercise of power, irrespective of the official orthodoxies of humanitarianism. This kind of work is also consequentialist in logic.

We should not exaggerate either the timing or the scope of the change. CARE, a humanitarian organization that began by delivering food packages during wartime, broadened its scope fifty years ago to work on reconstruction and conflict resolution. MSF acquired its distinctive identity through its commitment to *témoinage*, to stand as witness for those who could not speak for themselves. New organizations concentrate on human rights in war-torn societies but still consider themselves part of the humanitarian family. Others expanded the continuum from relief to development and struggle to make that transition as quick and as seamless as possible. None of this work was without controversy. All of it required an explicit political sensibility to complex interconnections in the societies in which practitioners worked, a willingness to temper a language of needs and rights with a language of consequences, and an ongoing iterative movement between principle and practice. Practice was refracting back through humanitarian principles that fit less and less neatly with what was happening on the ground. Accountability in all its aspects is a deeply political concept that refracts the complex power relationships within humanitarian space.

A Network Definition of Accountability

In an essentially contested field, has ALNAP been able to push forward toward a shared definition of accountability? The concept of effectiveness is at the core of the conversation about humanitarian accountability. What does effectiveness mean? How is effectiveness construed in the dialogue among humanitarians, states, donors, and war-torn communities? There is no single construction of effectiveness: it can refer, for example, to the global impact of humanitarian assistance on a community; to the specific impact of a specific project; to the efficiency with which resources are used—the relationship of inputs to outputs; and to the achievement of humanitarian objectives, however these objectives are established. Each of these choices is politically loaded, informed by the values and purposes of those who are setting the standard and each might well yield quite different conclusions within the same context. In any evaluation, the level of analysis matters as does the time span of evaluation. Even though the question is the same, results can differ across levels and over time.

How has the meaning of accountability been constructed? The narrowest construction of accountability looks, quite reasonably it seems, at whether humanitarian action achieves its objectives. Donors consider an evaluation that is limited to the objectives humanitarians set themselves as too narrow, overly subjective and self-referential, and "insufficiently rigorous." Consequently, the current discussion of accountability focuses on the more difficult and demanding criterion of the effectiveness of the outcomes of humanitarian assistance (Darcy 2005, 7).

Within this construction of accountability, the meaning of effectiveness defined within the conceptual architecture of "outcome" is bitterly contested among humanitarians. First, accountability defined as effectiveness forces a discussion about consequence. At its most extreme, it can substitute a logic— and an ethic—of consequence for an ethic of obligation. This is no longer cohabitation of the two logics, but the substitution of one for the other, a significant change in the terrain on which humanitarians stand. To draw the most extreme conclusion, a consequentialist logic would argue that humanitarians should only give assistance when it is effective, irrespective of whether it is needed.[5] This is no longer humanitarian assistance as a need, much less

5. De Waal (1997) comes close to this kind of argument. If the marginal value of humanitarian assistance is low, as he alleges, and there are significant negative consequences, then the

as a right, but assistance when and where it is effective. Put this way, this kind of proposition challenges the fundamentals of humanitarian identity. Arguably, consequentialist ethics always inform decisions to some degree when needs are great and resources are inadequate and scarce. Nevertheless, for most humanitarian organizations, needs and rights continue to trump the likely effectiveness of assistance in judgments that they make. The right to assistance bumps up squarely against accountability understood as an effective outcome.

Many within the humanitarian community would also resist the logic of "outcome" as a discrete result that can be separated and identified. Within a framework of needs and rights, humanitarians increasingly link project to program to system. More and more mindful of the interconnectedness of what they do to larger systems, they look not only at what they do but at how what they do fits into the larger ecology. In complex, interconnected systems, this larger perspective makes it even more difficult to link cause to effect neatly at discrete moments in time. The life of a single project—a single moment in time—is almost always arbitrary as a point of evaluation from a systems perspective. Yet it is often projects, rather than programs or systems, that are evaluated by funders and donors. Donors tend to narrow accountability to project evaluation precisely because evaluation of whether specific projects are effective in producing specific outcomes is far more tractable than the evaluation of programs that span longer time periods, and evaluation of programs is more tractable than an analysis of the trajectories of complex systems. There is, however, a price for this artificial concretization and reification of outcomes as specific and discrete within time frames that are arbitrarily demarcated. A great deal of what matters in complex societies goes missing in this kind of sectioned operation.

How does this fairly abstract argument translate into the work of ALNAP? Part of what ALNAP is about is bridging this gap between "donors and doers," between funders and humanitarian organizations. Both kinds of organizations are members of the network and shared membership in a network structure masks underlying power asymmetries and political difference as it gives voice to different sectors in determining the work program. Building consensus is easier in some contexts than in others. When causal knowledge is robust and the drivers are relatively insensitive to context, the effectiveness of an outcome can be fairly, easily, and appropriately measured. There is little controversy about the evaluation of the outcomes of projects to inoculate children against smallpox or programs to eradicate polio. As problems and programs become more complex, however, the criteria of effectiveness are infused with political values that shape policies and practices.

The argument about sustaining refugee populations in war-torn societies

---

logical conclusion is that humanitarian assistance should not be provided at all, irrespective of need.

exemplifies this kind of not-so-subtle process. Some proponents of effectiveness challenged the humanitarian assistance given to seven hundred thousand people who were forced out of the cities by the government of Robert Mugabe in Zimbabwe. The assistance provided by humanitarian organizations, the argument went, allowed Mugabe to consolidate power and continue to displace precisely those impoverished urban dwellers who posed the gravest threat to his regime (Wines 2005). As a last resort, this kind of argument suggests, humanitarians should withhold assistance from those without shelter or means. Implicit is the expectation that the dispossessed, those without food or shelter, would rise in a successful revolt against Mugabe. It goes without saying that the logic of this argument is not self-evident. Often, the poorest and the weakest are unable to mobilize the resources needed to overthrow a government. Withholding food aid would only further deprive those who are already badly deprived. The Humanitarian Policy Group disagreed strongly with those who propose targeting food aid. The argument about a dependency syndrome, it insisted, said more about the attitudes of donors than it did about the attitudes of those who received assistance.

ALNAP weighed in to this controversy about accountability measured through outcomes. It authorized and completed an evaluation of humanitarian action in Darfur, one of a series of evaluation reports, in 2004. ALNAP's report gave greatest emphasis to the failure of humanitarian organizations to mobilize earlier, more visibly, and more vocally, at night, when militias terrorized the local population, as well as during the day (ALNAP 2004). The report acknowledged that states and international organizations controlled the political and diplomatic resources for the kinds of intervention that were necessary to forestall the dislocation of hundreds of thousands of people caught in the cross fire. Nevertheless, humanitarian organizations and donors failed not through what they did do, but through what they did not do. A related study by MSF-Holland, an ALNAP member, reached the same conclusion: "The distinguishing feature of the Darfur crisis has been the lateness and inadequacy of the humanitarian response. It has been so serious that it amounted to 'systemic failure'" (MSF Holland 2005).

In its evaluation of humanitarian action in Darfur, ALNAP constructed accountability in the broadest possible way. It did not focus on specific outcomes, but rather on the failure to provide protection at an earlier stage of the crisis. When ALNAP balanced the risks of doing nothing—failing to try to protect and sustain—against doing something that might not be terribly effective, it weighed the costs of failing to try far more heavily. ALNAP constructed accountability directly within a normative concept of obligation. In so doing, it diminished the apprehensions of those humanitarian organizations that worried about an overly technical, formulaic, and outcome-based construction of accountability and bridged the political divide and the power asymmetries between the donors and the doers.

The danger, the ALNAP report continued, may be elsewhere. In a counterintuitive argument, ALNAP cautioned that it is possible that an emphasis on effective outcomes may lead to a reluctance by humanitarians to act at all. Although greater preoccupation with different dimensions of accountability is certainly positive, the ALNAP report concludes that in Darfur a preoccupation with accountability "undermined an essential aspect of humanitarian risk-taking" (ALNAP 2004). The emphasis on standards and codes of conduct was especially limiting, warned the Office of the Coordinator for Humanitarian Affairs in its report. Accountability taken too literally or too far represents "a strategy for humanitarian containment, not humanitarian action" (Broughyton, MacGuire, and Frueh 2005; Young et al. 2005).

ALNAP's reports reflected the deeply held normative concerns of humanitarian organizations in their discussion of accountability. Although its mission is to promote improved evaluation and accountability, the network through its reports warned early and loudly of the risks of an overemphasis on accountability defined exclusively as outcome. By reframing the problem in ways that were politically acceptable to humanitarian organizations delivering assistance, it masked the power of the donors and created a platform for shared work on the meaning of accountability. This broadly normative construction of accountability positioned the network as a credible interlocutor within the humanitarian community to take the discussion forward.[6]

Accountability How?

ALNAP faced a political challenge. There were substantial differences among its members on the meaning of accountability within the larger architecture of humanitarian principles and practice. As we have seen, there is an uneasy fit between the languages of humanitarianism and accountability, in large part because the normative principles of humanitarianism create a framework and template for doing good. ALNAP now had to deepen and broaden the discussion of "do good" to give meaning and content to accountability. It did so by changing the language.

ALNAP shifted the language from a heavy if not exclusive emphasis on accountability to a broader, more conceptually inclusive discussion of learning, evaluation, and participation as well as accountability. It defined accountability in a very straightforward way as "the means by which individuals and organizations report to a recognized authority, or authorities, and are held responsible for their actions" (ALNAP 2005a). The network then embedded accountability within the larger discussion of evaluation and defined evaluation of humanitarian action as

> a systematic and impartial examination of humanitarian action intended to draw lessons to improve policy and practice, and enhance accountability. It has the following characteristics: i) it is commissioned by or in cooperation with

6. Interviews by author with CARE International, Geneva, and World Vision.

the organization(s) whose performance is being evaluated; . . . iii) it assesses policy and/or practice against recognized criteria (e.g. efficiency, effectiveness/timeliness/coordination, impact, connectedness, relevance/appropriateness, coverage, coherence, and as appropriate, protection); and iv) it articulates findings, draws conclusions and makes recommendations (ALNAP 2005a).

It is not difficult to parse the political tensions and the compromises that are built into the definition. By changing the terrain, the ALNAP secretariat, working closely with key members, built the platform for a broadly defined concept of evaluation that included both the technical and the normative.

How has ALNAP gone about populating this broadly defined field of accountability? The network has created and sponsored a meta-evaluation project that annually reviews the evaluation reports submitted by members as well as those that are publicly available. The network has created a template and criteria for evaluation reports, and the results of the meta-evaluation are published annually in the *Review of Humanitarian Action*. In a politically strategic decision, ALNAP began by evaluating the evaluators and creating a shared platform on which evaluation now stands and, in so doing, helped to join up thinking across sectors on a complex problem and bring partners to the table. It was especially useful in the absence of strong theory—the absence of robust, reliable knowledge about the complex drivers of outcomes—to generate "joined-up thinking" on evaluation from multiple partners. ALNAP has built an evaluative reports database that is widely available to members and nonmembers. The searchable database is one of the primary vehicles for diffusing knowledge beyond network members. It also circulates to members "lessons learned" papers that often include additional material not available in formal evaluation reports.

How seriously are evaluation, guidelines, and standards taken by humanitarian organizations a decade after Rwanda? The ALNAP evaluation of Darfur found, contrary to expectation, that practitioners were seized with the need to measure up to professionally agreed-upon standards (ALNAP 2004, 113). A UN interagency review team visited Darfur in September 2004 and made explicit recommendations of where humanitarian organizations could do better in meeting standards; it returned to monitor these changes three months later. Evaluations were done during the mission, not after it was over, so that midcourse corrections could happen as quickly as possible. The ALNAP evaluation again went beyond the technical and found that codes of conduct were inhibiting and not very useful in helping individual organizations to learn. A parallel report by the Office of the Coordinator for Humanitarian Affairs (OCHA) observed a tendency, especially when uncertainty was high, to interpret standards as "absolutes, rather than indicators," to treat standards as targets that "can serve to inhibit rather than facilitate action" (Broughyton, Maguire, and Frueh 2005, 10–11).

At its best, ALNAP approximates "open source learning," modeled on the open-source software movement that is organized around a shared problem. ALNAP has succeeded best as a learning network that privileges a system of continuous feedback and iterative problem solving that builds on shared experience. The most successful mechanisms of accountability are likely to be those that build in the greatest possible opportunity for timely feedback and ongoing course corrections. When practitioners can see the immediate relevance to their work on the ground, they are more likely to be open to new research and new approaches.

Humanitarian organizations are committed, at least in principle, to drawing to the greatest extent possible on local knowledge as they seek better outcomes. Local knowledge is especially important when knowledge is contingent and context dependent. It is this constant checking against local knowledge that allows humanitarian organizations working on the ground to get early warning of missteps, suggestions for course correction and change, and validating information about performance. This kind of dialogue is important not only for corrective information about performance but also as an early warning system about unintended—and negative—consequences and as a rough causal map of interactions on the ground that are likely to influence outcomes.

Yet the study by OCHA in Darfur found little participation by beneficiaries of assistance in the management of issues that were of immediate and direct relevance to them (Broughyton, Maguire, and Frueh 2005, 11). Another way of framing that evaluation is that humanitarian organizations were demonstrating little accountability to the people on the ground that they were trying to help.[7] In a controversial report issued eight years after it was created, ALNAP joined the debate and unmasked some of the power asymmetries that were confounding the discussion of accountability. Its review concluded that a radical handover of responsibilities to local partners was unlikely as long as humanitarian organizations are held accountable by donors for their operational performance and are dependent on a funding structure that emphasizes what they themselves have accomplished (ALNAP 2004, 3). ALNAP identified as obstacles the absence of tools and guidance specifically designed to increase participation by affected populations and consequently began a study on consultation and participation in humanitarian action. In an effort to fill the gap, ALNAP issued a handbook for humanitarian practitioners (ALNAP 2005b; Grünewald 2007).

ALNAP's work identified real and visible trade-offs for humanitarian organizations in their accountability to different stakeholders. These trade-offs are

7. An evaluation by CARE International reported that CARE was successful in "setting up highly participatory water/sanitation committees within the IDP [internally displaced persons] camps that have taken an increasingly active role in site planning and latrine design." Other sector interventions by CARE have been less proactive in promoting empowerment (CARE 2004, 6, 17).

present in any architecture of accountability and cannot be designed away. The network hopes to make humanitarian leaders more self-conscious about their choices and to work with donors to structure different kinds of expectations.

The Norm and Practice of Accountability: Do Networks Matter?

I began this chapter by asking why donors chose to create a learning network around accountability. What advantages did a network—as opposed to other institutional arrangements—offer? The answer lies largely in the power asymmetries among members and in the politically charged conversation around accountability, in the contestation of the meaning of accountability, all in the context of a sense of urgency to pursue the conversation. The founding members of the network shared a sense of urgency, but came at it from very different perspectives. For humanitarian organizations it was the trauma of Rwanda, for national donor agencies it was the relatively new responsibilities that flowed from delegation, and for UN agencies it was their expanding re-mit in war-torn societies. A network offered a political opportunity to mask these differences, while allowing members to shape a mutually acceptable vo-cabulary to go forward. That is exactly what ALNAP did in its early years. It performed an essential political function in space that it created.

Closely related was ALNAP's capacity to veil the face of power and the asymmetries of power among its members. Donors are most obvious in their exercise of power; they condition the granting of funds on measurable per-formance. But UN agencies and humanitarian organizations, I have argued, also exercise power in the societies in which they work. They are less open and more uncomfortable than funders in their exercise of power, but they are powerful, albeit in different ways than donor organizations. They also strug-gle more openly with multiple accountabilities than do funders. ALNAP of-fered an opportunity to go around these asymmetries, to mask the face of power. In its early work, the network concentrated on the costs of inaction, on the harm of inaction rather than action. It tilted the conversation to educate donors on the searing costs of doing nothing, a lesson that humani-tarian organizations had learned painfully in Rwanda. Only after these para-meters had been set did the network begin to map the contested terrain of accountability.

The principal contribution of ALNAP in the early stages and the reason a network was acceptable to multiple stakeholders was its capacity to perform a quintessentially political function—to blunt the sharp edges of power and conceal its obvious dynamics. That ALNAP has only gradually expanded its membership is testimony to its sophisticated understanding of politics and power. This explicitly political dimension of networks is not given enough at-tention in the analysis of network effects.

I come to the second broad question. Did the emergence of ALNAP as a learning network matter? What impact did the network have as structure and as actor? ALNAP, like Amnesty International, bridges the divide between networks-as-actors and networks-as-structures.

Did ALNAP-as-actor have an impact on how the accountability of humanitarian organizations is constructed? Did the network-as-actor give specific meaning and content to the norm? The network is very young, in the early stages of the life cycle of a network, and it is difficult to draw strong inferences based on very limited evidence. Second, knowledge claims rest not only on what has happened but on what might have happened had ALNAP not been created. These kinds of counterfactual comparisons should always be tentative. At the most, I develop some plausible and tentative *ex post* explanations that can be evaluated against the similar study of Amnesty International by Lake and Wong in chapter 7.

I argue that the network-as-actor mattered to how accountability is constructed in the humanitarian community. I tell a story that is both different and similar to the story Lake and Wong tell about Amnesty International. Amnesty narrowed the meaning of human rights to a particular subset; it seeded only a small corner of a much larger field. ALNAP did the reverse: it broadened the meaning of accountability beyond the sectorally defined meanings of donor agencies, humanitarian organizations, and UN agencies. ALNAP bridged the political gap and then dealt with the asymmetries of power by changing the language and embedding accountability within a larger conversation about evaluation, participation, protection, and learning. Because the network included different political perspectives and reflected the asymmetries of power as well as capacity, it did not sharpen, narrow, exclude, and crystallize as did Amnesty; rather, it built a political consensus broad enough to encompass the divergent interests of donors and practitioners. In network language, the network created a collective voice that is louder than any of its members both within the network and outside. It is no surprise that the network doubled in size within a few short years and that it is under pressure to continue to admit new members.

The answer to a second question—did the network-as-structure help to diffuse the norm and practice of accountability?—is logically related to the first. The secretariat within ALNAP made strategic choices in the early design of its work that built consensus across political divides and allowed gradual expansion of membership within the network as the fear of donor control, deeply embedded within humanitarian organizations, began to recede. The new norms around accountability are a structural outcome, rather than the choice of any single set of members.

How widely and deeply has ALNAP diffused these new norms? The available evidence is limited to the reviews by OCHA and ALNAP of practice in the field, of the constraining impact of standards and guidelines, and of growing risk aversion. All this suggests that attention to accountability is greater than it was a decade ago. To attribute the change in practice largely to ALNAP is not warranted by the available evidence. However, ALNAP cohered as a network from multiple sectors and multiple interests because it transformed and transcended the debate about accountability. It framed accountability as an opportunity to learn, to reflect on the larger systems in which particular programs are embedded, to identify constraints, and to experiment with different ways of doing things. An environment of continuous learning across sectors helped to produce knowledge that is both contextualized and shared. ALNAP framed accountability both as the other face of power that humanitarian organizations exercise, and as a shield that can be used in the political battlefield that is now humanitarian space in war-torn societies. That space is triangulated as humanitarian organizations juggle their obligations to those they try to help and to those who fund their work even as they try to meet their own standards in the exercise of power.

In reframing the challenge of accountability, a concept that came directly out of the neoliberal global order, it became "easier" for humanitarian organizations to satisfy donors and "easier" for donors to compromise and broaden their understanding.[8] No donor compromised alone and no humanitarian organization ceded ground alone.

ALNAP has also become an essential and important, well-connected node in other accountability and humanitarian networks.[9] Through its mobilization of UN agencies, national and international donor agencies, humanitarian organizations, and independent consultants, ALNAP can be construed as an emergent governance network. It considers and develops standards of performance across a broad range of issues, evaluates the evaluators, develops best practices, and shares information through its members and its online accessibility. Governance is constructed through the practices of the network and disseminated through its members.

To put the argument another way, we would miss an important piece of global governance if we looked only at the members rather than at the relationships among them, and if we paid no attention to the relationship of this network to other networks. We would also miss an important part of global politics and of the global dynamics of power if we looked only at members and not at the network. In global politics today, networks tell an important story of power, politics, and governance.

8. Author's interviews, Office of the Coordinator for Humanitarian Affairs, New York, 2006.
9. ALNAP belongs to a loose grouping of organizations focused on improving quality and accountability in the humanitarian sector. These organizations meet regularly to ensure collaboration and coherence in their activities. The following organizations belong to this group: ALNAP, Coordination Sud, Groupe Urgence Réhabilitation Développement, People in Aid, and the Sphere Project.

PART IV

Networks and International Governance

9

Delegation, Networks, and Internet Governance

Peter Cowhey and Milton Mueller

Scholars have used the concept of networks to examine how informal systems of information exchange and coordination can organize actors globally, perhaps even at the expense of the authority of governments. But, as Kahler's introduction argues, the conditions for such developments are not well specified. Moreover, the form of network-as-actor is malleable and thus requires explanation. In this chapter we show how a combination of the literatures on principals and agents (the delegation literature) and on network economics can improve our understanding of the design of global governance. It applies this framework to the case of Internet governance, a realm often held up as an exemplar of the power of networks as actors, because of the networked structure that it coordinates.

The delegation literature looks at two related problems. When will an actor (the principal) conditionally grant power to an agent in order to gain the benefits of a division of labor to advance the principal's objective? And which mechanisms of control and monitoring allow the principal to remain reasonably certain that agents with some autonomy will continue to serve its purpose? The delegation literature suggests that it would be a surprise if network forms of organization in global governance truly escaped control by governments, much as Eilstrup-Sangiovanni (chapter 10) makes the same point about transgovernmental networks. But it also calls attention to the tensions between the interests of the principal and those of an agent. It analyzes choices about selecting an agent, the types of coordination (how hierarchical or centralized, for example), the role of direct government supervision of the institution, and the organization of decision making (e.g., the decision rules). Clearly, the nature of the task influences these trade-offs. When will governments delegate to networks as organizations? Delegation is about the network as an actor.

A less explored thread of networking theory in the international relations literature is the economic literature on telecommunications networks. This body of work can illuminate the kind of problems global governance networks must solve. It can explain the most likely areas of conflict and the type of networking activities that require coordination to claim large benefits. This literature treats the functional form and task of the network, the network-as-structure, as a source of hypotheses about the incentives driving the likely behavior of actors.

We examine Internet governance because transnational networked actors are particularly prominent. The Internet was set up in a way that ignored national boundaries. Much of its coordination depends on global technological communities that are not organized internally around formal hierarchies, national boundaries, or representation. These communities make decisions in ways that often rely on consensus led by a recognized authority. Many coordination points in the Internet, such as Internet addresses, reside in private nonprofit corporations, not governmental organizations. Additionally, Internet governance activities rely heavily on e-mail, online documentation, and other forms of networked collaboration made possible by the Internet itself. Finally, Internet governance has been influenced by the World Summit on the Information Society (WSIS), a global UN conference process that prominently featured networks of NGOs. Taken together, these factors seemingly favor a form of decentralized global governance, networks-as-actors, that goes well beyond national governments and seems relatively free of the traditional hierarchies of international organizations.

In contrast, network economics shows when hierarchies, points of vulnerability, and distributional clashes are likely to emerge as a consequence of the Internet as a network structure. Unlike some chapters in this book, which emphasize the way transnational actors achieve greater power *through* networked organization, our treatment emphasizes the ways in which power is exercised *over* networks. We show that the Internet's global governance often features a delegation of authority from governments (especially the U.S. government) to nonstate actors (some of which, but not all, operate as network forms of organization). In short, network economics show where and how governments and hierarchy likely intrude. Delegation theory then predicts when governments are likely to rely on delegation to nonstate actors, and when they are more prone to rely on traditional international organizations. As we show, the agents sometimes can manipulate the incentives created by the network as a structure to favor their authority.

We conclude that governments delegate most extensively to networks to reap efficiency gains, but exercise more direct authority over distributional problems. In mixed circumstances, delegation to nongovernmental authority may be to networks with elements of hierarchy that make it easier for governments to intervene.

We first review the two literatures, showing how the theories of delegation and networking have complementary strengths. We then apply delegation and networking theory to three distinct areas of Internet governance: a) the Internet Engineering Task Force (IETF) and its role in technical standards governance; b) the Internet Corporation for Assigned Names and Numbers (ICANN) and its role in making policy for Internet identifiers; and c) the conflict over international Internet interconnection arrangements.

Delegation and Network Economics

The literature on international institutions has imported theories of domestic politics about why political executives and legislatures (principals) grant powers to bureaucracies (agents), and how they assure compliance by these agents with the purposes of the principals over time (Hawkins et al. 2006).

For delegation in its purest form, the principal must be able to create and to rescind the grant of power (ibid., 7). However, the field of international relations addresses the issue of who has the authority in an anarchic environment (one lacking an acknowledged central authority). One property of networking is that collective action can easily be an emergent property of the network because the ease of interaction facilitates the emergence of informal and formal vehicles for collective action. This happened during the Internet's creation and created later choices about the terms of the decision network's authority.

Actors, like governments, delegate authority to international institutions (Lake and McCubbins 2006):

1. To create gains from specialization and expert knowledge possessed by agents (in international institutions such as the World Health Organization);
2. To improve the ability to address policy externalities affecting many states;
3. To grant agenda-setting power to agents that can ease paradoxes of collective decision making, and enhance policy credibility by yielding authority to agents with more extreme preferences (e.g., European Union officials are passionate advocates of the European Union); and,
4. To create a third party that can resolve disputes between principals (e.g., WTO trade dispute mechanisms).[1]

1. This list rewords and reorders the original passage in part and quotes the passage in part from Lake and McCubbins 2006.

Delegating authority means facing the risk that conflicts of interest between the principals and agents and the inevitability of asymmetric information (the agent knows more than the principal) will open the way to agents pursuing their own agenda ("slack"). Sometimes, the principal has to grant carefully defined, but real, autonomy to an agent to gain the desired goal (as in international dispute resolution mechanisms). However, principals have many tools to reduce the autonomy of agents, including some that may seem quite counterintuitive. These include "stacking the deck" in the agency's personnel system or in outside advisory processes to assure that people favorable to the goals of the principals have a disproportionate role. They also include reporting systems ("fire alarms") that encourage third parties to blow the whistle on the performance of agents.[2]

As long as the principals have enough information to judge the relative merit of an initiative compared to the status quo and some method of sanctioning the agent (e.g., a budget cut if the agent fails the principal), then a principal can profit from delegating power. Still, scholars of delegation recognize the potential for both unintended consequences and slack (Epstein and O'Halloran 1999).

When applied to international governance, a theory of delegation can do the following:

1. Identify the principals and the implications of the principals' median preferences for the chain of subsequent delegation (Broz and Hawes 2006). For example, the U.S. government is the ultimate principal for the Internet's ICANN. If other governments increase their influence over ICANN, the divergence of preferences among the principals would erode ICANN's autonomy.
2. Understand how the advantages to the principals influence the role of the agents. In a highly technical arena like Internet standards an agent will be an expert and require considerable discretion to be credible as a source of coordination decisions.
3. Illuminate how the challenges of monitoring and control shape the design of the delegated powers—who gets delegated power, what are the terms of reference, what are the decision processes. Transparency in Internet standards setting lowers the cost of monitoring and the high costs of personal commitment for standards leaders increase their expert credibility.

A theory of delegation cannot predict the design of governance because it cannot predict the incentives or options for the principals. In contrast, networking theory can illuminate design principles, incentives, and constraints

---

2. The concepts of "stacking the deck" and "fire alarms" are found, respectively, in Cowhey 1993 and McCubbins, Noll, and Weingast 1987.

for networked activities. This clarifies the challenges of delegation. In particular, the economic theory of networks explores the structure of networks and their consequences for performance and the distribution of benefits.[3] This approach is implicitly functionalist and treats the network as a structure. It shows how network structure creates trade-offs among different performance characteristics and identifies the key "strategic high grounds" that allow for control and manipulation of performance. These factors shape the choices about the delegation of authority for Internet governance.

Our discussion will omit some key design features of networks, such as the economics of congestion. Instead, we spell out the key implications of three features of networks for Internet governance.

Benefits

Any well-designed network should offer three benefits: network externalities, economies of scale, and economies of scope.

A network externality means that a network is more valuable when used by more people. The added value comes from the demand side, as the larger network offers any user who joins it more people, content, or services with which to interact. Hence, social welfare increases when others join the network.[4] But as recipients of spam and telemarketing calls know, the network externality does not go on forever; diminishing returns may set in (Noam 2001).

Supply-side economies of scale and scope are also important design considerations in networks. Scale economies refer to larger volumes on the same facilities, which reduce average costs per unit. They are achieved by aggregating traffic on shared facilities. Scope economies involve the performance of additional, complementary functions by the same network in a way that increases total efficiency. But, there are limits to the scale and scope argument. Many times, bigger is better for static economies. But bigger may also be slower and less innovative, and therefore less efficient in achieving dynamic economies (e.g., redesigning the network architecture radically). The growth of a network can also produce diseconomies of scale and scope (Mueller 1989). A linear increase in the number of participants in a network can produce an exponential increase in the number of possible interconnections or relationships, thereby requiring a disproportionate increase in the need for administrative coordination.

In sum, networks can reap benefits on these three fronts, but they are not exempt from laws of diminishing returns. Thus, the growing size of a trans-

3. This literature can also shed light on the design structure of noncommunications networks.

4. There can also be supply-side or production externalities, for example, when designers of equipment adopt the same standard because it raises the total capacity of the component supplier network. Shy 2001.

national network may make it less valuable to certain actors. And even if a network organization becomes more valuable as it increases in size, the increased complexity associated with continued growth may require structural changes in administration that fundamentally alter its character.

Scarce Network Resources and Hierarchy

Networking arguments in global governance emphasize their flat, decentralized structures. However, networks come in a variety of hierarchical flavors. Even the Internet—literally, the internetworking of networks—depends heavily on hierarchical structures. Thus, simply because elements are networked we cannot assume flat decentralization. Most important, probing when hierarchy is preferable gives us clues about the limits of decentralized, flat networks.

Hierarchy may be desirable when it conserves valuable, scarce network resources. The traditional telephone network, for example, was extremely hierarchical and very centralized at the top. This architecture conserved two scarce resources—transmission capacity and intelligent switching capacity. Born in an electrical-mechanical age, these resources were expensive to create and to expand. The Internet thrives by inverting the constraints of the telephone system. Bandwidth is relatively cheap and plentiful, and network intelligence or processing power has been doubling every year and a half for three decades. This has permitted a decentralized architecture that is relatively flat. But even on the Internet, scarcity leads to elements of hierarchy. One source of scarcity is a router's capacity to store and search Internet routing tables. As the number of networks on the Internet increases, the number of routes that packets can take grows exponentially. This fact imposes a hierarchical structure on routing and address assignment. Another is the administrative capacity to coordinate unique domain name assignments. As we shall see, the need for unique names produced a major coordination problem that only the introduction of hierarchy could resolve.

An important case of scarce resources driving the organization of networks is the essential (or bottleneck) facility, a node that is central to connections. These facilities are vital to the performance of core network services, but are expensive and difficult to duplicate or replace (usually requiring considerable time, effort, and sunk costs). Essential facilities are control points in the network, no matter how flat the network may generally be. They also are points of vulnerability for the network (as when telephone services crashed in Manhattan on September 11 because switching was concentrated around Wall Street).

The classic example of an essential facility in the phone network was the local access line (for phone or DSL broadband service) that went to residential homes. Digging trenches to lay cables to individual residences is expensive and time consuming; new entrants have a hard time replicating the capacity.

Thus, the entrant has to negotiate to rent access to the essential facility from the incumbent. This gives the incumbent the ability and the incentive to impose anticompetitive terms for access in a purely market negotiation.[5]

In sum, no matter how nominally flat and decentralized a network may be, a variety of elements—such as costs, physical limitations, coordination difficulties—may make the network both subject to hierarchical control and vulnerable. Scarce network resources—especially essential facilities—shape the design of networks, including the degree of hierarchy. Analysts of network organizations must carefully uncover the forms of scarcity driving design and performance.

Interconnection of Networks

Interconnecting competing networks (e.g., British Telecom sending traffic to Orange, or vice versa) is a critical design issue for networking. It is not easy to achieve effectively. Three issues are especially important.

The first problem is compatibility among networks. This is a technical issue, but it is also strategic. Networks may employ different standards for implementing the same functions. This may emerge out of the idiosyncratic history of a network, but incompatibility may also occur for strategic reasons, as it occurred in different global standards for the second generation of cellular telephone systems.[6]

The second aspect of interconnection is unbundling. Unbundling means breaking a network down into its component parts and allowing the parts to be rented and used by another network operator. Unbundling and interconnection have been central to the regulatory wars over telecommunications competition since the mid-1970s. Which network components are available under what terms and prices are the subjects of huge regulatory fights. This is not just a telecom story. Two NGOs cooperating may agree to exchange their mailing lists. But to what detail can you ask the other NGO to sort this data?

A third feature is reciprocal compensation. If you agree to exchange services with another network, on what basis will you be compensated? If traffic flows between two networks are usually about the same, or virtually zero, it may be easier to exchange on a reciprocal "courtesy" basis between the parties. If flows are regularly unbalanced what will be the compensation basis? Today, there are sometimes heated debates about what constitutes "equivalent" traffic flows among telecommunication networks. This has surfaced, for example, in debates about the flow of Web traffic over the global Internet. If more Web traffic enters the United States than goes out, how should U.S. and foreign carriers of Web traffic compensate each other, if at all?

5. For good surveys of the complete economics of the problem, see Gabel and Weiman 1998; Cave et al. 2006; Farrell and Weiser 2003; Bar et al. 2001.

6. Shapiro and Varian 1999 gracefully summarize the literature.

The lesson of interconnection is that there are economic incentives for networks to quarrel over networking. These quarrels are exacerbated by the network externality, which might make bigger networks unwilling to extend the benefits of their larger scope to smaller networks. Interconnection is hard; the terms for getting it right are not self-evident. The situation is ripe for strategic behavior by one or more parties. In the world of telecommunications this often leads to centralization of authority, in the form of regulatory agencies, to create stable expectations about the terms of interconnection (Shiman and Rosenworcel 2002). The insights of network economics are summarized below:

1. All network designs can deliver three benefits:
   - Network externalities
   - Economies of scale
   - Economies of scope
   - However, these benefits are subject to diminishing returns, diseconomies of growth, and trade-offs between static and dynamic efficiency
2. Networks vary in the degree of hierarchy among network elements and centralization of control
   - Scarce network resources often lead to hierarchical control
   - The sources of scarcity in a network can be surprising
   - Control of essential facilities can yield leverage over the whole network
   - Essential facilities are points of vulnerability for network performance
3. Interconnection among networks is a challenging task because
   - Technical standards/systems may vary among networks and there are mixed incentives for moving to homogeneous standards
   - Unbundling network elements for use by other networks is ripe for strategic behavior
   - Reciprocal compensation is contentious.

In summary, meshing the logics of networking and delegation suggests a strategy for analyzing networked governance. The theory of delegation can identify the principals, understand the implications of their preferences, examine the gains from delegation, and the mechanisms of control and monitoring. If governance structures are networks—or if networks are being governed—then the economics of networks can reveal structural features shaping actors' behavior involving scarce resources, bottlenecks, hierarchical structures, and interconnection tensions emerging from a network situation. Together, the approaches clarify both the design choices facing actors involved in the Internet and how Internet governance accommodates the strategic positions of governments. As the case studies show, authority is delegated to networks-as-actors as part of narrowly defined attempts to improve efficiencies. Hierarchical control by governments increases as the focus is distributional.

Application of Delegation and Networking Theory: The Challenge of Global Governance of the Internet

The Internet is often cited as a kind of "strange attractor" (to use a physics metaphor) for networking in governance as well as communications. So, it serves as a most likely case for new forms of networked governance. There are three interrelated tasks of established Internet governance, each with distinct characteristics.[7] For each task we first examine the networking story and then consider the delegation story.

The first task is the development of the technical standards. In this stage, adoption is voluntary and there are benefits from widespread compatibility, so there are incentives to cooperate but agreement is not always easy. The second is the allocation and assignment of exclusive resources, such as Internet addresses and domain names. This resource allocation resembles other domains, except that it requires technical knowledge and must fit within significant technical constraints; decisions on policies and procedures must contend with issues of scarcity, efficiency, equity, and the role of markets versus administrative planning. The third concerns the policies and procedures governing the interconnection of Internet service providers and their use of physical telecommunication facilities.

Standard Setting: The Networking Story

Technical standard setting is essential to interconnecting networks. The Internet protocols and standards emerged from a research community, not as a commercial development project. The U.S. military and later the civilian National Science Foundation funded the early researchers. The U.S. government did not create its own system of standard setting; it simply pursued robust data networking and the growth of computer science. It was content to let the computer science community provide the decision-making system for standards that evolved out of the incentives created by the network structure. The informal community of scientists that emerged from these projects evolved into the Internet Engineering Task Force (IETF).[8]

In its early days the IETF community was also a *model of the network as an actor.* As it evolved as an agent of a research community it reaped advantages from a decentralized structure of expertise and novel work methods. It was one of the earliest pioneers of the use of e-mail and e-mail lists to accomplish distributed collaboration and a set of nodes built around the work of respected research leaders. Its status as both production-level *user* and *designer*

---

7. We do not examine the efforts of governments to exercise censorship of Web content or sabotage websites precisely because there is little agreement on what content or practices are acceptable. Mathiason et al. 2004.

8. It had several prior names and structures, but the continuity is great enough to justify referring to the IETF throughout this discussion.

of Internet standards created the kind of self-correcting feedback and improvement incentives that account for much of its early success as a developer of standards and "running code." Its leadership did not always have a common agenda, but it had a dominant client in its formation (the U.S. government). It also was fiercely skeptical of any scheme for standards that interfered with innovation and experimentation. This experience corroborates the asserted advantages of the so-called network form of organization, and helps explain why the Internet protocols succeeded where the main alternative, the Open Systems Interconnection (OSI) protocols, failed. The OSI protocols relied on formal, face-to-face, bureaucratic development mechanisms and could not compete with the IETF's virtual collaboration and fusion of users and developers.

As the Internet became commercially significant, the potential conflicts of interest became greater. The IETF skillfully co-opted companies by including their best experts as long as they acted in their own individual capacity in the IETF work. The IETF also enlisted the U.S. and other governments as allies when its influence was challenged. The IETF acted strategically in exploiting the Internet as a structure in a manner similar to the secretariat of Amnesty International (described by Lake and Wong, chapter 7).

Standard Setting: The Delegation Story

During its early history IETF clearly was not an agent of any government. Nevertheless, we argue that it later became a "virtual agent" in a chain of delegation involving governments. The theory of delegation does not require a formal act of deliberative delegation by a principal (Hawkins et al. 2006, 7). Rather, a principal can become newly interested in an arena (such as credentialing doctors or certifying the safety of consumer products) where there is a preexisting "agent" who emerged for other reasons.[9] At that point, the principal, such as the U.S. government, can decide among three alternatives: (a) whether to accept the existing agent's activities as an acceptable embodiment of its interests; (b) move to modify the potential agent's identity, authority, or reporting relationship; or (c) try to substitute another agent for the existing one.

A major reason for delegation is to benefit from expertise, especially when there are large policy externalities. This includes granting (or accepting) agenda-setting power to highly committed, expert partisans of an approach that is preferable to other alternatives. Preexisting agents have already revealed their character through their pattern of actions. Even if no formal decision on delegation is ever made, the potential of government intervention can shape the prospective agent's pattern of conduct. The IETF represented a raucous community of prestigious experts with strong views on networking, prone to resist domination of technical design by government industrial poli-

9. See J. Mark Hansen's 1991 study of the Farm Bureau in U.S. politics.

cies or dominant firms. Moreover, the IETF's decision processes were totally transparent, had multiple steps (allowing for timely appeal if something went awry), and acted on a consensus guided by experts who were volunteering their time (Bradner 1996). This was a form of costly commitment by experts that enhances their credibility to principals (Lake and McCubbins 2006).

Did the IETF (and its antecedents) ever have to cement its role by establishing itself as a virtual agent of the U.S. or other governments? We argue that it did. The Internet protocol served a very useful function for the United States and its industry by providing a viable alternative to the standard-setting efforts of the International Telecommunication Union's International Telegraph and Telephone Consultative Committee (CCITT) and the domination of data networking by the proprietary standards of IBM (Abbate 1999, 167–77). The success of the Internet standards community rested on persuading major U.S. government agencies to support its efforts to "tip" the marketplace toward a particular approach to networking.[10] After that, the IETF had to keep delivering solutions faster than the alternatives.

By the time the Internet had emerged de facto as a commercially viable standard, no major government was anxious to argue with the large corporations who had embraced the Internet architecture. Just as important, retaining the IETF as the locus of standards governance allayed the worst fears of the three major industrial regions. For the U.S. government, the worry was that the European Union or Japan might belatedly engage in industrial policy to overcome the de facto boost to the U.S. computer industry emerging from the Internet computing revolution. For the EU and Japan, the IETF was an instrument for keeping the computer industry away from the consolidated dominance of Microsoft.[11] The real issue then became how to frame the IETF's influence in terms of broader principles that the industrial governments could support. They agreed to a principle found in many trade agreements: international standards should be "voluntary and industry led." This principle would deflect any government from intervening strongly in the marketplace to find competitive advantage for its firms. Thus, the IETF became accepted as the virtual agent of standards setting in data communication.

Resource Allocation/Assignment: The Networking Story

When it comes to Internet resources, the network-as-structure story revolves around essential facilities and bottleneck control. As user-friendly placeholders for numerical Internet Protocol (IP) addresses, domain names

10. Key IETF actors persuaded the U.S. military to distribute Transmission Control Protocol/Internet Protocol (TCP/IP) freely to universities and to fund "translator" gateways that allowed the interconnection of non-Internet and Internet networks. The adoption of TCP/IP by NSFNet in the 1980s was another crucial step. As late as 1990, however, some factions in the U.S. government still supported OSI over the TCP/IP protocols. Mahonen 2000.

11. Based on the notes of a participant in the U.S. government team that planned for the 1995 G8 Summit on the Information Society. Berners-Lee 2000 tells a similar story about the standards for the Web.

introduce two technical requirements. First, each name must be globally unique so that information going to or from a domain doesn't get confused. Second, during its use on the Internet each name must be bound to a numerical IP address, which is the "real" address as far as the Internet's packet-routing infrastructure is concerned (Mueller 2002b; National Research Council 2005).

The design of the Domain Name System (DNS) protocol provides for an inexhaustible number of domain names—there is no scarcity of identifiers. But any individual name must be assigned exclusively to a responsible user—that is, the uniqueness of assignments must be maintained. It was the need to *coordinate the uniqueness* of domain names that created the bottlenecks and scarcities that led to a hierarchical naming structure in DNS. One can understand the problem by imagining a totally flat name space in which every computer in the world connected to the Internet must somehow get a unique name. With tens of thousands of domains being added and deleted every hour, the process of compiling an exhaustive, authoritative, and accurate list of which names were already taken, and disseminating it to everyone who needed to reference it in a timely fashion, would be very difficult. Add to that the problem of names constantly changing their mapping to IP addresses as network configurations are modified.

DNS solves these coordination problems by making the name space and the mapping process hierarchical. A global central authority (ICANN) coordinates the registration and mapping of a small number of names at the top of the hierarchy (top-level domains or TLDs).[12] The root server system tells global Internet users which IP addresses are associated with those top-level names. Once names at the top of the hierarchy are assigned by the root administrator, the registries for each TLD (say, *.com*) can take over the task of assigning unique second-level names (say, *aol.com*), and operate their own name servers that match those second-level names to their proper IP addresses. Likewise, the unique second-level name holders can hand out unique usernames or third-level names (*peter@aol.com*), and so on.

With this hierarchy in place, administrators at the root level don't have to worry much about what happens below them, yet everything remains coordinated nevertheless. But the hierarchy also makes the DNS root an essential facility, and its administrator achieves substantial leverage over the industry and users. The critical facility here is the *DNS root zone file*, the authoritative source of information about which TLDs exist and which IP addresses they should be mapped to. Any computer on the Internet can distribute copies of the root zone file to users, so there are no restrictions on entry into the root server process. What leads to hierarchy is the question of who controls or coordinates the *content* of the root zone file.

12. Top-level domain names include the familiar *.edu, .com, .org,* and *.net,* as well as *.info, .mobi,* and all the two-letter country codes such as *.de* or *.mx.*

Whoever controls the root zone file also controls the supply of domain names at the top level, and can therefore manipulate value and control the distribution of benefits. Competitive entry into the market is affected by the root administrator's decisions, which also gives the root administrator the authority to regulate registries. The creation of new top-level domains, or the reassignment of the right to operate a major top-level domain such as *.org* or *.net*, involves wealth transfers representing hundreds of millions of dollars a year.

The DNS name space hierarchy was an impressive solution to scaling issues facing the coordination of unique naming in 1982, when its implementation started. As the Internet in general and domain names in particular became more valuable in the 1990s, the DNS's hierarchical structure created an essential facility at the top of the hierarchy, raising issues about who would control it (Mueller 2002b; Froomkin 2000; Shaw 1997). The bottleneck character of the root is reinforced by the presence of strong network externalities. If all computers on the Internet use the same name space, the easier it is for Internet users to interoperate efficiently using domain names. These network externalities, in turn, foster global convergence—and dependence—on a single, dominant root zone (Mueller 2002a; National Research Council 2005). Getting users to migrate en masse to a competing root is virtually impossible barring some major shift in technology.

Resource Allocation/Assignment: The Delegation Story

The institutional response to the emergence of the root as an essential facility is a classic example of delegation. We would expect a point of vulnerability in the Internet, such as the DNS root zone file, to generate special institutional mechanisms to protect it. We would also expect the centralization of power it represents to attract political interest but also substantial discretion for the agent (Hawkins et al. 2006, 26–27).

The U.S. Commerce Department's delegation to ICANN in 1998 allowed it to bypass the lengthy and difficult process of creating a new intergovernmental organization or of harmonizing territorial jurisdiction, instead creating a private corporation empowered to issue global contracts to address the governance problems. ICANN itself is a formally organized, hierarchical corporation, and its contracts are a binding form of governance. Many of its policy development processes, however, attempt to encompass informal, networked relations. Policy decisions are vetted through a relatively open system of corporatist representation involving functional constituencies—DNS service suppliers, the Internet technical community, multinational Internet service providers, civil society, trademark holders, and country code top-level domain (ccTLD) managers. Participation in most ICANN meetings and processes is open to anyone in the world, and its bylaws parse out seats on policy-making councils according to geographic representation rules. But, in a critical concession to European complaints, it created the Governmental Advisory Committee (GAC), which provides an interface between national sovereigns and the ICANN board. GAC has gradually grown in informal influence within ICANN, and further increases have resulted from the challenges of the World Summit on the Information Society.

This delegation tried to lock in a policy approach that coincided with U.S. preferences. The delegated agents are expert and partisan and the decision processes are relatively transparent to assist monitoring by key parties of interest to the United States. It was hoped that these features would co-opt enough support in the business and technical communities of Europe, in key governments, and in other technological centers that the control of ICANN over the root would be sustainable. But, for reasons predicted by networking theory, the root zone file and root server system, as essential facilities, remained subject to struggles for control and disputes over distribution.

The delegation to ICANN employs three instruments:

- A Memorandum of Understanding (MoU) between the U.S. Department of Commerce and ICANN with a list of specific tasks for ICANN and a set of specific priorities, milestones, or accomplishments. In September 2006, the MoU was changed to a somewhat more generalized Joint Project Agreement (JPA) that no longer lists specific tasks.
- A contract with the U.S. government to perform the so-called IANA functions (technical coordination of unique name and number assignments).
- A cooperative agreement between the U.S. Department of Commerce and VeriSign, Inc., controlling its implementation of root zone file modifications and defining its relationship to ICANN.

Under this arrangement the U.S. government retains policy authority over the root zone file; ICANN must submit any proposed changes to the Commerce Department for approval. VeriSign, a U.S. corporation and primary root server operator, is responsible for implementing U.S. government-approved decisions. The actual operation of the other root servers is performed by an informal and autonomous collection of engineering groups, a residue of the informal origins of the Internet. Three of the root servers are outside the United States. Contrary to the original intentions of the U.S. Commerce Department, most of the root server operators still have no contractual relationship with ICANN or any government. The root server operators have an established professional norm of not changing the content of the root zone file; they take it as a given and answer DNS queries only. Consistent with delegation theory, however, should one of these operators within the United States take actions that go beyond certain political parameters—for example, seriously undermining the ICANN regime or the stability of the Internet—one would expect it to trigger action by the government.

When creating ICANN, the United States stacked the deck in favor of its priorities. It disproportionately empowered the Internet technical community and intellectual property owners. The nonprofit corporation's board and policy development process, along with Commerce Department oversight, favored these communities. And its worldview led it to promote competition in the domain name registration industry, whittling away at the dominance of VeriSign. However, the United States favored regulation, and acted to prevent or slow competition, when such policies were needed to protect copyright and trademark interests. ICANN quickly implemented a system of eliminating domain name assignments that threatened the exclusivity of trademarked names, and prevented any expansion of top-level domain names that would drive up the costs of registering and protecting trademarks for major global companies (Weinberg 2002).

The terms of the delegation also assure that the composition of the board will not veer sharply away from the original median point. The accountability of the regime to the public and to domain-name consumers is weak. The original, radical idea of holding public, global elections to select half the ICANN board members, implemented experimentally in 2000, was not repeated when the results of the elections indicated that the distribution of power envisaged in the initial stacking of the deck might be threatened by the results of global board elections (Klein 2001).

From 2003 to the end of 2005, U.S. authority over the root became one of the flashpoints of the World Summit on the Information Society. Other countries, including the European Union, decried private-sector-led governance and the "pre-eminence" of one sovereign and demanded parity.[13] WSIS failed to resolve this conflict. Its only substantive action was to create a nonbinding, multistakeholder discussion forum, the Internet Governance Forum (IGF), to prolong but defuse the discussions.

In the IGF the interactions of states, civil society groups, and businesses equilibrated on a new kind of network governance organization. Transnational civil society networks who strongly disagreed with the policy preferences built into the ICANN regime welcomed WSIS as an opportunity to reopen contentious issues, such as ICANN's accountability and its impact on privacy, competition, and freedom of expression. In doing so, they strategically allied themselves with developing-country governments critical of ICANN and the United States, arguing together for a more equitable distribution of power and resources. The same civil society advocates, however, aligned themselves with private sector interests in supporting multistakeholder forms of Internet governance that limited the power of national states and gave parity to nonstate actors. In this respect the creation of an open, multistakeholder Internet Governance Forum was a small victory for civil so-

---

13. The UN Working Group on Internet Governance (WGIG) Report paragraph 48 says that "no single Government should have a pre-eminent role in relation to international Internet governance."

ciety. Whether this network model of governance can have any serious impact on the delegation-based regime remains an open question. Although the Internet Governance Forum is intended to apply only to transgovernmental and not multistakeholder networks, Eilstrup-Sangiovanni's contrast of the features of networks (chapter 10) suggests that the Forum would not be the preferred mode of operation for Internet issues that require strong levels of compliance, verifiability, and obligation.

Internet governance may eventually encompass a greater role for governments, even if ICANN remains in the hands of a nonprofit corporation. In response to WSIS, in 2005 the U.S. government issued a statement of principles formally asserting a U.S. right to retain policy authority over the root indefinitely.[14] U.S. business interests and the U.S. Congress overwhelmingly backed its claims. During the same period, the Bush administration responded to right-wing domestic political pressure by using the GAC to obstruct an ICANN decision creating a new top-level domain for pornography, *.xxx*. This was a classic example of sanctioning an agent that was using discretion unwelcomed by the ultimate principal. Although demands to move ICANN functions into the International Telecommunications Union (ITU) were taken off the table by WSIS, many state actors still insist on a distinction between "public policy" and "technical management," reserving to states the former and consigning ICANN and private sector actors to the latter. As a result of these developments, GAC has become much more influential in ICANN's policy process.

Given the wide divergence of preferences among states, an agreement to shift control over ICANN away from a U.S. principal would reduce the discretion granted to ICANN (Hawkins et al. 2006, 21, 27). Additionally, the importance of country codes seems to be growing. ICANN's initial attempt to incorporate ccTLDs into its private contractual regime, making them mere contractors on the same level of generic TLD registries like *.com* and *.org*, failed. National governments have viewed the assignment of these country codes to registries as implicating national sovereignty.[15] This creates an important national space within the global approach of the Internet design. In at least one case, that of China, a government has used its ccTLD to implement internationalized domain names in a way that impinges on ICANN's decision-making discretion.

Internet Interconnection and Telecommunication Facilities: The Networking Story

The third aspect of Internet governance involves the policy choices affecting the physical telecommunication infrastructure, and the negotiations

---

14. June 30, 2005, statement by the National Telecommunications and Information Administration, U.S. Department of Commerce.

15. ICANN GAC 2000. The sovereignty principle with respect to ccTLDs was formally recognized in the June 30, 2005, Principles issued by the U.S. government, and by the Tunis Agenda of WSIS.

among Internet service providers (ISPs) over the interconnection of those facilities. The key issue is *reciprocal compensation,* always a contentious problem.

In the United States, policy decisions favoring a competitive ISP market emerged between 1992 and 1995, prior to any delegation of U.S. authority to an international institution. A 1992 National Science Foundation report laid out the groundwork for introducing "network access points" into the architecture of the Internet. The network access points provided the infrastructure for interconnection among commercial rivals, thereby facilitating competitive provision of high-speed, backbone data transport. The Internet backbone in the United States switched to commercial provision in April 1995 when the NSF contracted out transport services to four commercial providers (Greenstein 2005).

Initially, competing Internet backbone networks in the United States exchanged traffic at no fee. Later, the carriers with the highest traffic volume and largest geographic scope (known as Tier One) began to recognize a hierarchy among carriers. With their Tier One "peers" they created private contracts to continue exchanging traffic at no cost. For smaller carriers, such as smaller regional or local ISPs, they charged a transport fee. Thus began a system of multitier pricing for interconnection. Despite complaints, U.S. regulators reasoned that enough competition existed in Tier One to keep pricing efficient and prevent harm to consumers.[16]

This sanguine view of backbone transport inside the United States did not extend to transport between the United States and the rest of the world. Until 1998 international telecommunication transport arrangements largely involved negotiations between multiple, competing carriers from the United States and monopolies (or systems with very limited competition) in other countries. Moreover, the rules for international interconnection of national networks, developed through the ITU, reinforced the monopoly pricing power for countries interconnecting with competitive markets. This system created a windfall for monopolists in developing countries who collected several billion dollars in profits annually from terminating the global traffic of U.S. carriers. The system also meant that global networks could not deliver their services inexpensively, a major liability in an information economy. So, the United States acted unilaterally in 1997 to cut what it paid to foreign monopolists for voice services—if voice prices declined, data prices would follow (Cowhey 2004). Thus, the United States unilaterally changed the terms for interconnection in international services.

The U.S. decision came just as the rise of the World Wide Web stimulated the volume of cross-border telecommunication traffic. Users around the world wanted to access the world's most popular websites, the majority of which were then in the United States. ISPs in other countries needed to con-

---

16. That is to say, there was no systematic ability to withhold capacity to raise prices on a sustained basis or limit the ability of others to enter the market: Greenstein 2005; Economides 2005. For a summary of the views of those worried about competitive problems, see Kesan and Shah 2001 and Benoliel 2003.

tract with U.S. carriers for Internet interconnection. U.S. carriers treated these foreign ISPs as the equivalent of Tier Two carriers—small and low volume. Therefore, they charged them for exchanging traffic. Moreover, the international transmission costs were not shared; foreign ISPs had to lease the entire circuit from their location to the U.S. exchange point.[17] In sum, foreign carriers had to assume a much larger share of the interconnection burden under this regime.

A major distributional conflict had emerged between the reciprocal compensation system worked out in the United States for Internet traffic and the ITU-based reciprocal compensation system that had existed for telephone communications. This led the United States to champion a shift in delegation, discussed below, while prompting supporters of the old system to make Internet interconnection an issue in WSIS.

Internet Interconnection and Telecommunication Facilities: The Delegation Story

The ITU had long been the delegated agent of governments for conducting policy work on international communications. During the 1990s, the United States and the other major industrial countries agreed that a part of the economic governance of telecommunications and information services should be shifted to the World Trade Organization.

By 1998 all of the Organisation for Co-operation and Development countries, plus Hong Kong and Singapore, had introduced competition in telecommunications services. (A number of large developing economies had also done so.) Together, these economies constituted the overwhelming preponderance of world telecommunications. After introducing competition into their internal markets, these countries wanted to enter each other's markets and to create cross-border networks as they deemed commercially feasible. However, they did not trust each other to open their markets unilaterally to foreign investors and suppliers, so they used the WTO to craft an agreement that set a higher common denominator for cross-border liberalization. In 1994, negotiations on what became the Basic Telecommunications Agreement were initiated in the WTO. The WTO agenda included commitments to allow foreign investment and provision of global networking infrastructure and services (Cowhey, Aronson, and Richards forthcoming).

The full membership of the WTO did not share the preferences of the countries involved in the Basic Telecommunications Agreement of 1997, but they were indifferent to the talks because the major markets did not ask them to participate. The active participants in the negotiations were satisfied to

---

17. Another problem was that U.S. companies also provided much of the transport linking different regions of the world. The route from Cairo to Jakarta usually ran through the United States until recently. For analyses, see Cowhey 2004 and TeleGeography 2000.

have commitments only from the core of the market. Their closely aligned incentives led to ambitious additional commitments on how to conduct their domestic regulatory regimes for telecommunications that were enforceable at the WTO (Cameron 2004). Thus, this delegation locked in both commitments and dispute resolution. The WTO delegation also was a costly and credible signal to other countries in the ITU that the major economies of the world wanted a change in the status quo. The WTO became a rival agent for international telecommunications and effectively gutted traditional ITU rules governing commercial arrangements for international transport. As predicted by delegation theory, the shift in the preferences of the governments of the largest markets in the world also had the consequence of pushing the ITU to revamp its approach to competition in order to not lose further ground.

The WTO's new jurisdiction limited the options for countries that objected to the new international contractual arrangements for Internet transport imposed by U.S. carriers. Under the WTO pact, if there was no failure in enforcing competition policy, there was no ground for a complaint by developing countries against the United States. In protest, the developing countries used WSIS to push for jurisdictional changes over the international pricing rules. Their proposals advocated a larger role for ITU jurisdiction and revised formulas for mutual compensation. As of 2008 they have not succeeded. This was a classic case of the choice about delegation of jurisdiction influencing the range of potential outcomes. The flash point for international debate—the distributional effects of reciprocal compensation—was predictable by any student of network economics. And significantly, on this contentious issue of distributional choice, governments kept decisions close to classic intergovernmental organizations.

The story of Internet governance shows how networking can influence the form of delegation. A new form of delegation emerged because lower costs of global networking (including more transparency of expert decisions) combined with great speed in action made it attractive for government principals to delegate to an IETF or ICANN rather than to intergovernmental agencies with specialized expertise. Moreover, these delegations to NGOs more reliably performed the agenda-setting goals of the key principal, the U.S. government, than would an international organization.[18] Thus, the ITU, a traditional intergovernmental organization, remains at the periphery of the Internet.

Still, the choice on delegation differed by function. Internet governance most closely approximates networked governance when it comes to technical standards functions. It takes full advantage of the potential for relatively de-

18. Cf. Eilstrup-Sangiovanni (chapter 10), who observes that international organizations usually trump transgovernmental networks if the goal is policy consistency.

centralized coordination that is more easily global and inclusive because of the low cost of networking. In the case of the IETF the coordination efficiencies led to a form of nongovernmental, networked governance serving the expert community. Nonetheless, the IETF's priorities were initially conditioned heavily by its grounding in the military and university research communities. Just as important, when commercial considerations finally arose over the intersection with phone networks and commercial data networks, key governments (especially the United States) chose not to push standards setting to alternative fora. At a minimum, the most powerful governments declined to substitute another agent for the IETF whose preferences were predictable and commercially neutral. And, crucially, the procedures of the IETF make it easy for governments to monitor the preferences and performance of the IETF.

Governments and hierarchy intrude more directly when decisions deal with scarce or exclusive resources and with the distributional issues tied up in reciprocal compensation for Internet connectivity. These resource and distribution questions touch a stronger political nerve, thereby producing a more direct government role, just as they did in the security policy questions considered in Eilstrup-Sangiovanni's discussion of government networks in international security issues (chapter 10). This is the story of ICANN and Internet transport policy. ICANN began as a delegation by the U.S. government to an NGO charged with finding a sweet spot of consent by global stakeholders, including foreign governments, while providing a high level of technical expertise. ICANN required hierarchy because it combined technical operations dealing with a hierarchic part of the Internet network structure and elaborate representational arrangements to legitimate choices on issues with distributional consequences. But these distributional implications also led to tinkering to allow more oversight by other governments. The heaviest hand of government fell on interconnection policy for data transport, because only like-minded governments acting officially could undo long-standing international rules that had inflated interconnection pricing. This required reengineering delegation from the ITU to the WTO.

The tale is not over. As the Internet has evolved, more of its operations have moved to a regional basis. This has created more functional robustness and localization (including in transport of data). The network characteristics of Internet governance may eventually lead to some elements of governance becoming more regionally decentralized. Even the most centralized function, the DNS root, could become more like a centralized module that enables global efficiencies while permitting more local control over names and numbers.[19] However, these efforts to facilitate distributed decisions have been overridden in many respects by strong political pressures to leverage hierarchical control of the root to achieve public policy goals, such as protecting

---

19. This fits the logic of software design suggested in a classic paper by David Parnas (1972).

trademarks, economic regulation, and preserving governmental oversight over domain names.

In short, the Internet has not escaped governments, but the governance systems have changed. Changes in the rules of decision making and the forms of stakeholder participation will drive outcomes in novel directions even if the parameters of choice still remain under the control of governments.[20]

20. We disagree with Goldsmith and Wu (2006) that Internet governance simply reaffirms the lesson that states retain control of global governance. This is like saying that it would not be important if a country switched from a presidential-congressional system to parliamentary democracy. Both allow voting publics to exercise control but changing the instrumental form of democracy has major implications for the path of public policy.

10

Varieties of Cooperation

GOVERNMENT NETWORKS
IN INTERNATIONAL SECURITY

Mette Eilstrup-Sangiovanni

Networks are at the heart of a vibrant debate in international relations studies about the role of the state and the changing nature of political authority. At least since the 1970s, scholars have foreshadowed the demise of the state in favor of global networks of corporations, criminals, and nongovernmental organizations that link their activities across borders and circumvent state authority (see Spiro 1995; Strange 1996; Matthew 1997; Naím 2003). Networking is not, however, confined to nonstate actors. A growing literature—spearheaded by international lawyers—points to the prominence of networks of government officials that share information and coordinate policies across borders (Picciotto 1997, 2000; Slaughter 1997, 2004a, 2004b; Zaring 1998; Raustiala 2002; Pollack and Shaffer 2001; Benvenisti 2006). Based on direct links among substate officials, and often operating without close supervision by either cabinets or chief executives, such transgovernmental networks (TGNs) provide an alternative to conventional interstate cooperation based on multilateral treaties and often coupled with formal international organizations.[1]

Government networks are not a new phenomenon. Specialized international organizations such as the International Telegraphic Union (1865), the International Postal Union (1874), the Food and Agriculture Organization (1945), and the World Health Organization (1948) have long been fora for

---

1. Some doubt that transgovernmentalism and intergovernmentalism are in fact distinct modes of collaboration (for example, Alvarez 2001). Although inter- and transgovernmental forms of cooperation overlap in important respects, I submit that they are functionally distinct and that understanding their differences can yield important insights into the nature of international cooperation. Other scholars that differentiate between trans- and intergovernmental cooperation include Keohane and Nye 1974; Slaughter 1997, 2004a, 2004b; Raustiala 2002; Bach 2003.

collaboration among domestic regulators and an object of study for social scientists (e.g., Mitrany 1932, 1943; Salter 1921, 1933; Claude 1956). What appears to be new, however, are the scale, scope, and strength of transgovernmental ties. By many accounts, TGNs are rapidly proliferating (Slaughter 2004b; Raustiala 2002, 4; Zaring 1998, 282; Bermann, Herdegen, and Lindseth 2000). From the global economy and finance to the environment, government officials increasingly collaborate with their functional equivalents abroad to address problems of a global scale. Prominent examples include the Basle Committee on Banking Supervision (1974), in which representatives of the world's most important central banks meet to regulate international banking markets, and the Financial Action Task Force (1989), where members of the G8 work together to combat money laundering. Within these function-specific networks, public officials exchange information and coordinate policies to strengthen enforcement. Due to their flexibility, speed, and low sovereignty costs many predict that government networks will be the primary vehicles for international cooperation in the twenty-first century, performing many of the functions of a world government—legislation, administration, and adjudication—only without the form (Slaughter 1997, 195; 2004b, 162; Reinicke 1999).

Yet, despite their promise as an emerging form of global governance, the dynamics of government networks are still insufficiently understood. So far, the literature on transgovernmentalism has mainly focused on demonstrating that government networks exist and have the capacity to influence policy outcomes. Getting this point across has taken precedence over rigorous analysis of why TGNs arise, and how they operate in particular settings. Moreover, both theoretical and empirical research on government networks has centered predominantly on areas of low politics—including financial regulation, securities, and antitrust—while other areas such as, for example, homeland and national security have received far less attention. We thus lack a fuller understanding of why TGNs develop and how they function across different policy areas.

In this chapter I seek to lay the foundation for an explanatory account of transgovernmentalism. My main question is under what conditions are TGNs likely to be a preferred vehicle for international cooperation as opposed to more traditional intergovernmental organizations (IGOs)? To many transgovernmentalists, government networks are a straightforward response to growing functional interdependence. As more policy problems have gone global, government officials have increasingly found it useful to deal directly with their foreign counterparts (Scharpf 1993b, 125; Raustiala 2002, 4). Moreover, "functional equivalency" (i.e., the proliferation of functionally similar regulatory practices within states) and developments in information and communication technology (ICT) make it both easier and more relevant for regulators and bureaucrats to cooperate across borders. Such explanations are, however, too indiscriminate. First, these developments are hardly new.

Domestic equivalency and functional interdependence were among the chief reasons cited by functionalist scholars in the early twentieth century in favor of a global technocracy. Second, if the proliferation of TGNs were a straightforward response to growing interdependence and advances in ICT, we would expect to see a general increase in networked cooperation. Yet government networks are not evenly distributed, either geographically or by issue area. Although some policy issues are characterized by informal, networked cooperation, others continue to be dominated by highly structured, formal treaty organizations. Existing literature leaves such organizational diversity largely unexplained.

In seeking to account for variation in TGNs versus IGOs, I focus specifically on international security cooperation as an area that has so far received scant attention from transgovernmentalist scholars. From the original theorizing of transgovernmental relations in the 1970s to the present, government networks have been seen to predominate in issue areas outside the realm of high politics (Keohane and Nye 1977). For example, Slaughter's manifesto for *A New World Order* foresees that even a world of disaggregated, networked states "would still feature states interacting as unitary actors on important issues, particularly in security matters" (2004a, 6). Yet, empirically, we see that many security issues—such as antiterrorism and antiproliferation—are today being dealt with by direct contacts between substate agents operating either within or alongside existing IGOs. These networks include militaries, national intelligence agencies, interior ministry officials, and police and law enforcement officials (Krahmann 2003, 2005; Webber et al. 2004). There are grounds, therefore, to broaden the focus of transgovernmentalist studies to include government networking in areas of high politics.

In what follows, I use the functional regime theory pioneered by Keohane (1984) and others to explain the presence of TGNs in international security. The basic premise of functional regime theory is that institutions exist to perform specific functions and that uncovering what function an institution serves is key to explaining its creation.[2] Transgovernmentalists, I contend, have generally paid insufficient attention to the particular functional attributes of networked organizations. Often TGNs are simply assumed to present an efficient solution to underlying cooperation problems, but the specific comparative advantages of networked cooperation remain obscure. To remedy this weakness, I draw on recent network studies in public policy, economics, and sociology to theorize the conditions under which states may opt to cooperate through TGNs. I find that, whereas standard regime theory— especially via its focus on the advantages of informal and soft law cooperation—can go some way toward explaining transgovernmental activity, the insights of regime theory need to be combined with a specific theory of networks in order to account for transgovernmentalism.

---

2. International regime theorists, who tend to focus on cooperation among unitary states, have largely overlooked TGNs consisting of substate actors/agencies.

My argument is developed in three stages. First, I describe the key features of TGNs and show how they differ from traditional IGOs. Second, I review some common claims by transgovernmentalists regarding the proliferation of government networks. I show that these claims are too general and indiscriminate to explain the proliferation of TGNs or to account for variation in their appearance across different issue areas. Instead, I draw on recent network studies to derive hypotheses about when we should expect TGNs to be a preferred instrument of governance. Third, I apply the argument to three cases of international security cooperation. Two cases—the Missile Technology Control Regime and the Proliferation Security Initiative—are informal government networks, while the third—the Chemical Weapons Convention —is a highly structured, formal IGO. This application is not intended to provide a full test of my argument. Nonetheless, I believe that investigating the proliferation of TGNs in an area where formal hierarchical cooperation is widely expected to be the rule can yield important clues about the allures of government networking.

Describing the Phenomenon: What Are Transgovernmental Networks?

To explain the proliferation of TGNs we must first identify what is distinct about this form of policy coordination. Robert Keohane and Joseph Nye first discussed the phenomenon of government networking at length in 1974. They distinguished three modes of international cooperation: *interstate* (or *intergovernmental*), *transgovernmental,* and *transnational.* Intergovernmental cooperation refers to diplomatic interactions among unitary, sovereign states— led by chiefs of government (CoGs) or foreign offices and consummated in multilateral treaties, which are often coupled with international organizations. This form is at the heart of the liberal international system that emerged during the nineteenth and twentieth centuries. Transgovernmental cooperation signifies "direct interactions among sub-units of different governments" that cooperate at the substate level rather than through chief executives (Keohane and Nye 1974, 43). This form is not based on international treaties but relies on informal, nonbinding agreements. Transnational cooperation, finally, refers to cooperation led by private nonstate actors, including business representatives, bankers, and NGOs, independently of states.[3]

Transgovernmentalism, by many accounts, is on the rise. Since the 1990s, observers have pointed to prima facie evidence for an increase in direct reg-

---

3. Transnationalism is heralded by many as the fastest growing and most significant form of international interaction, posing an acute challenge to state authority (Ohmae 1995; Strange 1996; Matthew 1997; Spiro 1995). I do not address transnational cooperation, although network theory clearly has much to say about this form, as other chapters in this book show. Rather my aim is to compare two forms of cooperation among state actors—trans- and intergovernmentalism—and to identify the conditions in which states prefer one to the other.

ulatory and legal cooperation among substate actors—including both high-level officials (ministerial level) and lower-level national regulators (Marin and Mayntz 1991; Slaughter 1997, 2004; Zaring 1998; Picciotto 1997, 2000; Picciotto and Mayne 1999; Reinicke 1999; Raustiala 2002; Benvenisti 2006). TGNs today encompass most spheres of governmental activity—from the global economy and finance to national security, environmental policy, and human rights—and include a variety of government agencies, such as central banks, antitrust regulators, national courts, police and customs authorities, and environmental protection agencies. They range from highly institutionalized organizations such as the Basle Committee or the G8 annual summits of leaders of the world's major economic powers, to more informal, or even secretive, bilateral or multilateral arrangements. TGNs may sometimes be housed within existing IGOs, as in the case of the OECD's Public Management committee (PUMA), the Financial Action Task Force (FATF), or the EU's web of expert committees (Trondal 2004), but even so, they are independent entities, separate from their IGO hosts.

How does cooperation in a transgovernmental mode differ from intergovernmental cooperation? International regime theorists have drawn important distinctions between formal versus informal agreements (Lipson 1991) and between "hard" versus "soft" law.[4] The differences between TGNs and IGOs overlap these distinctions but are not reducible to them. Indeed, reducing the difference between trans- and intergovernmental cooperation to a dichotomy between formal versus informal collaboration or soft versus hard law collapses together a variety of features of membership, negotiating, and implementing characteristics that separate these approaches and define their comparative advantage as means for pursuing collective policy objectives (SAIC 2001). The main differences between TGNs and IGOs pertain to membership, structure, and degree of obligation/legalization. It should be noted, however, that these are general differences to which individual exceptions can frequently be found. It should also be stressed that TGNs and IGOs are not mutually exclusive. Many IGOs are underpinned and complemented by TGNs. Yet, these forms represent distinct ways of organizing cooperation.

Membership

The most basic difference between inter- and transgovernmental cooperation is in the differing conception and representation of the state. The key actors in intergovernmentalism are unitary states. The intergovernmentalist image draws a relatively sharp distinction between the domestic and international realms of politics. International politics is the domain of foreign offices

---

4. See, e.g., Abbott and Snidal 2000; Kahler 2000. A special issue of *International Organization* (vol. 54, no. 3, 2000) is devoted to exploring issues of "Legalization and World Politics" and contains valuable perspectives on the benefits of soft versus hard law.

and is characterized by direct relations between executives. States are presumed to speak with one voice—a voice represented by either the head of state or the foreign minister. To the extent substate actors play any role in the formulation of international policy it is either through lobbying or advising executives at the stage of national policy formation or as agents implementing international agreements. International policymaking, however, remains dominated and controlled by executives (Pollack and Shaffer 2001, 24; Moravcsik 1998).

Transgovernmentalism, on the other hand, portrays the state as disaggregated rather than unitary (Keohane and Nye 1974, 44–48). To transgovernmentalists, the critical actors in international politics are not foreign ministries and CoGs, but high- and mid-level officials in subunits of national governments who coordinate policies across borders with only periodic supervision by foreign-policy establishments. Such coordination not only complements but also *substitutes* for cooperation at the executive level.

Structure

Interactions tend to be structured differently in TGNs and IGOs. Traditional international organizations (IOs) are often hierarchically structured. Action is based on high-level "political" decisions in the first instance, followed up by implementation by lower ties (Thompson 2003, 22–24; Sabel 1993, 71). By contrast, TGNs—like other networks—are characterized by lateral ties and decentralized decision making. Although power may be distributed unequally among network components, there are no formal, centralized lines of command. This flat organization implies "subsidiarity" (decisions tend to be worked out directly among the agents responsible for implementing them) and encourages the development of differentiated solutions to local problems rather than the imposition of centrally directed, uniform policies. It also implies the absence of a legitimate organizational authority to resolve disputes among actors.

Formality

A third difference pertains to how interests are coordinated. This difference, which is best characterized as a difference in degree rather than in kind, can be conceived along three dimensions: *legalization, obligation,* and *irreversibility.* Cooperation in an intergovernmentalist mode is often—but not always[5]—based on formal treaties, negotiated by executive branches and approved by formal legislative processes (Zaring 1998; Raustiala 2002; Slaugh-

5. Official international treaties do not always characterize intergovernmental cooperation. Governments can and frequently do opt for more informal executive agreements. Yet, a commitment made by a head of state is still a highly visible and credible sign of policy intentions and tends, therefore, to be more effective in binding national policies than commitments by lower-level bureaucracies. See, for example, Lipson 1991, 498–99.

ter 1997). Treaty-based cooperation often entails a high degree of obligation. Precise objectives are set out in detailed written agreements that provide clear definitions of acceptable and unacceptable behavior. Moreover, treaty-based agreements may be difficult to reverse. Although most treaties entail opt-outs and provisions for withdrawal, the high visibility and legally binding status of treaties means there may be high political costs to withdrawing or pulling back from implementing a specific initiative (SAIC 2001).

Transgovernmental cooperation, by contrast, tends to be informal and nonobligatory. TGNs are not constituted by treaty or ratified charter, they have few or no mechanisms for formal enforcement and implementation; indeed, nothing they do purports to be binding on states (Zaring 1998, 301–2; Slaughter 2004a, 48; Bermann, Herdegen, and Lindseth 2000, 1). The decisions of the Basle Committee, for example, are private and purely advisory (Raustiala 2002, 23). Transgovernmental agreements tend also to be less precise in terms of objectives and responsibilities, often leaving the terms of agreement vague (SAIC 2001; Zaring 1998, 301). Finally, the nonbinding status and low visibility of most TGNs means there are generally fewer costs to retraction from them than from formal, treaty-based agreements.

Relations among Units

The lack of a contractual foundation that can be relied on to settle disputes means that TGNs are critically dependent on expectations of generalized reciprocity. Hence, like all human networks, they typically depend on higher levels of trust than other organizational forms.[6] Whereas IGOs can rely on formal rules and administrative procedures to govern interactions, TGNs are based on direct personal contacts among professionals. As a result, they are often highly issue specific, composed of members with similar professional standards, interests, and values.

Decision Making and Implementation

A final difference pertains to decision making and implementation. IGOs are often (not always) configured as representational organizations, where formal votes are taken and majority rules may apply. Even when decisions are consensus based, the presence of a centralized bureaucracy implies an element of central agenda setting, which may constrain actors' choice. In TGNs, by contrast, decision making is predominantly consensus based (Zaring 1998, 281; Agranoff 2003, 21). The two forms also feature differing levels of support for implementation and compliance. Whereas IGOs often involve delegation to neutral agents that are empowered to interpret and enforce the rules, TGNs typically do not seek a common legal basis for action, but rely ex-

---

6. On the role of trust in networks see Powell 1990, 304; Thompson 2003, 43.

Table 10.1. Main characteristics of IGOs and TGNs

	IGO	TGN
Membership	Unitary states	Substate agencies/officials
Structure	Centralized/Hierarchical	Decentralized/Flat
Political visibility	High	Low
Legalization	High	Low
Obligation	High	Low
Irreversibility	High	Low
Unit relations	Rule-based	Trust-based
Scope	Broad	Narrow
Decision-mode	Consensus or (Q)MV	Consensus only
Support for implementation/ compliance	High	Low (self-enforced policies/voluntary compliance)

clusively on the capacities and willingness of individual members to implement agreements in accordance with national laws and practices and to monitor and verify the compliance of other members (Zaring 1998, 301).[7]

The main characteristics of these two types are summarized in Table 10.1.

Benefits and Drawbacks of the Network Form

The above characteristics of the network confer distinct benefits on social and political actors. In this section I focus on network benefits that apply specifically to TGNs and set them apart from other forms of international policy coordination.[8]

According to social network theory, a key advantage of the network is speed and efficiency of communication. In hierarchies, information must pass through a central processing unit, thereby increasing the risk of delays and information congestion. Moreover, it is often difficult to transmit information on local characteristics of problems and potential solutions to central decision makers (Scharpf 1993b, 135; Baker and Faulkner 1993, 844). By contrast, the network's flat structure implies that communication can flow unhindered between local nodes, thereby allowing for maximum speed and local initiative (Watts 2003, 280–81; Powell 1990, 325).

7. Decentralized enforcement is not unique to TGNs. Many IOs rely on national enforcement. For example, the Convention Against Torture requires governments to prosecute or extradite torturers. Yet, due to their formal, legal status, IGOs tend to have more detailed and intrusive verification and compliance regimes than TGNs do.

8. Some advantages of networking—such as enhanced prospects for learning through repeated interaction—are relevant to TGNs but do not clearly distinguish them from IGOs where learning also takes place.

Another advantage is low start-up costs. Due to their informal, noncontractual nature TGNs are faster and less costly to contract and implement than IGOs. IGOs often require considerable time and resources to establish in national or international law. After signing of treaties establishing IGOs, domestic political battles can result in ratification and implementation delays. By contrast, TGNs require no ratification and only limited implementing action.

Like other networks, TGNs exhibit both scalability and adaptability. Compared with IGOs, the scope and boundaries of TGNs are more easily redefinable. Much like the illicit drugs cartels or terrorist networks explored by Kenney and Kahler (chapters 5 and 6), nodes in TGNs are "loosely coupled" in the sense that they are not bound together by contractual agreements and have low political visibility. This implies that the costs—political as well as administrative—of adding new members are low. The practice of loose coupling also prevents "locking-in" of ineffective relationships. If a particular organizational link is not providing expected payoffs, actors can terminate the relationship at relatively low cost and replace it with alternative links (Thompson 2003, 144). The informal basis of TGNs also means that issues can be added to or dropped from the agenda with relative ease, allowing TGNs to adapt quickly to changes in their environment.

The network literature focuses overwhelmingly on network benefits. Yet, there may also be drawbacks to networked organization, which are often overlooked. First, while they promote fast communication, the lack of centralized leadership implies that networks may be subject to slow, complicated decision making as all members try to have their say (Thompson 2003, 46–47; Powell 1990, 318). Moreover, the flexibility associated with networks comes at a price. The possibility of frequent readjustment and modification of agreements may increase bargaining costs as individual members seek to adapt agreements to meet their short-term interests.

Second, networks such as TGNs may suffer from a credibility deficit. According to functional regime theory, a key reason for states to create international institutions is to enhance the credibility of agreements. Generally speaking, international institutions enhance credibility by lengthening the shadow of the future (Keohane 1984) and by solving second-order problems of monitoring and enforcement. This is particularly true of formal, treaty-based organizations where centralized verification and enforcement means there are high potential costs to reneging on agreements in the form of sanctions and reputation effects (Abbott and Snidal 2000, 427; Lipson 1991, 512). Yet, it is less likely to be true of TGNs. The decentralized implementation and verification associated with TGNs lends itself less well to raising compliance issues with other countries and seeking their resolution (SAIC 2001). Moreover, the low visibility of agreements administered by substate officials and regulators means there are fewer reputation costs to violating them.

A third potential problem is patchy implementation. The absence of centralized monitoring and enforcement means networks are often vulnerable

Table 10.2. Advantages and drawbacks to networked cooperation

Advantages	Drawbacks
Fast, efficient communication	Slow, complicated collective decision making
Low contracting and implementation costs	Low credibility/patchy implementation
Scalability	Limited scope due to reliance on trust
Adaptability	High bargaining costs due to frequent renegotiation

to free riders and that collective agendas can be easily undermined by parochial subunit goals (Powell 1990, 318).

Finally, the high premium on trust in networks may restrict the scope of participation (Raab and Milward 2003; Powell 1990, 300–26). It is well known that it is easier to generate trust and generalize expectations of reciprocity in small collectivities where actors are homogenous in values, perceptions, customs of action, and so forth. Hence, social and political networks may not expand as easily as proponents claim. Table 10.2 summarizes the advantages and drawbacks of network cooperation.

Explaining the Phenomenon: Accounting for the Proliferation in TGNs

Existing literature points to several reasons for increased transgovernmental activity. The most frequently cited cause is growing functional interdependence. According to transgovernmentalists, economic, social, and ecological interdependence is straining the capacity of the state to exercise control through centralized, hierarchical coordination: globalization undercuts the effectiveness of domestic regulatory institutions, creating new issues and problems, which can only be solved through collaboration with administrators in other states (Scharpf 1993b, 125; Finnemore 1996, 325; Keohane and Nye 1974, 41–42; Pollack and Schaffer 2001, 27; Raustiala 2002, 4). A second impetus for transgovernmentalism is the proliferation of functionally similar regulatory practices within states or "functional equivalency" (Raustiala 2002, 14, 21). States are increasingly organized in similar ways, not only in the sense that they are Weberian rationalist bureaucracies but also in the sense that there are closely corresponding functional divisions within state bureaucracies (Finnemore 1996, 325). Such similarities make it both easier and more relevant for regulators and bureaucrats in one state to cooperate with their functional equivalents abroad. Transgovernmental cooperation is further aided by the perception that many international policy issues are characterized by growing technical complexity and are therefore best controlled by a domestic regulatory agency rather than being guided by the foreign affairs bureaucracy (Raustiala 2002, 26; Keohane and Nye 1977, 210). Finally, scholars point to technological changes—in particular the revolution in ICT—that make cross-border networks easier and cheaper to maintain (Raustiala 2002, 13; Keohane and Nye 1977, 210).

It is quite evident that these trends contribute to the phenomenon of transgovernmentalism. As more policy problems transcend national borders and as policy issues become more technically complex, there is a growing need for cross-border cooperation involving policy experts. Yet, as noted, the above explanations are too indiscriminate. First, the cited factors are general, macrolevel phenomena. They may help to explain a *general* increase in transgovernmentalism (alongside other forms of international cooperation) but they are less useful for explaining variation in TGNs across different policy areas or between different groups of states (Whytock 2005). Second, they fail to isolate the specific advantages that arise from cooperation through TGNs as opposed to IGOs. After all, IGOs also address transborder issues and draw on national and international technical expertise. Third, none of these factors is new. It is noteworthy that the principal reasons cited by transgovernmentalists to account for the present growth in TGNs—functional interdependence, functional equivalency, technical complexity, and improvements in ICT— were also among the chief reasons cited by functionalist scholars in the early twentieth century to explain (and encourage) an expanding international technocracy.[9] We therefore lack answers to fundamental questions: Why do we witness a seeming proliferation of TGNs? Why among some states and not others?

In what follows, I consider the choice between TGNs and IGOs from the perspective of state executives rather than from that of individual public administrators. Most existing literature on transgovernmentalism rests on the premise that domestic regulators voluntarily seek each other out in order to improve the quality of domestic regulations or to avoid obsolescence in an increasingly globalized regulatory environment (see Colombatto and Macey 1996; Zaring 1998). Yet, there is reason to doubt this bottom-up perspective when it comes to high-politics areas such as national security. In such areas, networks continue to be underpinned by the power and authority of the state. Lower-level national officials may exchange ideas or reach informal agreements with their foreign counterparts on national security issues but they will only secure implementing action if it is in the interest of those who control state apparatuses. Moreover, the funds necessary for establishing and running TGNs usually must be approved by executives and, in some cases, by national parliaments.[10] With some simplification, we can therefore assume that, at

---

9. Like transgovernmentalists, functionalists hold that the best way to tackle universal socioeconomic problems is through administration rather than legislation. IGOs, they argue, are ill-equipped to deal with the complexities and fluidity of modern economic and social life. What are needed are function-specific networks of technocrats that can adapt more easily to constantly changing circumstances (Salter 1933 [1919]; Mitrany 1932, 1943, 35).

10. Although some transgovernmental initiatives, like the Proliferation Security Initiative

least in the security domain, executives can effectively choose (or prevent) the formation/employment of TGNs and set parameters for their activities.[11] This suggests that coordination through TGNs is best understood as a form of policy delegation by executives to lower-level officials. What prompts executives to delegate policy to lower-level national administrators who operate under few or no agreed rules, rather than to IGOs, which operate under a set of formally agreed rules and procedures? To answer this question I use a "rational design" framework: states, acting for self-interested reasons, are assumed to select institutions to minimize the costs and risk associated with achieving policy outcomes under different institutional arrangements (Koremenos, Lipson, and Snidal 2001a).

Conditions for Networked Cooperation

Small Group Size and Harmonious Preferences

We may hypothesize that TGNs are most likely among small groups with relatively homogenous preferences. Although a key benefit of the network is scalability, TGNs are likely to be best suited to cooperation among small groups with similar interests and values for two reasons. First, small groups are more likely to reap the benefits of speed and flexibility associated with networked cooperation. As noted, while networks facilitate fast and efficient communication, they can be subject to slow, complicated decision making due to a lack of centralized leadership and arbitration. This is less likely to be a problem among small groups with closely aligned preferences that will, ceteris paribus, have less difficulty in reaching consensus and will have less need for formal arbitration.

Second, networks are more likely among small homogenous groups due to credibility issues. As noted, TGNs do not offer centralized monitoring and verification and the terms of agreement are often ambiguous, increasing the risk of noncooperation. This is less of a liability among small groups with similar goals, since cheating among such groups is less likely and because effective peer-to-peer monitoring is more easily achieved among small numbers. Instead, small groups can benefit from the added flexibility and discretion en-

---

(PSI), do not require extra funding, most do. For example, funds for the Cooperative Threat Reduction Program, a transgovernmental program between the United States and USSR successor states, are included in the president's budget request for the Department of Defense and subject to the annual congressional appropriation and authorization cycle.

11. This interpretation is corroborated by Slaughter (2004b, 4, 7). She argues that TGNs function as a direct extension of the state. Although TGNs may arise outside formal international institutions they are composed of national government officials who are appointed by national governments and are subject to sanctions at home. The "top-up" view is also supported by Pollack (2005, 911–12). In his study of the regulatory networks associated with the New Transatlantic Agenda, he finds that "most of the transatlantic regulatory dialogues surveyed resemble not so much voluntarist romances undertaken independently of governments as much as 'shotgun marriages,' undertaken grudgingly under pressure from CoGs."

tailed in decentralized implementation and compliance. By contrast, the larger and more heterogeneous a group, the more likely members will seek to commit each other to a specific behavior and seek extensive monitoring and sanctioning mechanisms.[12]

> *Condition 1:* A first condition for governments to choose TGNs is small group size and relatively homogenous interests, which lessens the need for central arbitration and sanctioning.

Urgency and Time Horizon

Issues of timing may impact on institutional design in two ways. First, although urgency is not a necessary condition for networked cooperation in the way that small group size probably is (at least when it comes to sensitive areas such as national security), TGNs are particularly suited to cooperation in conditions where speed is a priority. TGNs are generally faster to set up than IGOs. As a result, reliance on TGNs should shorten the time between when a problem is identified and some form of collective action can be taken.[13]

Second, TGNs may be more attractive when time horizons are short. According to standard regime theory, a key reason why states create international institutions is to reduce the transaction costs of repeated cooperation: exchanging information, negotiating bargains, and codifying agreements (Keohane 1984; Keohane and Axelrod 1985). Formal IGOs do this by collecting and distributing information, by interpreting and enforcing rules, and by negotiating supplementary agreements. Institutions may also lower costs by resolving coordination dilemmas. In coordination dilemmas reaching an agreement is typically more important than precisely which policy is chosen (Stein 1982). In such cases, states can enhance efficiency by granting authority to an IO agent to propose policy or to adjudicate between alternative policies from a disinterested perspective.[14] TGNs are less likely to achieve these benefits. First, the noncontractual nature of TGNs implies they may fail

12. Some observers suggest the opposite, namely that TGNs are useful in cases where interests diverge too widely to be reconciled in a joint legal agreement (Benvenisti 2006). In such cases, TGNs can exploit bureaucrats' discretion under national laws to bridge the gaps. This rings true. Yet, I believe this logic is consistent with the idea that, for TGNs to work, there must be broad agreement on goals (if not on means) and no overwhelming fear of cheating. In such circumstances, TGNs can enable states to pursue shared goals while allowing for maximum flexibility in choosing specific means for reaching those goals.

13. Although there are examples of multilateral treaty agreements, such as the Convention on the Rights of the Child, that were negotiated with relative speed and garnered wide ratification in only a few years, and while some transgovernmental agreements may by contrast take longer to complete, informal, nonbinding agreements are, ceteris paribus, faster and less costly to implement.

14. Powers of proposal enable institutions to solve coordination problems because, so long as preferences do not diverge too widely, it is often cheaper for governments to accept an agent's proposal than to amend it.

to lock-in bargains but leave scope for frequent renegotiation, thereby increasing bargaining costs. Second, since TGNs do not empower administrative and judicial agents to propose, interpret, enforce, or extend broad legal principles, they are less likely than IGOs to solve problems of either coordination or "incomplete contracting." Of course, the transaction-cost benefits associated with centralized information gathering, arbitration, and enforcement in IGOs must be weighed against higher contracting costs. Delegation of monitoring and dispute-resolution functions to IOs requires protracted negotiation and contracting. Such an investment only makes sense if states anticipate that a cooperative relationship will endure over time. If time horizons are short, by contrast, the lower start-up costs associated with TGNs may be more appealing.

> *Condition 2a:* Governments are more likely to favor TGNs when speed is a priority.

> *Condition 2b:* Governments are more likely to favor TGNs when time horizons are short.

Uncertainty

A third factor, which gives preferentiality to TGNs, are the conditions of uncertainty surrounding many international policy issues. Conventional approaches to international relations tend to assume that states' self-interests are clear and the ways those interests may be most efficiently pursued are equally clear (Haas 1992, 14). The point of creating international institutions, in this view, is to hammer out mutually advantageous bargains and safeguard those bargains against defections by foreign governments or reversals by future domestic administrations. Yet, there may be situations in which states' interests are uncertain due either to inadequate information about the situation at hand or to doubt about the likely outcomes of different courses of action.

To judge the effects of uncertainty on institutional design we must distinguish between different *kinds* of uncertainty. "Behavioral uncertainty" arises when states are unsure about the actions taken by others—for example, when they have difficulty knowing whether others are complying with an agreement (Koremenos, Lipson, and Snidal 2001a, 778). "Uncertainty about preferences" arises when governments are unsure about others' intentions and motivations. Uncertainty about the "state of the world," finally, refers to states' knowledge about the consequences of their own actions or those of other states (ibid., 778–79). Such uncertainty may stem from rapid social, political, and economic change along with the increasingly complex and technical nature of many issues considered at an international level.

Different forms of uncertainty have different institutional implications. A frequent response to uncertainty about behavior or preferences is to create formal, legalized institutions, which can be used to monitor and report on behavior (ibid., 787–88) and whose stringent commitments may help to weed out uncommitted partners.[15] By contrast, uncertainty about the state of the world favors more flexible arrangements. A rapidly changing environment makes it difficult to anticipate the long-term consequences of cooperative measures. What are the most important future problems? Who are the most relevant allies in a given issue area? What are the distributive effects, international as well as domestic, of alternative agreements? How will measures to address a specific issue impact on other, related issues? Transaction cost theory suggests that in a constantly changing environment, actors will avoid binding large amounts of resources into formal, vertically integrated institutions that "lock-in" agreement. As Kahler (2000, 668) notes, delegation under uncertainty may be politically costly if a politician constrained by formal, legalized institutions is unable to compensate domestic groups affected by unexpected shocks. Instead they will seek institutional flexibility that can protect them against unanticipated costs or adverse distributional consequences (Rosendorf and Milner 2001, 831).[16] Of course, flexibility may be built in to formal treaties and soft law agreements. Yet, IGOs are on the whole less flexible than TGNs. Although many IGOs have escape clauses or veto options that allow members to respond to unanticipated shocks, the use of "opt outs," or veto power, is politically costly. Moreover, although IGOs may entail limited escape clauses, the underlying arrangements are not subject to change, except through renegotiation, which is likely to be slow and cumbersome. By contrast, the informal nonbinding status of TGNs means they can more quickly adapt to changing conditions.[17]

> *Condition 3:* Governments are likely to favor TGNs in conditions of uncertainty about "the state of the world," which creates doubt about the longer-term implications of agreements.[18]

Domestic Political Divisions

Governments are more likely to favor TGNs in the presence of domestic political opposition. It is well known that delegation to international institutions can be a vital tool for executives to strengthen their hand in domestic

15. According to Abbott and Snidal (2000, 429), the explicit rules and sanctioning mechanisms associated with formal organizations function as an *ex ante* sorting device: because explicit legal commitments impose greater costs on violators, a willingness to make them identifies one as having a low propensity to defect.

16. TGNs may also be cheaper to set up in conditions of uncertainty. Informal agreements make fewer informational demands on parties. Negotiators need not try to predict all future states and comprehensively contract for them. See Lipson 1991, 500.

17. For example, Beth Simmons finds that the use of nonbinding accords in the FATF has been an effective way to deal with rapidly changing financial practices and market conditions.

18. Flexibility can help states cope with uncertainty about states of the world but have no effect on reducing uncertainty about behavior or preferences. This is why small group size is an important condition for TGNs.

political struggles (Keohane and Nye 1974). By claiming their hands are tied at the international level, executives can resist pressure from legislatures and particularistic interests. TGNs are likely to enable executives to evade various domestic constraints to a *greater extent* than IGOs for several reasons. First, cooperation through TGNs reduces the weight of public debate. International treaties often require legislatures to vote directly on ratification and on implementing legislation. By contrast, TGNs require no ratification and only limited implementing action. In many cases they require no legislative action at all. They are therefore less likely to become captive to domestic disputes. Second, TGNs may reduce incentives for domestic groups to mobilize and pressure their governments to adopt specific policies that favor their interests. As Goldstein and Martin (2000, 604) argue, insofar as institutionalization entails a process of increasing rule precision, a more institutionalized regime will provide better information about the distributional effects of agreements. This in turn will affect the incentives of groups to mobilize for and against agreements. By contrast, the more ambiguous (and in some cases secretive) nature of many transgovernmental agreements may reduce domestic pressure by obscuring distributive effects. Third, the narrow technical scope of many TGNs means members can claim special scientific and technical expertise. As a result, their activities may be less exposed to scrutiny or intrusion by other agencies.[19]

> *Condition 4:* Executives are more likely to favor TGNs rather than treaties when they expect opposition to an international agreement from key domestic groups (legislatures, interest groups, and general publics).

Clubs and Exclusion of "Spoilers"

TGNs are useful for forming "clubs" of strongly committed states and for excluding "spoilers." Formal IOs, especially those registered with the UN, often aim at universality. Although a few states may be central to cooperation in a given area, the presumption is that all stakeholders can join as long as they pledge to uphold an agreement. The informal network approach, by contrast, allows a few committed parties to initiate an agreement without consulting others. This not only makes it easier to get cooperation off the ground but also has clear advantages when it comes to expanding agreements. By confining an initiative to a small group of highly committed states, "insiders" can set standards to which "outsiders" are later compelled to accede. If the initial group includes a majority of powerful states in an issue area, nonparticipating states may find they have to adapt to the rules set by the group, not be-

19. Evasion of domestic constraints has potential implications for such values as transparency and democratic control of foreign policy. I do not address these implications here, but the transparency and democratic legitimacy of TGNs has been the focus of intense debate elsewhere (see, for example, Howse 2000; Slaughter 2000, 2004b; Picciotto 1997, 2000; Raustiala 2002).

cause those rules bind them, but because insiders are able to deny them important privileges unless they comply. In this way, excluded states may find themselves forced to accept standards that they would not have contracted into as parties to formal multilateral negotiations.[20] We can make this more concrete with an example. Not all countries are party to the Financial Action Task Force (FATF).

The FATF, however, publishes a list of nonparticipating countries and territories, which, according to FATF standards, have critical deficiencies in their anti-money-laundering systems, and urges them to adopt recommended measures to improve their systems. If a listed state fails to comply with the recommendations, the FATF urges its members to "condition, restrict, target or even prohibit financial transactions with such jurisdictions." As a result, many states have joined the FATF (membership has grown from sixteen to thirty-one) and many more choose to comply with its guidelines even if they have not signed up to join the task force.

> *Condition 5:* TGNs are most likely among strongly committed and highly capable states that wish to exclude spoilers from cooperation.

Security Cooperation

Security is widely seen as an area dominated by intergovernmental cooperation under tight executive control. Although studies of transgovernmental relations in areas such as financial regulation, securities, and environmental protection abound, national security has so far received scant attention. This is an oversight. The aftermath of the cold war has seen significant changes in how security is governed. During the cold war, major international institutions such as the United Nations (1945), the North Atlantic Treaty Organization (1949), and the International Atomic Energy Agency (1957) were created to provide security. This period also saw the conclusion of such major arms-control treaties as the Partial Test Ban Treaty (1963), the Nuclear Non-Proliferation Treaty (1968), the Anti-Ballistic Missile Treaty (1972), the Bacteriological and Toxin Weapons Convention (1972), and the Strategic Arms Limitation Treaties (SALT I and II).

Since then much has changed. Although states continue to rely on formal

---

20. The fact that there are more bilateral and regional treaty agreements than multilateral ones might seem to contradict the idea that TGNs are better at excluding spoilers than treaty-based IGOs. Yet, while bilateral treaties may be perfectly acceptable in some cases, in areas with many obvious stakeholders it may be politically difficult to exclude states from gaining at least an observer status to formal negotiations from which they may influence the process. Moreover, formal treaty negotiations are more likely to run into objections from excluded states over their legitimacy under international law. Indeed, in some cases, such as the PSI, treaty-based cooperation would likely require amendments to international law, hence automatically drawing in a wider group.

treaties to govern security cooperation,[21] these have been complemented
(but not replaced) by a variety of transgovernmental instruments. For example, the early 1990s saw the creation of several TGNs between the United
States and the states of the former Soviet Union, including the Materials Protection, Control and Accounting Program, managed by the U.S. Department
of Energy and equivalent bureaus in former Soviet states, and the Cooperative Threat Reduction Program, managed by the U.S. Department of Defense
(SAIC 2001). There has been a proliferation of expert groups and task forces
among the G8, focusing on problems of nonproliferation, counterterrorism,
and nuclear safety.[22] More recently, the "war on terror" has led to intensified
information sharing among national intelligence agencies, interior ministry
officials, and police forces on both sides of the Atlantic (Webber et al. 2004,
16–17). What these initiatives have in common is that they are all informal,
nonbinding, highly flexible, and of relatively low political visibility.

What may account for these institutional developments? Four features
characterized the formal treaties that dominated cold war security cooperation: (1) they generally took a long time to negotiate and ratify;[23] (2) they typically had stringent verification procedures, which were a core concern for
the signatories;[24] (3) they required elaborate implementation measures; (4)
they had high political visibility, which made them subject to domestic and international audience costs (the difficulties confronting successive U.S. administrations in gaining relief from the ABM Treaty—and the international
visibility of this issue—is one example). These features were appropriate to a
cold war environment characterized by relative stability in strategic relations.
As Lipson (1991, 520) observes, strategic arms reduction agreements, which
were a major focus of cold war security cooperation, are rarely subject to sud-
den shocks or developments. Modern weapons systems require long lead
times to build and deploy. As a result, military capacity and technological advantages shift slowly within specific weapons categories. More generally, the
relative stability in strategic relations during the cold war meant that the costs
and benefits of formal treaty restraints could be projected with some confidence over the medium term. It also meant that rapid conclusion of agree-

21. The post–cold war period has seen the signing of major arms reduction treaties, including START I (1991), START II (1993), the Comprehensive Nuclear Test Ban Treaty (1996),
the Chemical Weapons Convention (1993), and the Mine Ban Treaty (1997).

22. Examples include the High Level Group on Nonproliferation, the Rome/Lyons Group
on Terrorism and Organized Crime, the Counter-Terrorism Expert Group, the G8 Nonproliferation Experts Group, the Nuclear Safety and Security Group, and the G8 Global Partnership
Against the Spread of WMD.

23. For example, START I (1991) and the CWC (1993) both took more than a decade to
negotiate. START II (1993) took seven years before entering into force, the CWC took four
years to ratify, and the Comprehensive Test Ban Treaty, signed in 1996, has still not entered
into force.

24. The major nuclear arms agreements between the United States and the USSR (SALT I,
SALT II, START I, START II, and the Limited Test Ban Treaty) all triggered intense debates on
verifiability (see SAIC 2001).

ments was not a major priority. Indeed, some suggest the slow pace of cold war treaty negotiations constituted a benefit insofar as it provided time to assess the implications of alternative actions, eased the difficulty of political adjustments, and allowed the parties to come to understand each other's perspectives on key issues (SAIC 2001). Instead, a priority was strong verifiability measures to ensure that cheating would be caught, and high political visibility to increase the cost of noncompliance.

Formal IGOs continue to offer advantages in many areas of international security cooperation as demonstrated by the conclusion of the Chemical Weapons Convention. Yet, today's security milieu differs from the cold war milieu in important ways. During the cold war, IGOs were used to establish credible commitments to a set of clearly defined long-term goals among fixed sets of actors. In contrast, present security goals are often short term and coalitions are constantly changing. Rapid political and technological change adds to uncertainty about the state of the world and makes it difficult for states to foresee the consequences of formal, legalized agreements. At the same time, it is widely believed that the end of the cold war has been accompanied by an increase in domestic constraints on foreign policy. Whereas foreign policy used to be controlled by a handful of executive leaders, international treaties are today subject to increasing scrutiny by legislatures and publics. These trends all favor TGNs by creating demand for flexibility and low visibility. Below I review three cases of security cooperation.

The Proliferation Security Initiative

The PSI responds to the growing challenge posed by the proliferation of weapons of mass destruction (WMD). Launched by President Bush in May 2003, the initiative aims to interdict the "transfer or transport of WMD, their delivery systems, and related materials to and from states and non-state actors of proliferation concern." The PSI's scope and objectives are set out in the Statement of Interdiction Principles issued in September 2003, which calls on participants to carry out cargo interdictions at sea, in the air, and on land to make it more costly and risky for proliferators to acquire weapons or related materials (U.S. Dept. of State 2003a). The principles further call on participants to adopt procedures for "rapid exchange of information concerning suspected proliferation activity," to review and strengthen national legislation, and to undertake specific cooperative actions, including coordinated training exercises designed to improve joint capacities to interdict WMD trafficking.

Organizational Structure: The PSI is an informal framework rather than a formal organization.[25] The initiative has no secretariat or coordinating body

---

25. PSI is described as "an activity, not an organization." U.S. Department of State, Chairman's Statement at the Fifth Meeting of the PSI, March 4–5, 2004, Lisbon, Portugal.

and no compliance mechanisms. It does not rest on a treaty agreement, which defines its scope and mandate. Instead, participants aim to share information "as appropriate" and to act when they consider it necessary to thwart illicit trade (Joseph 2004). The decision-making process relies on meetings of experts and representatives of participating governments (including foreign and defense ministry officials, national intelligence agents, military officials, customs inspectors, and law enforcement officers[26]), which are the only recognizable structures within the initiative. No specific budgetary authority or grant exists to support PSI activities.[27] In terms of legal authority, the PSI is based exclusively on the authority individual governments have under existing national and international laws (U.S. Dept. of State 2003a). As such, the initiative does not grant governments any new legal authority to conduct interdictions in international waters or airspace (Byers 2004, 529). Such interdictions may take place, but they must be confined to what is permissible under international law.[28]

The lack of an organizational framework and legal mandate is paralleled by a loose definition of goals and means of enforcement. PSI members remain vague in describing the types of shipments they are targeting, speaking only in general terms of "nuclear, chemical, or biological weapons, delivery systems and related materials." They have not offered definitions for these terms, and have declined to reference specifically the international conventions governing the possession of nuclear, chemical, and biological weapons (Joseph 2004). This leaves open a range of questions: How is the decision to interdict made? How is a state to be determined to be "of concern" and thus have its ships subject to interdiction? If a state is deemed "of concern" does this concern extend to commercial ventures trading with such a state? The ambiguity surrounding these issues is undoubtedly deliberate. As Joseph (2004) argues, not specifying items subject to interdiction allows participants maximum flexibility: the shipment of dual-use components carrying both military and civilian uses, for example, will be viewed differently depending on its ultimate destination.

Why a TGN? To explain the PSI's institutional design, we must first understand the nature of the problem it is responding to. Although it aims broadly

26. The PSI has been led in the United States by Undersecretary of State for Arms Control and International Security Jon Bolton. Assistant Secretary of State for Arms Control Steven Rademaker and Director of National Intelligence John Negroponte have also been closely involved.

27. The PSI has no joint budget and individual members have no earmarked funds for the project. In the U.S. context, the Pentagon maintains that existing U.S. capabilities can support PSI activities. See Joseph 2004; Richardson 2006.

28. International law does not prohibit the transfer of nuclear, chemical, and biological weapons, missiles, and related components, nor does it allow interdiction of WMD on the high seas. Under the 1982 UN Law of the Seas (LOS) Convention, ships owned or operated by a state shall, on the high seas, have complete immunity from the jurisdiction of any state other than the flag state. A ship can be stopped in international waters if it is not flying a national flag but it cannot be stopped simply because it is suspected of transporting WMD.

at WMD interdiction, most observers agree that the PSI is a reaction to the growing threat of proliferation to and from "rogue" states, specifically North Korea and Iran (Byers 2004, 526; Joseph 2004). The trigger for the initiative came in December 2002, when the United States intercepted the So San, an unflagged merchant ship traveling from North Korea to Yemen. An inspection revealed that the ship was carrying fifteen Scud-B missiles, fifteen warheads, and missile fuel oxidizer. However, the U.S. government found it was unable to seize the cargo due to the lack of provisions in international law allowing states to intercept and seize the cargo of foreign vessels in international waters.[29]

A second impetus came from the disclosure in the fall of 2002 that North Korea was pursuing a highly enriched uranium program to supply fissile material for nuclear weapons. To construct a working program North Korea would need to purchase many individual components from foreign suppliers, requiring multiple shipments via land, sea, and air (Joseph 2004). Interdiction of procurement shipments was thus an obvious way to block Pyongyang's program. But here also international law fell short: the United States had no jurisdiction to interdict vessels outside its own territorial waters and could not risk a formal blockade of North Korea since this would constitute an act of war and might invite condemnation from allies (Friedman 2003; Joseph 2004; Doolin 2004).

The predicament afforded two possible solutions. The first was to put forward a new treaty or a protocol to the Law of the Seas (LOS) Convention, which would alter the right of freedom of the seas and grant a legal mandate for interdiction of suspected WMD shipments in international waters or airspace. Several factors spoke against this solution. First, given the imminent threat of North Korea and Iran acquiring nuclear capabilities, speed was a priority (Condition 2a). An effort to change international law would likely be slow. The LOS took decades to write; changing it or negotiating a new treaty could be expected to take many years (Friedman 2003, 7). Even if a treaty were broadly signed and ratified, the states most likely to traffic in WMD, such as North Korea, would not become parties and their ships would not be subject to seizure (Byers 2004, 531; Friedman 2003). Second, a treaty-based approach was liable to founder on opposition from spoilers. China could be counted on to veto any UN resolution on interdiction,[30] and other states would likely raise concerns over what criteria would form the basis for forcible interdictions and how the resolution would be enforced to prevent overreaching (Joseph 2004). For cooperation to succeed, one would therefore need to find a way to bypass objections from "spoilers" (Condition 5).

---

29. The Law of the Seas Convention gives ships the rights of freedom of the seas and "innocent" passage through other states' territorial waters.

30. An attempt by the United States in September 2003 to insert a provision authorizing high-seas interdiction into UNSC Resolution 1540, which calls on states to strengthen domestic controls over WMD manufacture and possession, was blocked by the threat of a Chinese veto. See Friedman 2003, 4; Richardson 2006, 13.

A third factor that militated against the formal route was uncertainty about how a multilateral treaty would affect the interests of the United States and its close allies (Condition 3). The principle of exclusive "flag state" jurisdiction is beneficial to the United States. As Byers (2004, 527) notes, the LOS regime forms the legal foundation for the global mobility of U.S. forces. The United States has a keen interest in safeguarding the transfer of weapons and technology to its armed forces abroad and to foreign allies. The same is true of other states with which the United States is likely to cooperate in antiproliferation efforts. Hence, the United States and its partners are not willing to surrender the requirement of flag state consent on an irrevocable basis (ibid., 540). The requirement of flag state consent also protects merchant vessels legitimately carrying goods to or from U.S. territory. An international agreement extending reciprocal stop-and-search powers could risk being biased in unforeseen ways against domestic commercial interests, as foreign states could cut off U.S. shipments when it served their purposes (Friedman 2003, 2). Indeed, Byers (2004, 545) speculates that U.S. shipping interests and perhaps even the U.S. Navy defended the requirement of flag state consent, thus implying domestic opposition to a more wide-ranging agreement (Condition 4).

Given these constraints, what was needed was an informal agreement that would (a) bypass domestic and international objections, (b) address the proliferation threat promptly, and (c) be sufficiently flexible to avoid imposing unwanted constraints on the legitimate (or indeed illegitimate) business of the United States and its allies. The PSI fulfils these requirements. Instead of changing international law, the PSI uses an aggressive and innovative approach to the enforcement of existing national regulations to thwart WMD trafficking (Rice 2005). According to Joseph (2004), PSI members use minor legal violations (such as a technical customs violation) as a rationale to inspect and seize illicit shipments. They also take advantage of national laws to search suspected vessels while they are docked in members' ports. This informal strategy has several advantages. First, due to the lack of a legal framework, the initiative was adopted and implemented with great speed. Only a handful of plenary sessions were held before the launch. In the first year of its operation, ten interdiction-training exercises were scheduled, improving working relationships among the navies, coastal authorities, customs officials, and law enforcement agents of PSI participants, and partners cooperated in several interdiction efforts. Second, the secrecy surrounding PSI operations and the fact that no budgetary funding has been sought for the initiative minimizes domestic controversy and reduces pressure from parties claiming that it violates international law.[31] Third, PSI entails a high degree of flexibility, which

31. A frequent criticism has been that by inviting interdictions "on land, at sea, and in the air," the PSI defies the inviolability of international waters and the right of "innocent passage" within other nations' territorial waters, which is considered customary law and enumerated under Article 19 of the LOS Convention. The United States has not ratified the LOS, but every other PSI member has.

safeguards members' individual interests. PSI participation does not generate any automatic commitments. On any given interdiction activity, only those members who choose to involve themselves will do so.[32] More important, there is great selectivity with respect to targets of enforcement. The initiative does not aim to track all illicit shipments of WMD and dual-use goods but is limited to seizing shipments by countries or nonstate actors that are viewed as posing a security threat to PSI participants, such as North Korea and Iran. In an interview in November 2003, Undersecretary of State for Arms Control and International Security John Bolton responded to a question on whether PSI should also focus on Israel, India, and Pakistan: "There are unquestionably states that are not within existing treaty regimes that possess WMD legitimately. We're not trying to have a policy that attempts to cover each and every one of those circumstances. What we're worried about are the rogue states and the terrorist groups that pose the most immediate threat."[33] Critics have asserted that the selective focus on "shipments to and from states and nonstate actors of proliferation concern" is inherently discriminatory and subjects some states to an unfair scrutiny of their trade and commerce (Joseph 2004). For example, China has expressed concern that the PSI could infringe on the right of innocent passage for Chinese ships through the territorial waters of PSI member states and could be used as a pretext to seize legal Chinese missile and arms exports (Richardson 2006, 8–9). Yet, so long as PSI members operate within the bounds of existing international law they are free to engage in selective enforcement. By narrowly targeting a few states, the PSI avoids alienating countries that are not of proliferation concern. At the same time, selective enforcement allows participants to quickly adjust the focus of the initiative in response to political and military developments. This is a level of flexibility that could not have been achieved within a formal, treaty-based agreement, which would have had to offer a clear definition of the conditions under which a state would be targeted for interdiction.

A final strength of the PSI is the small number of participants (Condition 1). The PSI began as an initiative among eleven states—all close American allies.[34] Today there are twenty members.[35] Many more countries have expressed support for the PSI.[36] Yet, initial members have chosen not to pursue an aggressive expansion of membership. Instead, other nations are asked to participate in PSI activities on a case-by-case basis, insofar as they can contribute to a particular operation. The decision to restrict membership to a

32. U.S. Dept. of State 2003b.
33. Quoted in Joseph 2004.
34. Australia, France, Germany, Italy, Japan, the Netherlands, Poland, Portugal, Spain, the United Kingdom, and the United States.
35. Since its creation the PSI has been expanded to include Russia, Canada, Norway, Singapore, Denmark, Argentina, Iraq, Georgia, and Turkey.
36. At the first anniversary of the PSI, sixty-two countries plus the EU and NATO were represented, evidencing the growing support for the initiative. U.S. Department of State, Chairman's Statement at the Fifth Meeting of the PSI, March 4–5, 2004, Lisbon, Portugal.

small, close-knit group seems to reflect a desire to keep the initiative flexible and free of the constraints on decision making associated with a larger and more diverse group (Joseph 2004). It may also be indicative of the desire to exclude spoilers from influence. By confining the initiative to a small group of closely allied states, PSI members have acquired a potent tool with which to pressure outsiders to aid their antiproliferation efforts. By unilaterally targeting other states' ships and commerce, PSI members can pressure them to grant legal rights of reciprocal stop-and-search and cooperate in searches of third-party vessels. Indeed, the United States has used PSI as a basis for signing a series of bilateral ship-boarding agreements with key flag, coastal, or transit states.[37] Due to such agreements, more than half the global commercial shipping fleet is subject to rapid boarding, search, and seizures by the United States or a PSI member (Richardson 2006, 15; Roston 2004). The key to success, however, is to secure the cooperation of states that control large ports at strategic chokepoints or own large merchant fleets. PSI members are therefore likely to target countries such as China and Indonesia through whose waters North Korean vessels are likely to pass, to pressure them to enact legislation allowing them to stop and search North Korean ships (Doolin 2004).

How effective is the regime? Although information regarding interdictions is generally kept secret, there have allegedly been numerous successful interdictions since the PSI was launched.[38] On the other hand, critics point to notable interdiction failures such as an alleged Iranian purchase of a mobile crane, probably intended for a missile program, from Germany (Roston 2004). Clearly, the fact that the PSI has not succeeded in halting proliferation in all cases does not mean it is ineffective. Yet there are clear limitations to a narrow transgovernmental regime. By choosing not to pursue a UN resolution, PSI members have not secured a right to interdict on the high seas. This means that potential interceptions by PSI coastal states of vessels exercising the right of transit passage through international shipping straits or innocent passage through national waters could raise thorny legal issues. Byers (2004,

37. The United States has signed bilateral treaties with Belize, Croatia, Cyprus, Liberia, the Marshall Islands, and Panama. Such agreements allow U.S. officials to board ships registered under these flags anywhere in international waters if they are judged to pose a proliferation danger. Panama and Liberia are the two countries with the most foreign vessels registered under their authority. Cyprus is sixth and the Marshall Islands is seventh.

38. In 2003, the United States allegedly intercepted aluminum tubes bound for North Korea's nuclear program, a combined Franco-German effort intercepted sodium cyanide likely bound for North Korea's chemical weapons program, and details were released about the interception of a ship carrying components for uranium centrifuge tubes destined for Libya (Joseph 2004; Rice 2005). Media reports indicate that in 2004 German authorities intercepted twenty-four long-distance detonators and South African police seized eleven shipping containers holding components of a centrifuge uranium enrichment plant. In 2005 German authorities apparently seized four low-voltage motors destined for a nuclear power plant in Iran, and in May 2005 authorities in Antwerp intercepted a shipment of charged aluminum plates bound from Hamburg to Iran.

543) speculates, however, that if they should perceive an urgent need to do so, PSI members would prefer to break international law. The occasional breach of the rules may be preferable, he argues, to seeking a change in international law. If a high seas interdiction is judged necessary, members will not claim a right under international law. This will allow them to break the rules without advancing strained and potentially destabilizing legal justifications.[39]

Another potential weakness is that membership remains patchy. Although the PSI includes some of the world's leading military and economic powers, key players such as China, India, Indonesia, Singapore, and Thailand, who control major strategic ports in the Asia-Pacific region, have not signed on (Doolin 2004). The PSI is still young, though. Given their political and economic clout, continued pressure by PSI members may succeed in tightening the cordon around the world's proliferators.

Missile Technology Control Regime

The MTCR is an informal agreement made by the G7 partners in 1987 to limit proliferation of nuclear-capable missiles and missile technology. The regime is based on adherence to a common export control policy (the "Guidelines") applied to a list of controlled items (the "Equipment and Technology Annex"), which includes virtually all key equipment and technology needed for missile development, production, and operation—whether military or dual use. The regime also provides for the sharing of intelligence and technical expertise. The MTCR originally targeted nuclear-capable missiles only, but in 1993 its objective was expanded to cover delivery systems capable of delivering all types of WMD, and in 2003 the mandate was further widened to preventing terrorists from acquiring missiles and missile technology. The regime today has thirty-four members, including most of the world's key missile manufacturing states, and a number of countries unilaterally observe its guidelines.

Organizational Structure. The MTCR is not an international organization or treaty-based regime but an informal association among countries sharing a common interest in controlling missile proliferation (U.S. Dept. of State 2003c). The regime has no headquarters or secretariat (the French foreign ministry serves as an informal point of contact) and the decision-making process is minimally structured. The partners hold an annual plenary meeting chaired on a rotational basis. Intersession consultations take place monthly through point of contact meetings in Paris, and technical experts meetings

---

39. If the PSI continues to prove its value without provoking charges of misuse then a United Nations Security Council resolution may eventually become a feasible option. In the long run, this could turn out to be a case where a TGN becomes an IGO.

are held on an ad hoc basis. All meetings are closed to the public due to the sensitive nature of the discussions and intelligence materials being shared.

Like the PSI, the MTCR entails a high degree of ambiguity and discretion with respect to means and goals of enforcement. Items included in the Equipment and Technology Annex are not subject to an export ban but may be transferred at the discretion of individual members, on a case-by-case basis. Before transferring controlled items, exporting governments are invited to obtain credible assurances from recipients that the items will be used for acceptable purposes (U.S. Dept. of State 2004; Arms Control Association 2004). However, these guidelines are voluntary and implemented by governments in accordance with national export control legislation and practices. Because the decision to export is the sole responsibility of each member, the MTCR has no penalties for transfers of controlled items. Instead, members impose their own penalties. For example, U.S. law mandates that Washington sanction entities (whether individuals, companies, or governments) that export MTCR-controlled items to certain countries identified as proliferators or potential threats to national security. It does so irrespective of whether these entities are a state or operate within a state that is a member of the MTCR. Typically, Washington prohibits the charged entity from signing contracts, receiving aid, or buying arms from the U.S. government for a period of two years (Ministry of Foreign Affairs, Canada 2005).

Why a TGN? The origins of the MTCR are similar to the PSI. The regime emerged in reaction to a perceived growing threat of global proliferation of nuclear-capable missiles and technology. In the early 1980s, evidence of long-range missile development and proliferation among several developing countries, including Libya, Egypt, Syria, Iraq, Iran, and Saudi Arabia, strengthened the resolve of the G7 to tighten controls on proliferation (Halevy 1993). Yet several considerations militated against creating a binding international treaty that would restrict the right to—or contribute to an international norm against—international transfers of missiles and missile technology. First, strategic interests demanded that the G7 partners remain free to transfer technology among themselves and to select third parties. A formal, binding agreement might risk constraining partners in unwanted ways (Condition 3). Second, there were powerful domestic actors (including the military, the national security bureaucracy, and nationally based manufacturers) who could be counted on to oppose a binding regime that placed a comprehensive ban on international transfers of missiles and related technology (Condition 4).

Like the PSI, the MTCR avoids these problems by adopting a highly flexible and discriminatory approach. The regime does not seek a general ban on the transfer of missiles and related technology. The narrow objective of export licensing is to prevent transfers that may contribute to the proliferation of WMD. But controls are not intended to impede peaceful aerospace programs or to restrict access to technologies necessary for economic development (U.S. Dept. of State 1993). More important, the MTCR, like the PSI, does not provide a multilateral instrument that draws a clear line between acceptable and unacceptable missile activities. Rather, it condemns specific activities on a case-by-case basis (Ministry of Foreign Affairs, Canada 2005). As such, the guidelines are not offensive to domestically based manufacturers. Indeed, far from restricting trade, the MTCR Guidelines may enable it by building confidence among suppliers that they can provide access to technology without it being diverted to WMD delivery system programs. Nor does the program hinder technology or hardware transfers to third-party governments with whom the partners wish to cooperate militarily.[40]

The MTCR also provides a clear example of the benefits of TGNs when it comes to excluding spoilers and setting standards to which others can later be pressured to accede (Condition 5). The initiative started among a small group of states with homogenous interests. These included the world's foremost producers of missiles and missile technology. By confining the initiative to a core group, members excluded potential spoilers from influence at the drafting stage. Yet, the potential for the ad hoc application of sanctions meant that members could later pressure nonmembers to abide by the guidelines. Because of their control over advanced technology and equipment (commercial as well as military) MTCR members have the ability to deny privileges to nonmembers unless they give credible assurances that they will counter proliferation.[41] Core members have repeatedly called on nonmembers to apply the MTCR control list and guidelines. This strategy is particularly evident with respect to China, who is seen as a major proliferation source. The United States and other MTCR partners opposed Chinese participation in the process of drafting the guidelines due to their concern that China might gain access to sensitive missile design information (Center for Nonproliferation Studies 1998). Members then proceeded to sanction China for breeches of the MTCR Guidelines. In 1991 the United States imposed sanctions on China for allegedly exporting M-11 missile technology to Pakistan. The sanctions were lifted the following year after China gave written assurances that it would adhere to the MTCR Guidelines (Center for Nonproliferation Studies n.d.; Halevy 1993). The United States has since sanctioned Chinese entities for allegedly engaging in missile proliferation with Iran and other countries of concern. China denies the charges and is in discussion with MTCR members about joining the regime. Another suspected proliferator, Russia, joined the

40. Membership decisions are equally arbitrary. Although the regime intends to ban missiles with more than 300km range and 500kg payload, this criterion is waived for some members. When Ukraine joined in 1998 it retained the right to produce offensive missiles and was allowed to keep its Scud missiles—the type of rocket the MTCR is specifically designed to counter—in return for ending its nuclear commerce with Iran. See Pande 1999.

41. For example, the United States has made China's Most Favored Nation status conditional on better performance on nonproliferation. China, in turn, has accused the MTCR of discrimination on the part of states already possessing missile technology. Other states have raised similar objections. See Ministry of Foreign Affairs, Canada 2005; McDougall 2002.

MTCR in 1995, after being sanctioned for having sought to transfer cryogenic rocket engines to India (Pande 1999). Several other countries have chosen unilateral compliance. For example, India announced in 2005 that it intended to adhere unilaterally to the MTCR Guidelines (Center for Nonproliferation Studies n.d.) and Israel and South Africa have also chosen to observe the guidelines voluntarily (Pande 1999).

The MTCR is widely believed to have contributed to a reduction in missile proliferation. The regime has been credited with stopping a joint Condor II ballistic missile program among Argentina, Egypt, and Iraq, and with persuading Brazil, South Africa, South Korea, and Taiwan to abandon missile or space-launch-vehicle programs (Pande 1999). Poland and the Czech Republic are also said to have destroyed their ballistic missiles, in part, to better their chances of joining MTCR (Arms Control Association 2004). Still, the regime has clear limitations. Among members, the application of voluntary export controls has been uneven. Companies or individuals in France, Germany, Italy, Japan, and the United States have reportedly transferred entire systems, components, materials, or technological information to other countries engaged in missile development (Pande 1999). The MTCR has failed to prevent (or halt) the development of missile programs by at least five countries: India, Israel, Pakistan, Iran, and North Korea.[42] These countries continue to advance their missile programs and, as nonparties to the MTCR, continue to supply technology to other states. The limitations of the MTCR do not consist in having failed to persuade these countries to join the regime: clearly states with an interest in proliferation are unlikely to sign up to any agreement—formal or informal—that aims to thwart their ambition. However, an international treaty-based regime with broad participation and strong verification and sanctioning mechanisms might have done more to dissuade these countries from advancing their missile programs in the first place.

The PSI and the MTCR offer good illustrations of the conditions favoring TGNs. The two cases appear to support conditions 1, 3, 4 and 5. Both networks emerged among small groups with highly homogenous interests and values (Condition 1). In both cases, there was a clear need for flexible standards and easy escape. On the one hand, this need arose from general uncertainty about how cooperation would influence the long-term strategic interests of member states and from concerns about potentially adverse effects on key domestic groups (Condition 3). On the other hand, it derived from a straightforward desire to engage in selective enforcement. This militated against spelling out clear definitions of acceptable and unacceptable activities and favored a flexible approach that would allow members to continue certain practices while working to curb the same practices among foreign

42. Israel, of course, was never a target state. And the indigenous character of India's missile program makes the MTCR practically redundant in the context of that country.

states. Both cases also featured domestic opposition to a constricting agreement (from shipping interests and the military in the PSI and from domestically based producers in the MTCR) (Condition 4). Finally, in both cases there was a desire to exclude potential spoilers from the drafting stage (Condition 5).

The effects of urgency (Condition 2a) are less clear. Although speed was certainly a priority in drafting the PSI it is not clear that pressure for a quick solution was any greater in this case or in the case of the MCTR than for most issues of international security cooperation. The relationship between time horizons and institutional form (Condition 2b) is also ambiguous. The MTCR has been operational for more than twenty years and shows no signs of disappearing, yet it has not been formalized. The PSI may be expected to be relatively short-lived in its current form. However, a short time horizon in this case may be the result of a highly informal, flexible, and adaptable institutional structure as much as a precondition for it.

The Chemical Weapons Convention

The Chemical Weapons Convention (CWC) is a multilateral arms control agreement outlawing the production and use of chemical weapons. The treaty was signed in Paris in January 1993, after more than a decade of painstaking negotiations, and entered into force on April 29, 1997.[43] The Convention is the second multilateral disarmament agreement to provide for the elimination of an entire category of WMD.[44] The Convention prohibits all development, production, acquisition, stockpiling, transfer, and use of chemical weapons. It further establishes a comprehensive export control regime that applies not only to scheduled chemicals but also to all the elements that make up the definition of a chemical weapon (toxic agent, munitions, and delivery system) (Feakes 2001, 46). Since its entry into force, 183 states have become parties to the CWC.

Organizational Form. The CWC has an extensive formal organization. It is administered by the Organization for the Prohibition of Chemical Weapons (OPCW), which is responsible for implementing its provisions. The OPCW consists of three bodies: the Conference of the States Parties, a policymaking organ of all member states that meets once a year; an executive council consisting of forty-one states, which oversees implementation; and a technical sec-

43. Negotiations on provisions for eliminating chemical weapons began in 1962 within the Conference of the Committee on Disarmament and continued within its successor institution, the Conference on Disarmament.

44. The 1972 Convention on the Prohibition of the Development, Production and Stockpiling of Bacteriological and Toxin Weapons (BWC), which took force in 1975, was the first multilateral agreement to eliminate an entire category of WMD. The BWC at present contains no provisions for monitoring or verification of compliance or implementation.

retariat that analyzes data and conducts inspections. Implementation requirements are stringent. At the national level, members are required to pass legislation making the provisions of the treaty binding on their citizens and companies; to implement national export controls on controlled chemicals; and to establish a "national authority" to communicate with the OPCW (Tucker 2001). Rules and obligations are very specific: an annex lists all the prohibited substances and is updated regularly to keep up with technological developments. Strict verifiability criteria are in place: OPWC inspection teams conduct routine inspections of military and industrial plants in all member states, and each member has a right to request inspection of a facility—declared or undeclared—on the territory of another member state suspected of violating the treaty.

Why an IGO? Our framework suggests several reasons why control of chemical weapons is tackled through a highly legalized IGO rather than a TGN. First, verifiability measures are of central importance to controlling the production of chemical weapons. Chemical weapons are notoriously difficult to monitor (more so than transfers of missiles or missile technology) due to problems of dual-use substances that can serve as precursors for chemical weapons. Hence, an elaborate regime is needed to permit close monitoring of compliance. Second, new developments in the chemical industry require constant adaptation of the industry verification regime (Kelle 2003). As a result there are clear benefits to having a centralized secretariat, which can gather, analyze, and synthesize information and keep up with technical developments. Third, broad participation is of central importance. Any nation with a developed chemical industry has the potential to make chemical weapons. Moreover, there are growing concerns over the involvement of non-state actors in the production and use of chemical weapons. Unlike in the cases of interdiction of nuclear weapon components or control of WMD-capable missiles, therefore, it does not suffice to target select countries of special proliferation concern.

At the same time, many factors that favored reliance on TGNs in the case of WMD interdiction and antimissile proliferation were absent with respect to controlling chemical weapons. First, flexibility, either in the form of easy escape from the regime or in the form of the possibility for selective enforcement or double standards, was not a major concern. The United States and other major proponents of the CWC are not heavily reliant on chemical weapons. Hence, there is less need for ambiguity in defining acceptable conduct or for flexibility with respect to enforcement. Second, although private commercial interests were widely affected, this did not create a domestic lobby against a treaty regime. The potential negative effects of the Convention were narrowly concentrated on a single domestic group: the chemical industry. Rather than oppose a treaty agreement, industrial leaders chose to collaborate in the elaboration of a formal regime that would increase public confidence that chemical companies have no connection to weapons (Burgess 2001).

The reasons for the collaboration of the chemical industry are instructive: until 1984 trade in dual-use chemicals was unregulated. In 1984 it was discovered that Iraq's production of chemical weapons had relied extensively on precursors and production equipment supplied by Western companies. In response, several countries imposed national export controls and licensing measures on chemical weapon precursors, including Canada, the European Community, Japan, New Zealand, and the United States (Feakes 2001). Since they were unilateral and voluntary these measures had the effect of disadvantaging industries in countries in which they were adopted vis-à-vis foreign competitors. Hence, the chemical industry had an incentive to cooperate with governments to get out-and-out bans lifted and to extend export control measures, to which they were already subject, to other countries.

The harmful effects of unilateral export controls explain the absence of domestic opposition to a formal, binding regime in major Western countries. But how do we explain support for the CWC among other countries? Ironically the explanation seems to lie in the formation of a small transgovernmental alliance. In 1985, a group of states created an informal mechanism to harmonize national export controls on dual-use chemical weapon precursors and production equipment (Feakes 2001, 45). This group, which is known as the Australia Group (AG), includes the world's most advanced producers and consumers of industrial chemical components.[45] Nonmembers have widely seen it as a discriminatory cartel that harms their economic development by impeding legitimate trade in chemicals and equipment (ibid., 47). Brazil, Cuba, India, Iran, Malaysia, China, and Pakistan have all been highly critical of the AG, accusing it of being "a white man's club" that practices "apartheid." Yet, the AG has provided an incentive for other states to agree to a formal multilateral export control regime. By acceding to the CWC they hope to undermine the rationale and legitimacy of the AG and to gain access to matériel and equipment necessary to advance their chemical industrial capacity. Article 11 of the CWC treaty states that "the Convention shall not hamper the economic and technological development of states parties and shall instead promote chemical trade among states parties for peaceful purposes." When Cuba, Iran, Pakistan, and Sudan submitted their CWC ratifications to the UN secretary-general, they attached statements critical of the AG. Together with India these countries have created a Non-Aligned Movement, which calls for "the removal of all and any discriminatory restrictions that are contrary to the letter and spirit of the [CWC]" (Feakes 2001, 46). In response to the creation

45. The AG consists of thirty-two states plus the European Commission: Argentina, Australia, Austria, Belgium, Bulgaria, Canada, Czech Republic, Cyprus, Denmark, Finland, France, Germany, Greece, Hungary, Iceland, Ireland, Italy, Japan, Republic of Korea, Luxembourg, Netherlands, New Zealand, Norway, Poland, Portugal, Romania, Slovak Republic, Spain, Sweden, Turkey, the United Kingdom, and the United States.

of the CWC, AG members have in turn pledged to remove export controls from "states parties to the Convention acting in full compliance with their obligations under the Convention."

The CWC is highly credible. Since its entry into force in 1997, five members have declared that they possess chemical weapons (the United States, India, Russia, South Korea, and Albania) and have begun destruction activities. However, the CWC also highlights the downsides of a formal treaty approach. First is the refusal of several known and suspected chemical proliferators to join the treaty, including North Korea, Egypt, Iraq, and Syria. Second, stringent verification procedures do not guarantee success: a number of states parties continue to lag behind in national implementing legislation (Kelle 2003). Partly as a result of such patchy implementation, the AG is still operational and core members of the group such as the United States and the United Kingdom continue to defend its existence as a necessary tool to deal with noncompliance under the CWC.

The concept of "political networks" offers a useful framework for conceptualizing recent developments in international security cooperation. While international security cooperation takes place both through IGOs and TGNs, observers point to a growing reliance on transgovernmental networks (Krahmann 2003; Webber et al. 2004). In this chapter I have sought to account for this trend by combining international regime theory with an explicit theory of networks. Although international regime theory, via its account of rationales for informal and soft law cooperation, offers a good starting point for explaining transgovernmental activity, a satisfactory explanation of transgovernmentalism requires us to incorporate additional insights from theories of networked cooperation. Drawing on recent network studies in public policy, economics, and sociology, I have identified several unique features of networked organizations that help explain the proliferation in TGNs. For example, the flat organizational structure associated with networks promotes differentiated local solutions to common problems. This is important in an area, such as security, where sovereignty concerns are high. Also, the informal, noncontractual nature of TGNs means they can adapt quickly to conditions of uncertainty and rapid change, which characterize many areas of international security. Due to their noncontractual nature and low visibility, networks are also well suited to allowing executives to evade domestic constraints on policy. This is a useful asset in a political context in which gaining domestic approval of international treaties is widely thought to have become increasingly difficult.

One advantage of networked cooperation deserves specific highlighting. As we have seen, TGNs allow states to limit cooperation to small groups of like-minded states, with the group being easily expanded once momentum has been achieved. By making informal rules and enforcing them unilaterally, insiders can change the incentives facing outsiders and compel them to comply with rules they would not have agreed to as parties to formal, multi-lateral treaty negotiations. Although I have shown this logic at work in the area of security cooperation, there is reason to believe it generalizes to other areas of international cooperation.

In this chapter I have demonstrated how network theory can help us understand recent trends in international security cooperation. By taking into account the specific features of networked cooperation we can differentiate between TGNs and IGOs in terms of the functional benefits they bestow on states. At the same time, an analysis of government networking suggests important refinements to network theory as it is presently used by international relations scholars. The existing literature on networks focuses overwhelmingly on network benefits. Due to their flexibility and adaptability networks are often claimed to be uniquely adapted to cooperation in a fast-changing, global world. As we have seen, however, although there are clear benefits to networked cooperation, there are also important drawbacks, which are often less well understood. A focus on government networks serves to illuminate both the advantages and drawbacks of the network form. As Kathryn Sikkink notes in the conclusion, governments, unlike other international actors—for example, criminal or terrorist groups—are often free to choose between different forms of cooperation. A focus on networking among governments is therefore likely to be particularly useful in highlighting the comparative advantages of networks vis-à-vis other organizational forms.

One final issue needs addressing. The TGNs analyzed in this chapter are in important respects reflections of U.S. foreign policy. The PSI and the MTCR were both initiated by the United States and their continued success depends crucially on American support and leadership. The same is true of TGNs in other areas: the initiative for the FATF, for example, came primarily from the United States in cooperation with a few close allies. One might speculate, therefore, that increased cooperation through TGNs is not a general trend but evidences a specifically American predilection for informal means of international cooperation. This predilection may be explained in part by America's hegemonic position. As hegemon, the United States can afford unilateral enforcement of small-scale regimes. Hence it is less likely to value centralized sanctioning. It may also be explained in terms of a specifically American preference for avoiding international legal constraints. Since the end of the cold war the United States has backtracked from a number of formal treaty commitments, including the ABM Treaty and the Comprehensive Test Ban Treaty. It has also been reluctant to proceed with negotiation of a verification protocol for the Biological Weapons Convention. Growing reliance on TGNs may thus be interpreted partly as an American attempt to redefine multilateralism and create a system of international cooperation that is more flexible and places fewer constraints on American national interests. Such an interpretation would, I believe, be overly narrow. Although the United States has been the main driving force behind several prominent

TGNs, reliance on transgovernmental cooperation is by no means exclusive to the United States. To give just one example, police cooperation within the EU has developed along predominantly transgovernmental lines in the last decade and serves as a vivid illustration of how an informal networked approach can circumvent many hurdles of sovereignty, which previously hindered cooperation in this area.

11

The Power of Networks in International Politics

Kathryn Sikkink

Networks are ubiquitous in social life. But this book highlights political networks, in the sense that they have either political causes or political effects or both. Likewise, the authors focus on transnational political networks where network membership or network effects, or both, stretch across national borders. The strength of this book is that it brings together a discussion of a wide variety of transnational political networks that have previously been considered separately. In doing so, it allows us to ask and answer theoretical and empirical questions about the general role of networks in global politics.

In chapter 1, Kahler presents the main conceptual and definitional issues, and discusses the broad relevance of network research to key debates in international relations. The conclusions focus on summarizing the answers that the chapters provide to a more focused set of research questions about networks. Many of these answers are related to how power is exercised by and in networks, which is the main theme of this final chapter. Specifically, I will address: (1) how and why networks emerge, scale-up, and proliferate; (2) under which conditions networks can have influence or be effective; and (3) how networks contribute to global governance, and how to address questions of accountability. The answers to these questions often vary, however, with the different types of networks discussed in the book, so a brief discussion of types of networks precedes the exploration of these research questions.

Types of Networks

The authors in this book use two main approaches to networks: network-as-structure and network-as-agent (or unintentional and intentional networks).

Despite these labels, structure is a constant for all networks. But networks-as-actors are thick intentional networks that are simultaneously both structures and agents, while networks-as-structures are thinner, uncoordinated networks that only exist as structures. These two approaches may actually signal two end points on a continuum with fully intentional networks on one side and purely unintentional networks on the other; many of the actual networks we study may combine conscious and unintentional elements and fall at some midpoint on the continuum. The distinction is nevertheless important for many of the answers to the questions discussed here.

An additional way to categorize networks-as-actors is to focus on the main type of actors involved, their main purposes, and their main tactics. Networks-as-actors are purposeful, often strategic actors, while networks as structures are not purposive actors, and thus cannot be characterized either by the main purposes of their enterprise or by their tactics. Within the category of networks-as-actors, the purpose of the network and the types of actors involved may influence in very important ways its tactics and dynamics. For example, the differences are quite stark between Kenney's drug networks (chapter 5), where the purpose is the promise of fantastic profits and the political power necessary to facilitate that personal enrichment, and Yanacopulos's justice network (chapter 4), where the purpose is to reduce debt payments for impoverished countries.

Many different types of actors use network forms of organization; while networks are the organizational vehicle of choice of small nonstate actors, they are also used by states and business groups. Networks often bring together diverse types of actors, but most networks are dominated or characterized by a particular type of actor. Transgovernmental networks are made up exclusively of state actors, drug networks are dominated by illicit business groups, while nongovernmental organizations and social movements play a central role in transnational advocacy networks. Epistemic communities are networks where scientists and experts, both inside and outside of governments, are key players, and armed insurgents dominate terrorist networks. But in addition to thinking about the dominant types of actors involved in networks, it may also be useful to think about the main actors behind the formation of networks. The networks discussed by Stein (chapter 8), Eilstrup-Sangiovanni (chapter 10), and Cowhey and Mueller (chapter 9) are all *government organized networks,* even though in the case of humanitarian networks and Internet networks, many of their members are nongovernmental. Human rights networks and debt-relief networks, on the other hand, are networks mainly *of* nongovernmental actors organized *by* nongovernmental organizations.

Networks are motivated by different purposes. Every network has multiple motivations, including its own survival, but we can still identify the main purpose of most networks. Some networks form mainly to pursue economic gain (like drug networks) while others pursue policy coordination and implementation (such as the TGNs discussed by Eilstrup-Sangiovanni). Advocacy networks form to promote principled ideas, while many humanitarian networks devote most of their energies to the delivery of humanitarian services. All use network forms of organization, but the main purpose shapes the particular form the networks take and the tactics they use. Network purpose is intimately related to the issues of power discussed here, because it clarifies the question of the purposes for which network power is exercised. Network power is usually not an end in itself but a tool to achieve purposes, and thus the consideration of network purpose must go hand in hand with an exploration of network power.

Another important distinction between different networks is the distinction between those networks that engage in clandestine or illicit activity and thus often use violent tactics, such as the drug and terrorist networks, and those networks that engage in public or legal activity and use nonviolent tactics. For the public/legal networks, especially advocacy networks, the search for publicity is the driving force behind their formation and functioning. For the clandestine networks, as Kenney says, "secrecy is the driving force behind organizational structure." If, as network theorists argue, network structure helps explain the functioning and outcomes of networks, and if secrecy is the driving force behind network structure in clandestine networks, we expect that clandestine networks will be quite different than public ones. In secret networks communication within and across cells is fairly limited. Most other networks don't limit information, but take advantage of one of the main characteristics of networks—their ability to move large amounts of information quickly and easily.

Despite these differences in types of networks, almost all of the chapters in this book stress some common characteristics of networks: (1) their voluntary nature and thus the possibility of exit; (2) the central role of information and learning; (3) their ability to build trust and confidence among network participants, and (4) their flexibility and adaptability compared to other organizational forms.

Many chapters stress the voluntary nature of the networks they study. For networks-as-actors, network nodes choose whether to participate in networks. This gives networks their informal nature and means that you can't "lock-in" either actors or commitments. Thus networks must create benefits for network members, what many authors refer to as network externalities, in order for networks to continue to exist. These benefits may be of a very diverse sort—but because networks are voluntary, nodes will exit if they do not perceive benefits, and seek out other kinds of arrangements.

All the chapters also stress the informational role of networks. One of the most striking characteristics of networks is that they are "particularly apt for circumstances in which there is a need for efficient reliable information" (Powell 1990). Because networks are based on trust and reciprocity they encourage people to exchange information, not just purchase it. Networks provide access to tacit knowledge that is difficult to codify and resides in the heads of experienced practitioners (Kenney, chapter 5). Eilstrup-Sangiovanni (chapter 10) stresses that the lack of hierarchical organization in the transgovernmental networks she studies contributes to the speed and efficiency of communication, as well as more opportunities for local initiative. The centrality of the transfer of reliable information is a characteristic of both the networks-as-actors and the networks-as-structures examined in this book. Learning- and information-based adaptation are primary characteristics of Elkin's constitutional network (chapter 3). Stein also argues that the ALNAP has been a source for learning internally and in the larger networks of the humanitarian sector (chapter 8).

A third shared characteristic of the networks-as-actors examined in this book is the ability to build trust and confidence among participants to facilitate coordination and collective action. So, for example, Eilstrup-Sangiovanni considers trust-based relations as one of the four characteristics of networks that are important for political coordination. She argues that networks are "more dependent on trust than other organizational forms." The role of trust in networks also derives from the fact that many political networks are embedded in broader social networks. In most political networks, these broader social networks are useful for both recruiting people of confidence and for linking networks to the outside political actors that they hope to influence. These social networks seem to be even more important in the case of illicit networks (at least they are mentioned more explicitly in the chapters by Kenney and Kahler).

Finally, all networks appear to have greater flexibility and adaptability than other organizational forms. They can both expand freely, and they can decouple more easily. Slaughter (2004a), discussing TGNs, stresses that because networks are more flexible and have low sovereignty costs, they are often the vehicles of choice for international cooperation. Networks can "adjust quickly to new problems or unanticipated changes in their environment" (Eilstrup-Sangiovanni, chapter 10). The downside of this flexibility, however, is that this increases bargaining costs and creates more potential for conflict. Kenney (chapter 5) also stresses organizational flexibility as one of the attributes that favors networks over hierarchies.

But despite these similarities and commonalities among different kinds of networks, the differences among networks are so striking that we need to be careful not to overemphasize the similarities and ignore the differences, especially the differences between networks-as-structures and networks-as-actors.

How and Why Have Networks Emerged and Grown?

The authors take up many issues about the life cycle of networks, especially questions of why and how networks are born or emerge, how they grow or "scale-up" and why some networks disappear or die. Here we will focus in particular on the issue of network emergence and growth.

The chapters focusing on networks-as-structures and networks-as-actors differ in their approach to the issue of network emergence. Those who put more emphasis on agency stress how "networks are built" while those who focus on the networks-as-structures stress how "networks happen." These two approaches are not always mutually intelligible. Hafner-Burton and Montgomery (chapter 2) conclude that a network automatically forms when states join a type of international treaty organization called a preferential trade agreement (PTA). But such a definition makes Eilstrup-Sangiovanni's main question superfluous. She asks why states form networks *instead of* forming international treaty organizations. We can only make sense of these differences when we understand the differences between these two understandings of networks. States choose whether to form a TGN (a network-as-agent) or an international treaty organization (ITO). Inadvertently, upon joining an ITO, they may also form a network-as-structure, even if they are not aware of it.

Thus, for Hafner-Burton and Montgomery, the decisions of many states to join a preferential trade agreement in turn *create* a network. But to say that the PTA creates the network suggests that there is some agency to create a network. It would be more appropriate to say that when many states join a PTA, a network happens or emerges.

Existing literatures pose various hypotheses to explain the growth in transnational networks. There are different "origin stories" for networks. One prominent explanation for network emergence is a delegation account. Networks exist because other actors, mainly states but also international organizations, have created them and delegated authority to them (Cowhey and Mueller, chapter 9). These networks can be seen as examples of delegation from executives to lower-level officials (Eilstrup-Sangiovanni, chapter 10), or from states to nonstate actors like the Internet Engineering Task Force acting on behalf of states to carry out policy coordination and standard setting (Cowhey and Mueller, chapter 9), or delegation by states to nongovernmental organizations to deliver services (Stein, chapter 8). This delegation model is clearly more useful in explaining the emergence of government-organized networks than the emergence of networks organized by nongovernmental organizations.

Another key explanation for network emergence is simply that growing functional interdependence has led to the growth of all forms of international association, of which networks are simply one example. Yet another explanation is that technological change and increasing complexity have contributed to the kinds of connections essential to the formation and sustaining of networks (Eilstrup-Sangiovanni, chapter 10). These hypotheses are relevant to the formation of all the networks considered here, both networks-as-structures and networks-as-actors.

Most of these explanations are macrolevel phenomena that may help explain the overall increase in transnational networks, but are less useful for explaining why networks emerge around some issues, but not others, or with some members and not others. Also, most of these explanations have been used to explain the rise of international institutions more generally; thus, they can't always explain why actors prefer networked forms of organization as compared to other forms (Eilstrup-Sangiovanni, chapter 10).

The authors propose additional hypotheses that focus on explaining why networks emerge instead of some other organizational form. Both state and nonstate actors may choose network forms of organization because they allow actors to preserve autonomy. Actors surrender less autonomy in network forms of organization because no formal commitments are made, and the exit option continues to be open to network participants. Stein lists the desire for autonomy as part of the reason networks emerge in the area of humanitarian assistance. But it is exactly this characteristic of networks that may make them less desirable in other situations, as Eilstrup-Sangiovanni reminds us. When actors prefer to lock-in commitments and lower the risk of defection, they will be less likely to choose networks.

Both Kenney and Eilstrup-Sangiovanni suggest that the rise of one form of network generates the need for the rise of "networked responses." The rise of transnational networks of nonstate actors (especially illicit or violent ones) may generate networked responses on the part of governments. Various chapter authors ask explicitly why and when networks emerge instead of some type of hierarchy. Their answers focus on the specific benefits actors receive through networked cooperation. Both Kahler and Stein, for example, link the issue of network growth to the effectiveness of networks. Kahler (chapter 6) says that networks are more likely to emerge when they are likely to be more successful than hierarchies at promoting collective action. In the case of humanitarian organizations, Stein argues that it was their success in delivering goods and services that led to increased demands for such organizations. Second, she argues, the withdrawal of states from this area of direct service delivery at the same time as states increased their funding for humanitarian assistance has led to increased demand for humanitarian networks.

Eilstrup-Sangiovanni proposes a persuasive argument about why governments choose to form TGNs instead of international treaty organizations. Governments are more likely to choose networked forms of organization when (1) issues call for quick action; (2) uncertainty is pronounced; (3) their preferences differ from rival domestic agents; and (4) there is a desire to avoid spoilers.

One question is how well this argument travels to help explain the formation of other forms of networks. The first two points above relate to the nature of the issue area. There is some evidence from the chapters that the nature of the issue area does influence whether or not actors choose networks. Terrorist groups and drug networks may choose networks because they can act quickly and are easier to keep secret and under the radar screen. But advocacy groups may choose networks because they are efficient tools for getting public information out to a wider audience. Although these may seem contradictory, they are both consistent with aspects of what we know about the characteristics of networks.

In other ways, Eilstrup-Sangiovanni's argument doesn't travel. She makes an argument about the opportunity costs of different organizational forms for different actors. An opportunity-cost argument depends on the organizational alternatives or menus that actors have available to them. Since only states can be full members of international treaty organizations, only states choose between networks and ITOs. Eilstrup-Sangiovanni's argument will be most useful to understand government-organized networks such as TGNs, or those described in the chapters by Stein and Cowhey and Mueller.

Nongovernmental actors are not able to choose between creating either a network or an international treaty organization. Transnational advocacy organizations often participate in international treaty organizations, but they cannot create them. The human rights networks described by Lake and Wong (chapter 7) see their networks as complements to, not as alternatives to, human rights treaty organizations. For many nonstate actors, the *alternatives* they have open to them are either to build their own hierarchical international nongovernmental organization or to pursue networked forms of organization. Our dark networks also have this choice open to them, but the costs of a hierarchical organization may be even greater for drug or terrorist networks than for advocacy networks or epistemic communities. When the costs of building hierarchical nongovernmental organizations are large for nonstate actors, the choice of networked forms of organization may be more obvious for them than it is for states.

For networks-as-structures, and particularly as examples of uncoordinated interdependence, it is not appropriate to say that actors choose to form a network. Governments may choose to adopt practices similar to those adopted in other countries (constitutional provisions, for example, in the case of Elkins, chapter 3), but they don't choose to form or join a network-as-structure. The network emerges as a result of their uncoordinated policy choices. Networks happen when countries do the same thing (not necessarily by being in contact with one another). In order to explain why networks-as-structures emerge and grow, we need to explain why countries do the same thing. This is the central question for both the sociological institutionalist literature and the diffusion literature. Synthesizing some of these literatures, Elkins proposes that the networks he is writing about emerge and grow through processes of adaptation and learning, especially through cultural norms, support groups, competition, information cascades, learning from available models, and learning from reference groups.

Under What Conditions Can Networks Have Influence? Network Effects and Network Effectiveness

Defining Effectiveness

Networks-as-structures are unintentional and uncoordinated, and thus do not act collectively. In the networks-as-structure approach, authors stress networks' effects rather than effectiveness, and clarify that such effects can be suboptimal or functional and efficient (Elkins, chapter 3). In this sense, we could say that some networks have "influence" but are not necessarily "effective" in the sense of meeting specific goals.

Networks-as-actors, on the other hand, are often consciously designed to act collectively to further specific goals. In this approach, the notion of effectiveness involves change or collective action in the direction of network goals. If the network produces changes contrary to its goals, we would say the network failed. This book, however, explodes the notion that network effectiveness might always involve some public good. For terrorist networks or drug networks, effectiveness implies the ability to reach their goals, which would include the ability to create terror or to expand the production and distribution of drugs.

This raises issues about what we mean by effectiveness. The authors in the book are concerned with effectiveness at three different levels: (1) agenda setting and information provision; (2) policy and discursive change; and (3) behavioral change by key actors.

Some chapters focus mainly on the effectiveness of networks in setting agendas within networks and outside of the networks in the policy sphere. This is the main focus of the chapter by Lake and Wong (chapter 7), which stresses that Amnesty International helped set the agenda for the whole human rights network to work on a small set of civil and political rights. Kahler is also concerned with agenda setting within networks and outside of networks, and argues that one of the main successes of al Qaeda was its ability to shift its focus to the far enemy, the United States.

Stein points out that humanitarian service organizations have multiple understandings of effectiveness, but all the definitions are ultimately concerned with behavioral change in the field of both the givers and the recipients of aid. In the case of humanitarian organizations, and perhaps other service delivery organizations, effectiveness involves the delivery of services, not simply the setting of agendas or discursive change of key actors.

Documenting Effectiveness

It is difficult to research and document network effectiveness. Arguments about effectiveness are often counterfactual, in that they argue that networks are effective compared to what existed before networks, or what would have existed without networks (this is the essence of Yanacopulos's arguments on the campaign for debt relief, chapter 4). Second, some argue that networks are effective compared to other forms of organization, especially hierarchies, including states and formal international organizations. Some authors discuss effectiveness in relation to ideals. The critique of humanitarian organizations is often a critique of their effectiveness (or accountability) compared to an ideal of what they should do. These ideals may be those of the organizations themselves, in their mission statement, or those of the publics they serve, or of the donors.

The chapter by Yanacopulos is focused primarily on the issue of effectiveness. For her, the networks were effective at different levels. She is first concerned with the "ability to raise awareness about the issue," and get the debt cancellation issue onto the agendas of the G8, the international financial institutions, and the media. Indeed, the campaign was apparently so effective in influencing the discursive positions of the British government under Tony Blair that it made network members uncomfortable that there were too many similarities between their demands and the government's positions, at least on paper. But Yanacopulos is also concerned with behavioral change on the part of key target actors—for example, whether the Jubilee 2000 campaign actually led to debt reduction or cancellation. She argues that there was more progress on reducing debt and increasing development aid than there would have been in the absence of the network campaigns. Kahler (chapter 6) is also interested in behavioral change, and gauging whether terrorist networks produce "successful" collective actions; in his particular case, an increase in global terrorist activity by network partners.

Eilstrup-Sangiovanni considers TGNs to have been effective in some cases. She argues that the TGNs she studies contributed to a reduction in missile proliferation and made possible some interdictions of materials for nuclear proliferation. But she also points to the limitations of these networks. Their major strength appears to be in setting standards that nonmembers can later be pressured to adopt. But the one formal treaty organization in her study, the Chemical Weapons Convention, is also credited with being effective in leading to the destruction of existing chemical weapons. The argument is not that networks are more or less effective in the abstract than ITOs. Rather Eilstrup-Sangiovanni argues that networks and ITOs have different merits, and in some cases, like the case of chemical weapons, TGNs can provide a practical and conceptual foundation for later treaty-based cooperation. For Stein, effectiveness is one of two central dimensions of accountability. She directs our attention to how criteria involving outcomes are consequentialist, as opposed to the rights-based criteria previously used in many advocacy and service organizations. The ability of organizations to deliver services on the ground is an essential measure of both effectiveness and accountability.

Explaining Effectiveness

But even when we can establish to our satisfaction that some networks were indeed effective, we still need to be able to try to find explanations for effectiveness. Because the definition of what constitutes effectiveness varies in different networks, it is hard to specify what features contribute to the effectiveness of diverse networks. For example, Kahler points out that in clandestine networks, the maintenance of secrecy is essential for effective action. Thus, the need for "concealment of illicit activities" may mean that "sparse and decentralized networks are more effective" at evading law enforcement. But planning complex tasks, such as the destruction of the World Trade Center, requires centralization. Thus even within a single network, there is no single recipe for success. Kahler points out that a central tension within terrorist networks is that they are simultaneously criminal networks (in that they carry out illegal activities and thus require secrecy) and advocacy networks, and thus require publicity for their political success.

Despite these difficulties, the chapters in this book propose or suggest some possible explanations for effectiveness. For example, it is possible that the *nature or structure of the networks themselves* contribute to effectiveness. One question is to what degree the various ways networks are structured will help us explain the effectiveness of political networks. In particular, do the various network structures discussed in this book help explain which networks are more effective?

Not all the chapters specify the type of network structure, and as a result we can't fully evaluate the argument about the link between network structure and effectiveness. Relatively little precise research has been done about the exact structure of international political networks (in part because the research needed to establish exactly the network type of large international networks spread across the globe is hugely time consuming). We don't actually know the structural characteristics of many transnational networks.

In general, network theory predicts that dense networks are likely to be more effective than thin networks. But other network characteristics may also be relevant. For example, do the predictions about efficiency and robustness from network theory (see Lake and Wong for a summary) help us understand which networks will be more effective than others? Networks with a scale-free structure are in general highly efficient and relatively robust, but vulnerable to the failure of central nodes. The definitions of efficiency in network theory are very limited (ability to transmit information across the network quickly) and the concerns about effectiveness in this book go well beyond the movement of information to include agenda setting and collective action. Still, it is interesting to ask whether the type of structure makes the network more effective in the broader sense.

Kahler (chapter 6) argues that three features of networked organization contributed to the successful promotion of collective action in the case of al Qaeda: its embeddedness in existing social networks; the degree to which the network is able to provide scarce resources to its members, of a material (the operation of training camps) or nonmaterial kind (legitimacy or status); and the nature of the network structure. He argues that al Qaeda's structure and its ability to evolve organizationally contributed to its effectiveness. In particular, al Qaeda was a hybrid of network and hierarchy—a network with a hierarchical node—the Central Staff of al Qaeda leadership. This gave it a high degree of flexibility, as it could produce tightly run operations conceived by the leadership, or dispersed operations where local groups took the initiative. Kenney (chapter 5) also suggests that network structures matter for effectiveness. He says that while wheel networks were more "ruthlessly efficient," the chain networks have nevertheless helped maintain Colombia's leading position in the drug industry in the face of hostile drug enforcement efforts. This suggests that different network structures have different strengths: while wheel networks were more efficient at production or export, chain networks may be better at secrecy.

Second, the *nature of the issue area* may affect network effectiveness. International relations theorists have long understood that coordination games may be easier to solve than cooperation games; to the degree that certain issue areas resemble coordination games, networks in these issues may be more effective. Other issues, with characteristics such as the need for speed or the degree of complexity, may lend themselves more to network solutions (Eilstrup-Sangiovanni, chapter 10). Peter Haas (1992) argued that particular kinds of problems, with high levels of complexity and uncertainty, were areas where epistemic communities, one of the basic kinds of networks, were likely to form. It could be that these are also issues where networks are likely to be more effective.

There is also the possibility that certain issues lend themselves more to network activity because of the *intrinsic appeal of certain issues or ideas*. Kahler (chapter 6) suggests that we can't understand the power of al Qaeda without understanding the power of identity appeals. For example, Keck and Sikkink (1998) argue that transnational advocacy networks are more likely to be effective on issues involving bodily harm to vulnerable populations with short causal chains and on issues involving equality of opportunity. Yanacopulos (chapter 4) also suggests that some issues may be perceived as "easier" to organize around than other issues. Some claim that the debt cancellation is "cheap" for states and thus more politically tractable, since the main cost is borne by the international financial institution, not by states themselves.

How Is Power Exercised within Networks?

The most important contribution that some of the chapters make to network theory is to directly incorporate considerations of power into our analysis of networks. Lake and Wong argue that network theory must be modified if it is to help us tackle the issues of power in political networks. In particular, they argue that network theory must recognize that in real social networks (1) nodes are cognizant actors able to formulate and make utility-improving choices; (2) alternative outcomes have distributional implications for nodes, favoring some over others; and (3) nodes vary in the power or influence they possess. They argue that these fairly basic political assumptions must be added to network theory in order to make it useful to political scientists.

Hafner-Burton and Montgomery (chapter 2) are also interested in using social network analysis to understand power dynamics within networks and the international system, but they argue that social network analysis already contains the necessary tools to reveal "social power" within networks. Hafner-Burton and Montgomery define the social power (or prestige) of a state in a network as the sum of a state's ties to other actors in the system. Thus, as for Lake and Wong, nodes in the network vary in the power or influence they possess. But Hafner-Burton and Montgomery use a different definition of power than many other authors in the book, one consistent with their network-as-structure approach. Social power is an attribute of the place in the network, not of an action or an outcome.

Lake and Wong and Kenney provide additional hypotheses about how certain kinds of networks, given their structures, lend themselves to different forms of exercises of power. So, for example, a scale-free network, or a wheel network, gives lots of power to central nodes, because if they exit, the whole thing falls apart. But distributional networks, small-world networks, and chain networks don't give this same power to central nodes.

Lake and Wong's argument that "power is an emergent property of networks themselves" rests on the threat of exit in hub networks. As they recognize, the threat of exit depends on the opportunity cost of exit. Different actors face different opportunity costs for exit from networks. If Lake and Wong are correct that the threat of exit in scale-free networks is a major source of power within networks, then we need to know more about which networks have what structure, and about the opportunity costs of exit in different networks. For many advocacy groups, participating in a network is not very costly and there are benefits associated with it. Exit from the network may involve costs to advocacy organizations' core values and identities. So for example, Stein shows that the humanitarian sector has the power of exit, but to exercise that power often runs contrary to the self-identity of humanitarianism. Stein gives the example of Zimbabwe, where many feel that humanitarian organizations should exit because their presence lends support to the Mugabe regime and its policies. But to exit could lead to more suffering in rural areas, and for many organizations exit is not acceptable under these conditions.

For advocacy networks, especially with a strong membership base, the decision to exit from popular campaigns or networks may be costly in terms of alienating members. At the same time, the opportunity costs of exiting are high because few good alternatives are available to most NGOs who exit a network, and those alternatives may be costly. As Yanacopulos said about the J2K campaign, when one member organization was asked whether disaffected members of the coalition could quit, she answered that there were "powerful reasons for organizations not pulling out, namely that to do so would go down very badly with one's own supporters and do one's own image a lot of damage." Nevertheless, exit from advocacy networks does occur. In the case of the J2K campaign, NGOs from countries in the global South exited from J2K and formed an alternative network (Jubilee South). What gave the southern groups power was not the structure of the network per se. These southern groups were not at the center of a wheel and hub network. Their power didn't come from their structural position. Their power came from the nature of legitimacy in their advocacy networks. Many development, debt, and human rights advocacy networks gain legitimacy from their claim to speak on behalf of the powerless and the disenfranchised, especially in the global South. Thus, the NGO network nodes from the South have power because if they exit from the network, they undermine one of the network's main claims to legitimacy—its claim to speak on behalf of the powerless. Network exit is often less credible for advocacy groups, and what gives groups power is not necessarily their central location in the network structure, but their central location in the legitimacy claims of the network. Thus power is not always exercised in the same way in advocacy networks as in other networks. A key source of advocacy network power is the legitimacy of their claims.

Thus, power doesn't only reside in the structural position or material resources of network nodes, but it also relates to the purposes of networks. When discussing power within and outside networks, for networks where ideas (causal or principled) are a main purpose, our understanding of power must consider "epistemic power"—the power of ideas. At least, we can't unproblematically import models of power from network theory, or models of power that just focus on the first and second face of power, but we need to also look at what Barnett and Duvall (2005) have called "productive power" or the power to constitute social subjects through knowledge and discursive practices. How and why does one understanding of human rights or the "free flow of ideas" win out over another, and what does that tell us about the operation of power within networks and in society more generally?

In epistemic communities, where the purpose has to do with causal and technical knowledge, groups will have power in part because they have unique access to such causal or technical knowledge. Cowhey and Mueller clarify how the unique technical knowledge of members of the IETF community gave them power within the network. In religious networks, where the purpose has to do with the spread of doctrine, individuals most closely associated with doctrine will have power (thus the power of the clergy in fundamentalist religious networks). In groups whose main purpose is profit, the most wealthy or profitable nodes will have exceptional power. Groups with money have power in all networks, of course, but they have more power in networks whose sole or main purpose is the accumulation of profit. In groups whose main goal is the spread of a principled idea, association with the legitimacy of that idea is a central source of power.

When discussing how power is exercised within networks, it should be mentioned that in Kenney's drug networks, and often in other illegal networks as well, the threat of violence or intimidation is one of the tools used to exercise power within the network, an option that is not on the menu of most legal networks. Kenney's networks are willing to use *plomo* (lead bullets) as well as *plata* (money) to persuade actors to trade favors to carry out the network's goals. Likewise, the use of violence is one of the main ways that political authorities interact with illicit networks. This may seem so obvious as to be banal, but it once again emphasizes important differences between the way that legal and illicit networks function internally and interact with their environment.

Stein is one of the few authors who addresses the possibilities of abuse of power within or by networks. In general, the whole existence of the accountability network in the humanitarian sector is a recognition of power, and an effort to have that power made accountable. But ALNAP is a response not only because powerful donors imposed their criteria on humanitarian organizations—it also served to generate internally accepted understandings of power and risk within the humanitarian sector.

Power is exercised in quite traditional ways among states in TGNs, although with somewhat greater flexibility than in international treaty organizations. The U.S. government's perceived security needs were behind the Proliferation Security Initiative network, and one of the purposes of the network was to permit it to develop nonuniversal and nonreciprocal procedures to deal with rogue states that would not be extended to the United States. One goal of the network was to avoid imposing unwanted constraints on the legitimate or illegitimate activities of the United States and its allies, an exercise of power that would have been more difficult in an international organization (Eilstrup-Sangiovanni, chapter 10).

How Do Networks Contribute to Global Governance?

Networks both participate in existing intergovernmental global governance arrangements and at times provide alternative and/or complementary forms of global governance, what we call "networked" forms of governance. By global governance, we refer to the formation and functioning of rules, institutions, and practices through which international actors maintain order and achieve collective goals (Rosenau 2000). In these governance tasks, networks have been particularly involved in standard setting and in the implementation of standards, especially through monitoring. Chapters by Eilstrup-Sangiovanni, Cowhey and Mueller, and Stein all explicitly discuss network contributions to global governance. Illicit networks don't provide governance, but they provoke governance responses, some networked and some more hierarchical. The ability of networks to participate in global governance or to provoke governance responses is yet another indicator of the emerging power of networks in global politics.

Most other chapters mention networked forms of governance. Cowhey and Mueller (chapter 9) ask why certain forms of network governance have emerged and how they have evolved. Their answer, informed by the delegation literature, suggests that networked forms of governance are often the result of government decisions not to form alternative governmental or intergovernmental forms of governance.

One of the main ways that networks engage in governance, according to Cowhey and Mueller, is through setting standards. The role of networks in setting standards was also highlighted by Lake and Wong, Stein, and Eilstrup-Sangiovanni. Cowhey and Mueller argue that the form of governance that emerges in an issue area may be path dependent and idiosyncratic to the nature of the issue area. If so, it may be difficult to generalize about network contributions to global governance. Eilstrup-Sangiovanni (chapter 10) would appear to agree, since she argues that TGN network governance encourages "decentralized, differentiated solutions to local problems rather than the imposition of centrally directed, uniform policies." She uses the concept of "subsidiarity" to describe transgovernmental network forms of governance. This involves "the making and implementation of decisions and policies by those who are directly involved or affected." If we think about networks as sometimes engaged in global governance structures, it expands our understanding of the nature of governance and the actors involved. Networks can expand the number and type of actors involved in governance, especially by getting nonstate actors involved in governance tasks. But as Eilstrup-Sangiovanni has also shown, some network forms of governance may also function as a way to exclude actors, such as rogue states or spoilers.

Stein (chapter 8) argues persuasively that ALNAP is an "emergent governance network." This is one of the best examples in this book of how the functions of governance are carried out by the network itself—developing standards, conducting evaluation, and sharing information that leads to changed practices in the field. Governments could have pressured for more formal organizational responses to the issues of the governance of humanitarianism, within the UN, for example, but they chose not to do so. Humanitarian organizations could have resisted more strenuously these efforts to limit the autonomy of their actions. But the network nevertheless succeeded in coming up with new understandings of accountability that were useful to network members in terms of giving them tools to conduct their work on the ground. ALNAP's ability to be a learning network seems to have allowed it to play this governance function. Stein argues that we are more likely to see networked forms of global governance when networks "allow pragmatic solutions to develop without requiring ideological concessions. These pragmatic solutions blunted sharp conflicts of interest and strengthened the capacity of the network to attract new members and to broaden the agenda."

How Do Networks Contribute to Accountability and How Can Networks Be Held Accountable?

Networks contribute to holding other actors accountable. Increasingly, though, questions are being raised about how networks themselves should be held accountable. The discussions above have highlighted the ways in which networks wield and exercise power in global politics. Systems of accountability are essentially constraints on abuses of power (Grant and Keohane 2005). The demand for accountability of networks is thus simultaneously a recognition of the increasing power of networks. Theorists have pointed out that accountability works in different and more complex ways in the international realm than in the domestic realm. It may be even more difficult to define how accountability works in a networked world than in the general world of international politics. And even if we can define what accountability of and in networks means, systems of network accountability may be particularly difficult to implement.

Information and transparency are necessary preconditions for accountability. Exactly because networks are particularly suited to situations that require rapid and reliable information, they may be particularly apt participants in processes of global accountability. The provision of information is one key way in which most networks contribute to accountability. Human rights advocacy networks, for example, have long specialized in the provision of detailed information about human rights violations by governments, information that was previously secret. This information then can be used by networks, other governments, and international organizations to try to hold these governments accountable.

We also need to ask how networks themselves can be held more accountable. Since we recognize that networks are increasingly powerful actors in international politics, it is important to understand how such actors are held accountable. Stein makes clear some of the problems with thinking about accountability in a networked transnational space. It is not always clear to whom different actors should be accountable. For Stein, accountability is directly linked to effectiveness, since she conceives of accountability along two dimensions: representativeness and effectiveness. In terms of representativeness, humanitarian organizations struggle with multiple accountabilities. Particular tension may arise between being accountable to donors and being accountable to the people humanitarian organizations aim to help.

Stein argues that network accountability in the humanitarian sector, at least, will be measured in large part by how effective the network is in meeting its goals. A major humanitarian criteria is "do no harm," which is "deeply consequentialist" if minimalist in terms of effectiveness. But Stein also asks why networks are suddenly concerned with accountability, and why they have chosen a network to help them address the question. As states retreat from direct service delivery in the area of humanitarian assistance and take on the role of donors, they have become "increasingly present as regulators interested in outcomes and accountability." So, in this case, we see that the emergence of a principal-agent relationship between states and humanitarian organizations contributed to greater demands for accountability. Although some demands for accountability also came from within humanitarian organizations, particularly in the wake of Rwanda, there has been "an allergy to accountability" within humanitarian organizations, in part because it is difficult for organizations to acknowledge they are powerful and that they are political actors. This may also be true about a wider range of nongovernmental organization and advocacy networks, motivated as they are by principled ideas. Some humanitarians interpret the demand for accountability "as an implicit allegation of failure or even worse, as a charge of immorality," and thus it strikes at the very identity of humanitarians. Despite this allergy to accountability, the humanitarian ALNAP network has been quite effective in developing better understandings and practices of accountability.

What Are the Policy Implications of This Work?

The policy implications of this work are potentially very great. For example, the issue of when to form networks is of obvious interest to states and nonstate actors. The question of effectiveness is also very important for policymakers. In the case of the dark networks, more information about the conditions under which they can be effective may be important because policymakers will want to disrupt those very characteristics of networks that make them most effective. Kahler's argument about the features of networked organization that contributed to al Qaeda's successful promotion of collective action potentially provides both a road map for future terrorist groups and for government agencies fighting terrorism to both evaluate their past actions and plan future ones. If, as Kahler argues, the training camps in Afghanistan were essential to the effectiveness of al Qaeda, then breaking up those training camps was an important step in weakening the network.

There are huge policy implications of much of the work discussed here but these are not always completely fleshed out. For example, what are the policy implications of Stein's argument that certain demands for accountability could lead to more risk-averse behavior by certain networks? If flexibility and innovation have been one of the hallmarks of networks, it could be that greater demands for accountability in the network sector will limit its more unique organizational contributions. Kenney's research is clearly of great interest to drug enforcement agents, but scholarly research cannot often be easily distilled into clear policy directives. Reading Kenney's work, it is not clear whether states should fight networks with networks or fight networks with state hierarchies. A DEA agent might say that the move from a wheel network to a chain network was a mark of success in the war against drugs, because it reduced the supply of drugs to the marketplace.

Transnational political networks are an increasingly important feature in global politics. Scholars of international relations can no longer fully understand most current developments in the international system without taking political networks into account. These networks have not replaced the state but exist as an alternative organizational form alongside of states, international organizations, and markets. International relations scholars will continue to study the important hierarchies (states, international organizations, and international nongovernmental organizations) in international politics, but they will want to understand how political networks integrate and interact with these actors. Past studies of transnational political networks have tended to focus on a single type of network: for example, transnational advocacy networks or transgovernmental networks. Network studies from other disciplines provide useful concepts and tools, but they have tended to ignore the politics of networks, a central concern for any political scientist.

This book, in contrast, explores a wide range of networks and explicitly focuses on the political issues of power, effectiveness, accountability, and governance by and within networks. In particular, the conceptualization of two types of network analysis—networks-as-structures and networks-as-actors—is an important clarification that helps us categorize diverse forms of research. These are ideal types, of course, and most networks "embody elements of agent and structure simultaneously" (Keck and Sikkink 1998, 5). The authors in this book relate network theories to big theoretical debates in the field of international relations, especially long-standing debates in international relations about the primacy of structure or agency in global politics, and related debates about the nature and exercise of power. Scholars who focus on networks-as-structures, not surprisingly take an approach to power that sees it emanating from the structural properties of or position in the network. Such an understanding of structural power, such as Hafner-Burton and Montgomery's definition of social power or prestige, however, often remains primarily definitional. Scholars who focus on networks-as-actors, on the other hand, are more likely to focus on the specific abilities of networks to set agendas or influence the policy goals they advocate.

To further advance the study of transnational political networks, it might be useful to end this book by posing key questions for future research. An important avenue for future research in the networks-as-structures approach is to test whether the definitional properties of network power and prestige actually translate into successful behavioral exercises of power. Does a certain position in a network permit observable exercises of power? Are certain network nodes able to affect the behavior of other actors as a result of their position in the network? For example, can states that join many trade agreements and thus have many ties to other states use this formally defined social power to get other actors to change their behavior in line with what the prestigious state wants? To answer these questions, researchers will need to seek more information about the actions of states and outcomes and not just about their position in the network.

Sometimes the differences between networks-as-structures or the networks-as-actors are not dictated by the subject matter per se, but by the methods used by the researcher. In other words, the emphasis on one side or another in the agent-structure debate may be an issue of focus and method. Certain forms of network analysis may not permit the researcher to interrogate whether or not agency is at work, or whether actions are in fact being coordinated. Network analysis may not lead the researcher to gather the qualitative information necessary to see agency or coordination. Likewise, certain forms of research on networks as actors may presume agency, in the form of coordinated action, and be inattentive to the possibility of "uncoordinated interdependence." One can always find agency if one is looking for it, but the bulk of the dynamic at work may be uncoordinated interdependence rather than a network working as an agent coordinating outcomes. Thus in future research it may be increasingly important to combine methods so that researchers study both the structural and the agentic qualities of networks. In this book, this effort to combine methods is best exemplified by Elkins's work on constitutional networks.

In this book, the authors propose a series of more specific hypotheses about the conditions under which networks emerge and proliferate, under what conditions they can be effective, and how they contribute to global governance. On all these issues, networks are seen to exercise power, but their power does not always take traditional forms nor is it exercised in standard ways. In each of these areas, more research is needed. For example, we could use more research on the question of why networks emerge in some issue areas but not in others. There is some evidence, for example, from this book that the nature of the issue area influences whether or not actors choose networks, but this evidence is far from straightforward, and further research is needed to generate more persuasive arguments. Finally, much more research needs to be conducted on the conditions under which networks can be effective, and in particular on how network structures and properties relate to network effectiveness.

Among the virtues of this book is that it is among the first by international relations scholars to study the wide range of different types of transnational political networks. Second, the book explicitly reincorporates the study of power into network analysis. Each chapter in the book examines either the power of networks or power within networks, or both. The book also makes an important contribution to the study of international politics by conceptualizing the network phenomena more clearly: defining political networks, discussing the various approaches to networks, and describing different types of networks and the particular forms they take. Much more research remains to be done to provide satisfactory answers to the questions we pose, but we believe this book provides an essential basis for such future research.

References

9/11 Commission. 2004. *The 9/11 Commission Report: Final Report of the National Commission on Terrorist Attacks upon the United States.* New York: W. W. Norton.

Abbate, Janet. 1999. *Inventing the Internet.* Cambridge: MIT Press.

Abbott, Kenneth, and Duncan Snidal. 2000. "Hard and Soft Law in International Governance." *International Organization* 54 (3): 421–56.

Abuza, Zachary. 2002. "Tentacles of Terror: Al Qaeda's Southeast Asian Network." *Contemporary Southeast Asia* 24 (3): 427–65.

Adamson, Fiona B. 2005. "Globalization, Transnational Political Mobilization, and Networks of Violence." *Cambridge Review of International Affairs* 18 (1): 35–53.

Agranoff, Robert. 2003. "A New Look at the Value-Adding Functions of Intergovernmental Networks." Paper presented at the National Public Management Research Conference, Georgetown University, Washington, D.C., October.

Albini, Joseph L. 1971. *The American Mafia: Genesis of a Legend.* New York: Appleton-Century-Crofts.

AJIL. 2004. "Proliferation Security Initiative for Searching Potential WMD Vessels." *American Journal of International Law* 98 (2): 355–57.

ALNAP. 2001. "Humanitarian Action: Learning from Evaluation." *ALNAP Annual Review 2001.* London: Overseas Development Institute.

——. 2002. "The Vision for ALNAP." London: Overseas Development Institute.

——. 2004. *ALNAP Review of Humanitarian Action in 2004.* Available at http://www.alnap.org. Accessed April 4, 2008.

——. 2005a. "The ALNAP Quality Proforma 2005." Annex 1. London: Overseas Development Institute, February 3.

——. 2005b. *The Global Study on Participation and Consultation of Affected Populations in Humanitarian Action.* London: Overseas Development Institute.

Alvarez, Jose. 2001. "Do Liberal States Behave Better? A Critique of Slaughter's Liberal Theory." *European Journal of International Law* 12: 183–246.

Anderson, Mary. 1996. *Do No Harm: Supporting Local Capacities for Peace through Aid.* Cambridge, Mass.: Local Capacities for Peace Project.

Andreas, Peter. 2000. *Border Games: Policing the U.S.-Mexico Divide.* Ithaca: Cornell University Press.

———. 2003. "Redrawing the Line: Borders and Security in the Twenty-first Century." *International Security* 28 (2): 78–111.

Anonymous [Michael Scheuer]. 2002. *Through Our Enemies' Eyes: Osama Bin Laden, Radical Islam, and the Future of America*. Washington, D.C.: Brassey's.

———. 2004. *Imperial Hubris: Why the West Is Losing the War on Terror*. Washington, D.C.: Brassey's.

Arango, Mario, and Jorge Child. 1984. *Narcotráfico imperio de la cocaína*. Medellín, Colombia: Editorial Percepción.

Argyris, Chris, and Donald A. Schön. 1996. *Organizational Learning II: Theory, Method, and Practice*. Reading, Mass.: Addison-Wesley.

Arlacchi, Pino. 1986. *Mafia Business: The Mafia Ethic and the Spirit of Capitalism*. Translated by Martin Ryle. London: Verso.

Arms Control Association. 2004. "Fact Sheet: The Missile Technology Control Regime at a Glance." Available at http://armscontrol.org/factsheets/mtcr.asp. Accessed April 4, 2008.

Arquilla, John, and David Ronfeldt. 2001. "The Advent of Netwar (Revisited)." In *Networks and Netwars: The Future of Terror, Crime, and Militancy*, edited by John Arquilla and David Ronfeldt, 1–25. Santa Monica, Calif.: RAND.

Asch, Solomon E. 1951. "Effects of Group Pressure upon the Modification and Distortion of Judgment." In *Groups, Leadership, and Men*, edited by H. Guetzkow. Pittsburgh: Carnegie Press.

Bach, David. 2003. "Varieties of Cooperation: Domestic Politics and International Market Governance." Paper presented at the annual meeting of the American Political Science Association, Philadelphia.

Bachrach, Peter, and Morton S. Baratz. 1962. "The Two Faces of Power." *American Political Science Review* 56: 947–52.

———. 1971. *Power and Poverty*. Oxford: Oxford University Press.

Bagley, Bruce M. 2004. "Globalisation and Latin American and Caribbean Organized Crime." *Global Crime* 6 (1): 32–53.

Baker, Wayne E., and Robert R. Faulkner. 1993. "The Social Organization of Conspiracy: Illegal Networks in the Heavy Electrical Equipment Industry." *American Sociological Review* 58 (December): 837–60.

Bandura, Albert. 1977. *Social Learning Theory*. Englewood Cliffs, N.J.: Prentice-Hall.

Bandy, J., and J. Smith, eds. 2005. *Coalitions across Borders: Transnational Protest and the Neoliberal Order*. Lanham, Md.: Rowman and Littlefield.

Bar, Francois, Stephen Cohen, Peter Cowhey, Brad deLong, Michael Kleeman, and John Zysman. 2001. "The Next Generation Internet." In *Tracking a Transformation: E-Commerce and the Terms of Competition in Industries*, Berkeley Roundtable on the International Economy, 435–73. Washington, D.C.: Brookings Institution Press.

Barabási, Albert-László. 2002. *Linked: The New Science of Networks*. Cambridge, Mass.: Perseus Publishing.

———. 2003. *Linked: How Everything Is Connected to Everything Else and What It Means for Business, Science, and Everyday Life*. New York: Plume.

Barabási, Albert-László, and Réka Albert. 1999. "Emergence of Scaling in Random Networks." *Science* 286 (5489): 509–12.

Barnett, Michael. 2007. "Humanitarianism." In *Humanitarianism in Question: Politics, Power, and Ethics*, edited by Michael Barnett and Tom Weiss. Ithaca: Cornell University Press.

Barnett, Michael, and Raymond Duvall. 2005. "Power in International Politics." *International Organization* 59 (1): 39–75.

Beckfield, Jason. 2003. "Inequality in the World Polity: The Structure of International Organization." *American Sociological Review* 68 (3): 401–24.

Benford, R., and D. Snow. 2000. "Framing Processes and Social Movements: An Overview and Assessment." *Annual Review of Sociology* 26: 611–39.

Benjamin, Daniel, and Steven Simon. 2003. *The Age of Sacred Terror.* New York: Random House.

Benoliel, Daniel. 2003. "Cyberspace Technological Standardization: An Institutional Theory Retrospective." *Berkeley Technology and Law Journal* 18 (4): 1259–1340.

Benvenisti, Eyal. 2006. "Coalitions of the Willing and the Evolution of Informal International Law." In *Coalitions of the Willing: Avant-Garde or Threat?*, edited by T. Stoll, Christian Calliess, and G. Nolte. Cologne: Carl Heymans Verlag.

Bermann, George, Matthias Herdegen, and Peter Lindseth. 2000. *Transatlantic Regulatory Cooperation: Legal Problems and Political Prospects.* Oxford: Oxford University Press.

Berners-Lee, Tim. 2000. *Weaving the Web.* New York: Harper Business.

Betancourt, Dario, and Martha L. García. 1994. *Contrabandistas, marimberos y mafiosos: Historia social de la mafia colombiana (1965–1992).* Bogotá: Tercer Mundo Editores.

Bhagwati, Jagdish. 1993. "Regionalism and Multilateralism: An Overview." In *New Dimensions in Regional Integration,* edited by J. de Melo and A. Panagariya, 22–51. Cambridge: Cambridge University Press.

Bikhchandani, Sushil, David Hirshleifer, and Ivo Welch. 1998. "Learning from the Behavior of Others: Conformity, Fads, and Informational Cascades." *Journal of Economic Perspectives* 12 (3): 151–70.

Block, Alan A. 1979. "The Snowman Cometh: Coke in Progressive New York." *Criminology* 17 (1): 75–99.

———. 1980. *East Side, West Side: Organizing Crime in New York, 1930–1950.* Cardiff, UK: University College Cardiff Press.

Blok, Anton. 1974. *The Mafia of a Sicilian Village, 1860–1960: A Study of Violent Peasant Entrepreneurs.* Oxford: Basil Blackwell.

Bonacich, Phillip. 1987. "Power and Centrality: A Family of Measures." *American Journal of Sociology* 92 (5): 1170–82.

Borgatti, Stephen P., and Martin G. Everett. 1999. "Models of Core/Periphery Structures." *Social Networks* 21 (4): 375–95.

Borgatti, Stephen P., and Pacey C. Foster. 2003. "The Network Paradigm in Organizational Research: A Review and Typology." *Journal of Management* 29 (6): 991–1013.

Borrus, Michael, Dieter Ernst, and Stephan Haggard. 2000. *International Production Networks in Asia: Rivalry or Riches?* New York: Routledge.

Bourdieu, Pierre. 1986. "The Forms of Capital." In *Handbook of Theory and Research for the Sociology of Education,* edited by J. G. Richardson, 241–58. New York: Greenwood Press.

Bradner, S. 1996. "The Internet Standards Process—Revision 3." RFC 2026, Network Working Group, IETF. Available at ftp://ftp.isi.edu/in-notes/rfc2026.txt. Accessed April 4, 2008.

Brady, Henry, and Paul Sniderman. 1985. "Attitude Attribution: A Group Basis for Political Reasoning." *American Political Science Review* 60: 880–98.

Brams, Steven J. 1969. "The Structure of Influence Relationships in the International System." In *International Politics and Foreign Policy: A Reader in Research and Theory,* 2nd ed., edited by J. N. Rosenau, 583–99. New York: Free Press.

Broughyton, B., S. Maguire, and S. Frueh. 2005. *Inter-Agency Evaluation of the Humanitarian Response to the Darfur Crisis.* New York: UN Office for the Coordination of Humanitarian Affairs, February.

Broz, Lawrence, and Michael Brewster Hawes. 2006. "Congressional Politics of Financing the International Monetary Fund." *International Organization* 60 (2): 367–99.

Bull, Hedley. 1977. *The Anarchical Society: A Study of Order in World Politics.* London: Macmillan.

Burgess, Richard. 2001. "Chemical Industry and the CWC." In *Chemical Weapons Convention: Implementation Challenges and Solutions,* edited by J. B. Tucker. Washington, D.C.: Monterey Institute of International Studies.

Burke, Jason. 2003. *Al-Qaeda: Casting a Shadow of Terror.* New York: I. B. Tauris.

——. 2004. "Al Qaeda." *Foreign Policy* (May–June): 18–26.

Burt, Ronald S. 1992. *Structural Holes: The Social Structure of Competition.* Cambridge: Harvard University Press.

——. 2001. "Structural Holes versus Network Closure as Social Capital." In *Social Capital: Theory and Research,* edited by Nan Lin, Karen Cook, and Ronald S. Burt, 31–56. New York: Aldine de Gruyter.

Butts, Carter T. 2007. SNA: Tools for Social Network Analysis (R package version 1.5). Software. Available at http://erzuli.ss.uci.edu/R.stuff. Accessed April 4, 2008.

Byers, Michael. 2004. "Policing the High Seas: The Proliferation Security Initiative." *American Journal of International Law* 98 (3): 526–45.

Byman, Daniel L. 2003. "Al-Qaeda as an Adversary: Do We Understand Our Enemy?" *World Politics* 56 (October): 139–63.

Cameron, Kelly. 2004. "Telecommunications and Audio-Visual Services in the Context of the WTO: Today and Tomorrow." In *The WTO and Global Convergence in Telecommunications and Audio-Visual Services,* edited by Damien Geradin and David Luff, 21–33. New York: Cambridge University Press.

Cao, Xun. 2006. "Convergence, Divergence, and Networks in the Age of Globalization: A Social Network Analysis Approach to IPE." Paper presented at the Inaugural Meeting of the International Political Economy Society, Princeton University, November 17–18.

CARE. 2004. "CARE International's Humanitarian Response to the Darfur Crisis, Real-Time Evaluation." Phase 2, December.

Castells, Manuel. 1996. *The Rise of the Network Society.* Malden, Mass.: Blackwell.

Castillo, Fabio. 1987. *Los jinetes de la cocaina.* Bogotá: Editorial Documentos Periodísticos.

Cave, Martin, Luigi Prosperetti, and Chris Doyle. 2006. "Where Are We Going? Technologies, Markets and Long-Range Public Policy Issues in European Communications." *Information Economics and Policy* 18: 242–55.

Center for Nonproliferation Studies. 1998. *Missile Technology Control Regime.* Monterey, Calif.: Monterey Institute of International Studies.

——. N.d. "Inventory of International Nonproliferation Organizations and Regimes." Available at http://cns.miis.edu/pubs/inven/. Accessed April 4, 2008.

Centola, Damon, and Michael Macy. 2007. "Complex Contagions and the Weakness of Long Ties." *American Journal of Sociology* 113 (3): 702–34.

Cervantes, José. 1980. *La noche de las luciernágas.* Bogotá: Plaza y Janes.

Chambliss, William J. 1988. *On the Take: From Petty Crooks to Presidents.* 2nd ed. Bloomington: University of Indiana Press.

Clark, Ann Marie. 2001. *Diplomacy of Conscience: Amnesty International and Changing Human Rights Norms.* Princeton: Princeton University Press.

Clark, J. 2003. *Globalizing Civic Engagement.* London: Earthscan.

Claude, Inis. 1956. *Swords into Plowshares: The Problem of Progress of International Organization.* London: University of London Press.

Coleman, James S. 1961. *The Adolescent Society.* Glencoe, N.Y.: Free Press.

——. 1990. *Foundations of Social Theory.* Cambridge: Harvard University Press.

Coll, Steve. 2004. *Ghost Wars: The Secret History of the CIA, Afghanistan, and Bin Laden, from the Soviet Invasion to September 10, 2001.* New York: Penguin Press.

Collins, Carole, Zie Gariyo, and Tony Burdon. 2001. "Jubilee 2000: Citizen Action across the North-South Divide." In *Global Citizen Action,* edited by Michael Edwards and John Gaventa. London: Earthscan.

Colombatto, Enrico, and Jonathan Macey. 1996. "A Public Choice Model of International

Economic Cooperation and the Decline of the Nation-State." *Cardozo Law Review* 18 (3): 925–56.

Convention on the Prohibition of the Development, Production, Stockpiling and Use of Chemical Weapons and on Their Destruction (A/RES/47/39). United Nations General Assembly. Available at: http://www.un.org/documents/ga/res/47/a47r039.htm.

Cooley, Alexander. 2004. "The Marketplace of Humanitarian Action: A Political Economy Perspective." Paper presented to the Social Science Research Council, New York, November 9.

Correlates of War Project. 2005. "State System Membership List, V2004.1." Available at http://correlatesofwar.org/. Accessed April 4, 2008.

Cowhey, Peter. 2004. "Accounting Rates, Cross-Border Services, and the Next WTO Round on Basic Telecommunications Services." In *The WTO and Global Convergence in Telecommunications and Audio-Visual Service,* edited by Damien Geradin and David Luff, 51–82. New York: Cambridge University Press.

Cowhey, Peter, Jonathan Aronson, and John Richards. Forthcoming. *The Four Trillion Gamble: The Political Economy of Communications and Information Markets in the Twenty-first Century.* Cambridge: MIT Press.

Dahl, Robert A. 1957. "The Concept of Power." *Behavioral Science* 2 (3): 201–15.

Dahrendorf, Ralf. 1990. *Reflections on the Revolution in Europe.* London: Chatto and Windus.

Darcy, James. 2005. "Thoughts on the Effectiveness of Humanitarian Action." Paper presented to the Social Science Research Council, New York, April 12.

Darton, A. 2006. "Comic Relief 'Public Perception of Poverty' Omnibus Survey." Wave 5 Findings, Summary Report.

David, Paul. 1985. "Clio and the Economics of QWERTY." *American Economic Review* 75: 322–37.

Davis, Gerald F., and Henrich R. Greve. 1997. "Corporate Elite Networks and Governance Changes in the 1980s." *American Journal of Sociology* 103: 1–37.

Deutsch, Karl Wolfgang. 1953. *Nationalism and Social Communication: An Inquiry into the Foundations of Nationality.* Cambridge: Technology Press of the Massachusetts Institute of Technology; New York: Wiley.

de Waal, Alex. 1997. *Famine Crimes: Politics and the Disaster Relief Industry in Africa.* Oxford: James Currey.

Diani, Mario. 2003a. "Leaders or Brokers? Positions and Influence in Social Movement Networks." In *Social Movements and Networks: Relational Approaches to Collective Action,* edited by Mario Diani and Doug McAdam, 105–22. Oxford: Oxford University Press.

———. 2003b. "Networks and Social Movements: A Research Programme." In *Social Movements and Networks: Relational Approaches to Collective Action,* edited by Mario Diani and Doug McAdam, 299–319. Oxford: Oxford University Press.

Donnelly, E. 2002. "Proclaiming Jubilee: The Debt and Structural Adjustment Network." In *Restructuring World Politics: Transnational Social Movements, Networks, and Norms,* edited by S. Khagram, J. Riker, and Kathryn Sikkink. Minneapolis: University of Minnesota Press.

Doolin, Joel. 2004. "Operational Art for the PSI." Unpublished manuscript, Naval War College, Newport, R.I.

Dorussen, Han, and Hugh Ward. 2008. "Intergovernmental Organizations and the Kantian Peace: A Network Perspective." *Journal of Conflict Resolution* 52 (2): 189–212.

Dowlah, Caf. 2004. *Backwaters of Global Prosperity: How Forces of Globalization and GATT/WTO Trade Regimes Contribute to the Marginalization of the World's Poorest Nations.* Westport, Conn.: Praeger.

Drury, A. Cooper. 1998. "Revisiting Economic Sanctions Reconsidered." *Journal of Peace Research* 35: 497–509.

Economides, N. 2005. "The Economics of the Internet Backbone." In *Handbook of Telecommunications Economics*, vol. 2, edited by Sumit T. Majumdar, Ingo Vogelsang, and Martin E. Cave, 375–413. Amsterdam: North-Holland.

Elkins, Zachary. 2003. "Designed by Diffusion: International Networks and the Spread of Democracy." PhD diss., Department of Political Science, University of California, Berkeley.

Elkins, Zachary, and Thomas Ginsburg. 2006. "The Comparative Constitutions Project." Available at http://www.comparativeconstitutionsproject.org. Accessed July 29, 2008.

Elkins, Zachary, Thomas Ginsburg, and James Melton. Forthcoming. *The Lifespan of Written Constitutions*. New York: Cambridge University Press.

Elkins, Zachary, Andrew Guzman, and Beth Simmons. 2006. "Competing for Capital: The Diffusion of Bilateral Investment Treaties, 1959–2000." *International Organization* 60 (4): 811–46.

Elkins, Zachary, and Beth Simmons. 2005. "On Waves, Clusters, and Diffusion: A Conceptual Framework." *Annals of the American Academy of Political and Social Science* 598: 33–51.

Elster, Jon. 1995. "Forces and Mechanisms in the Constitution-Making Process." *Duke Law Journal* 45 (2): 364–96.

Emirbayer, Mustafa, and Jeff Goodwin. 1994. "Network Analysis, Culture, and the Problem of Agency." *American Journal of Sociology* 99: 1411–54.

Epstein, David, and Sharyn O'Halloran. 1999. *Delegating Powers*. New York: Cambridge University Press.

Evans, Peter. 1997. "Eclipse of the State? Reflections on Stateness in an Era of Globalization." *World Politics* 50: 62–87.

Farrell, David M. 2001. *Electoral Systems: A Comparative Introduction*. New York: St. Martin's.

Farrell, Joseph, and Philip Weiser. 2003. "Modularity, Vertical Integration, and Open Access Policies," *Harvard Journal of Law and Technology* 17 (1): 85–134.

Feakes, Daniel. 2001. "Export Controls, Chemical Trade, and the CWC." In *The Chemical Weapons Convention: Implementation Challenges and Solutions*, edited by J. B. Tucker, 45–52. Washington, D.C.: Monterey Institute of International Studies.

Fearon, James D. 1998. "Bargaining, Enforcement, and International Cooperation." *International Organization* 52: 269–305.

Felter, Joe, Jeff Bramlett, Bill Perkins, Jarrett Brachman, Brian Fishman, James Forest, Lianne Kennedy, Jacob N. Shapiro, and Tom Stocking. 2006. *Harmony and Disharmony: Exploiting al-Qa'ida's Organizational Vulnerabilities*. West Point: United States Military Academy Combating Terrorism Center.

Festinger, Leon. 1950. *Social Pressures in Informal Groups: A Study of Human Factors in Housing*. Stanford: Stanford University Press.

Finnemore, Martha. 1996. *National Interests in International Society*. Ithaca: Cornell University Press.

Finnemore, Martha, and Kathryn Sikkink. 1998. "International Norm Dynamics and Political Change." *International Organization* 52: 887–917.

Firebaugh, Glenn. 1999. "Empirics of World Income Inequality." *American Journal of Sociology* 104 (6): 1597–1630.

Fiske, Susan T., and Shelley E. Taylor. 1991. *Social Cognition*. 2nd ed. New York: McGraw-Hill.

Fowler, A. 1997. *Striking a Balance*. London: Earthscan Publications.

Frankel, Jeffrey A., ed. 1998. *The Regionalization of the World Economy*. Chicago: University of Chicago Press.

Friedman, Benjamin. 2003. "The Proliferation Security Initiative: The Legal Challenge." Bipartisan Security Group Policy Brief, Washington, D.C., September.

Froomkin, Michael. 2000. "Wrong Turn in Cyberspace: Using ICANN to Route around the APA and the Constitution." *Duke Law Journal* 50: 17–184.

Gabel, David, and David Weiman. 1998. *Opening Networks to Competition: The Regulation and Pricing of Access.* New York: Kluwer Academic Press.

Gerges, Fawaz A. 2005. *The Far Enemy: Why Jihad Went Global.* Cambridge: Cambridge University Press.

Gilpin, Robert. 1987. *The Political Economy of International Relations.* Princeton: Princeton University Press.

Glennie, Jonathan. 2006. "The Myth of Charity: A 2005 Reality Check." *Globalizations* 3: 258–60.

Goddard, Stacie E., and Daniel H. Nexon. 2005. "Paradigm Lost? Reassessing Theory of International Politics." *European Journal of International Relations* 11 (1): 9–61.

Goffman, E. 1986. *Frame Analysis: An Essay on the Organization of Experience.* Boston: Northeastern University Press.

Goldsmith, Jack, and Timothy Wu. 2006. *Who Controls the Internet? Illusions of a Borderless World.* New York: Oxford University Press.

Goldstein, Judith, and Lisa Martin. 2000. "Legalization, Trade Liberalization, and Domestic Politics: A Cautionary Note." *International Organization* 54 (3): 603–32.

Gould, Stephen Jay. 1989. *A Wonderful Life: The Burgess Shale and the Nature of History.* New York: W. W. Norton.

Granovetter, Mark S. 1973. "The Strength of Weak Ties." *American Journal of Sociology* 78 (6): 1360–80.

——. 1978. "Threshold Models of Collective Behavior." *American Journal of Sociology* 83: 1420–43.

Grant, Ruth, and Robert Keohane. 2005. "Accountability and Abuses of Power in World Politics." *American Political Science Review* 99 (1): 29–43.

Greenberg, Karen J. 2005. *Al Qaeda Now: Understanding Today's Terrorists.* Cambridge: Cambridge University Press.

Greenstein, Shane. 2005. "The Economic Geography of Internet Infrastructure in the United States." In *Handbook of Telecommunications Economics,* vol. 2, edited by Sumit T. Majumdar, Ingo Vogelsang, and Martin E. Cave, 289–374. Amsterdam: North-Holland.

Grünewald, François. 2007. *The Participation Handbook Involving Crisis-Affected People in Humanitarian Action.* London: Oxfam.

Gulati, Ranjay, Dania A. Dialdin, and Lihua Wang. 2002. "Organizational Networks." In *The Blackwell Companion to Organizations,* edited by Joel C. Baum, 281–303. Oxford: Blackwell.

Gunaratna, Rohan. 2002. *Inside Al Qaeda: Global Network of Terror.* New York: Columbia University Press.

Gutiérrez Sanín, Francisco. 2000. "Politicians and Criminals: Two Decades of Turbulence, 1978–1998." *International Journal of Politics, Culture, and Society* 14 (1): 71–87.

Haas, Peter. 1992. "Introduction: Epistemic Communities and International Policy Coordination." *International Organization* 46 (1): 1–35.

Hafner-Burton, Emilie M. 2005. "Trading Human Rights: How Preferential Trade Agreements Influence Government Repression." *International Organization* 59 (3): 593–629.

Hafner-Burton, Emilie M., Miles Kahler, and Alexander H. Montgomery. Forthcoming. "Network Analysis for International Relations." *International Organization.*

Hafner-Burton, Emilie M., and Alexander H. Montgomery. 2005. "War, Trade, and Envy: Why Trade Agreements Don't Always Keep the Peace." Paper presented at 46th annual convention of the International Studies Association, Honolulu, Hawaii, March 1–5.

——. 2006. "Power Positions: International Organizations, Social Networks, and Conflict." *Journal of Conflict Resolution* 50 (1): 3–27.

——. 2008. "Power or Plenty: How do International Trade Institutions Affect Economic Sanctions?" *Journal of Conflict Resolution* 52 (2): 213–42.

Halevy, Tammy. 1993. "Chinese Compliance with the Missile Technology Control Regime: A Case Study." *National Security Quarterly* 3: 14–23.

Hamilton-Hart, Natasha. 2005. "Terrorism in Southeast Asia: Expert Analysis, Myopia, and Fantasy." *Pacific Review* 18 (3): 303–25.

Hansen, J. Mark. 1991. *Gaining Access: Congress and the Farm Lobby, 1919–1981.* Chicago: University of Chicago Press.

Hart, Stephen. 2001. *Cultural Dilemmas of Progressive Politics.* Chicago: University of Chicago Press.

Hawkins, Darren C., David A. Lake, Daniel Nielsen, and Michael Tierney, eds. 2006. *Delegation and Agency in International Organizations.* New York: Cambridge University Press.

Heckmann, Friedrich. 2004. "Illegal Migration: What Can We Know and What Can We Explain? The Case of Germany." *International Migration Review* 38 (3): 1103–25.

Hirschman, Albert O. 1945. *National Power and the Structure of Foreign Trade.* Berkeley: University of California Press.

Hodkinson, Stuart. 2005. "Make the G8 History." *Red Pepper* online blog. Available at http://redpepper.blogs.com/g8/2005/07/index.html. Accessed April 4, 2008.

Hopf, Ted. 1998. "The Promise of Constructivism in International Relations Theory." *International Security* 23 (1): 171–200.

Hopgood, Stephen. 2007. "The Professionalization and Bureaucratization of Humanitarian Action." In *Humanitarianism in Question: Politics, Power, and Ethics,* edited by Michael Barnett and Tom Weiss. Ithaca: Cornell University Press.

Howard, Rhoda E., and Jack Donnelly. 1986. "Human Dignity, Human Rights, and Political Regimes." *American Political Science Review* 80: 801–17.

Howse, Robert. 2000. "Transatlantic Regulatory Cooperation and the Problem of Democracy." In *Transatlantic Regulatory Cooperation: Legal Problems and Political Prospects,* edited by George Bermann, Matthias Herdegen, and Peter Lindseth. Oxford: Oxford University Press.

Huckfeldt, R. Robert, and John D. Sprague. 1995. *Citizens, Politics, and Social Communication: Information and Influence in an Election Campaign.* New York: Cambridge University Press.

Hufbauer, Gary Clyde, Jeffrey J. Schott, and Kimberly Ann Elliott. 1990. *Economic Sanctions Reconsidered: Supplemental Case Histories.* 2nd ed. Washington, D.C.: Institute for International Economics.

Humanitarian Accountability Project (HAP). 2001. *Humanitarian Accountability: Key Elements and Operational Framework.* Geneva: HAP.

Ianni, Francis A. J., with Elizabeth Reuss-Ianni. 1972. *A Family Business: Kinship and Social Control in Organized Crime.* New York: Russell Sage Foundation.

ICANN Governmental Advisory Committee. 2000. "Principles for the Delegation and Administration of Country Code Top Level Domains." Available at http://gac.icann.org/web/docs/cctld/cctld.pdf. Accessed April 4, 2008.

Ingram, Paul, Jeffrey Robinson, and Marc L. Busch. 2005. "The Intergovernmental Network of World Trade: IGO Connectedness, Governance, and Embeddedness." *American Journal of Sociology* 111 (3): 824–58.

International Crisis Group (ICG). 2003. "Jemaah Islamiyah in Southeast Asia: Damaged but Still Dangerous." ICG Asia Report No. 63. August 26.

———. 2007. "Colombia's New Armed Groups." Latin American Report No. 20. May 10.

Jackson, Matthew O. 2005. "A Survey of Network Formation Models: Stability and Efficiency." In *Group Formation in Economics: Networks, Clubs and Coalitions,* edited by Gabrielle Demange and Myrna Wooders. New York: Cambridge University Press.

James, Scott, and David A. Lake. 1989. "The Second Face of Hegemony: Britain's Repeal of the Corn Laws and the American Walker Tariff of 1846." *International Organization* 43: 1–29.

Joseph, Jofi. 2004. "The PSI: Can Interdiction Stop Proliferation?" *Arms Control Today* (June). Available at http://www.armscontrol.org/act/2004_06/Joseph.asp. Accessed April 4, 2008.

Kahler, Miles. 2000. "Conclusion: The Causes and Consequences of Legalization." *International Organization* 54 (3): 661–83.

Kahler, Miles, and David A. Lake. Forthcoming. "Economic Integration and Global Governance: Why So Little Supranationalism?" In *Explaining Regulatory Change in the Global Economy*, edited by Walter Mattli and Ngaire Woods. Princeton: Princeton University Press.

Kahneman, Daniel, Paul Slovic, and Amos Tversky. 1982. *Judgment under Uncertainty: Heuristics and Biases.* Cambridge: Cambridge University Press.

Katz, Michael, and Carl Shapiro. 1985. "Network Externalities: Competition and Compatibility." *American Economic Review Papers and Proceedings* 75: 424–40.

Katzenstein, Peter J., ed. 1996. *The Culture of National Security: Norms and Identity in World Politics.* New York: Columbia University Press.

Katzenstein, Peter J., and Takashi Shiraishi, eds. 1997. *Network Power: Japan and Asia.* Ithaca: Cornell University Press.

Kaufman, Edy. 1991. "Prisoners of Conscience: The Shaping of a New Human Rights Concept." *Human Rights Quarterly* 13: 339–67.

Keck, Margaret E., and Kathryn Sikkink. 1998. *Activists beyond Borders: Advocacy Networks in International Politics.* Ithaca: Cornell University Press.

Keet, Dot. 2000. "The International Anti-Debt Campaign: A Southern Activist View for Activists in 'the North' and 'the South'." *Development in Practice* 10 (3–4): 461–77.

Kelle, Alexander. 2003. "The CWC after Its First Review Conference: Is the Glass Half Full or Half Empty?" *Disarmament Diplomacy* 71 (June–July). Available at http://www.acronym .org.uk/dd/dd71/71cwc.htm. Accessed April 4, 2008.

Kenney, Michael. 2005. "Drug Traffickers, Terrorist Networks, and Ill-Fated Government Strategies." In *New Threats and New Actors in International Security,* edited by Elke Krahmann, 69–90. New York: Palgrave Macmillan.

——. 2007. *From Pablo to Osama: Trafficking and Terrorist Networks, Government Bureaucracies, and Competitive Adaptation.* University Park: Pennsylvania State University Press.

Keohane, Robert O. 1984. *After Hegemony: Cooperation and Discord in the World Political Economy.* Princeton: Princeton University Press.

Keohane, Robert O., and Robert Axelrod. 1985. "Achieving Cooperation under Anarchy: Strategies and Institutions." *World Politics* 38 (1): 226–54.

Keohane, Robert O., and Joseph Nye. 1974. "Transgovernmental Relations and International Organizations." *World Politics* 27 (1): 39–62.

——. 1977. *Power and Interdependence: World Politics in Transition.* Boston: Little, Brown.

Kesan, Jay P., and Rajiv C. Shah. 2001. "Fool Us Once Shame on You—Fool Us Twice Shame on Us: What We Can Learn from the Privatizations of the Internet Backbone Network and Domain Name System." *Washington University Law Quarterly* 79: 89–220.

Khagram, Sanjeev, James V. Riker, and Kathryn Sikkink, eds. 2002. *Restructuring World Politics: Transnational Social Movements, Networks, and Norms.* Minneapolis: University of Minnesota Press.

Kim, Jang Hyun, and George A. Barnett. 2007. "A Structural Analysis of International Conflict: From a Communication Perspective." *International Interactions* 33: 135–65.

Kim, Kyungmo, and George A. Barnett. 2000. "The Structure of the International Telecommunications Regime in Transition: A Network Analysis of International Organizations." *International Interactions* 26 (1): 91–127.

Klein, Hans. 2001. "Global Democracy and the ICANN Elections." *Info* 3 (4): 255–57.

Klijn, Erik-Hans, and Joop F. M. Koppenjan. 2000. "Public Management and Policy Networks: Foundations of a Network Approach to Governance." *Public Management* 2 (2): 135–58.

Knoke, David. 1990. *Political Networks: The Structural Perspective.* Cambridge: Cambridge University Press.

Koremenos, Barbara, Charles Lipson, and Duncal Snidal. 2001a. "The Rational Design of International Institutions." *International Organization* 55 (4): 761–99.

———. 2001b. "Rational Design: Looking Back to Move Forward." *International Organization* 55 (4): 1051–82.

Korey, William. 1968. *The Key to Human Rights Implementation*. New York: Carnegie Endowment for International Peace.

———. 1998. *NGOs and the Universal Declaration of Human Rights: "A Curious Grapevine."* New York: St. Martin's Press.

Krahmann, Elke. 2003. "Conceptualizing Security Governance." *Cooperation and Conflict* 38 (1): 5–26.

———. 2005. "Security Governance and Networks." *Cambridge Review of International Affairs* 18: 19–34.

Krasner, Stephen D. 1991. "Global Communications and National Power: Life on the Pareto Frontier." *World Politics* 43: 336–66.

Krauthausen, Ciro, and Luis Fernando Sarmiento. 1991. *Cocaína y Co.: Un mercado ilegal por dentro*. Bogotá: Tercer Mundo Editores.

Krebs, Valdis E. 2002. "Mapping Networks of Terrorist Cells." *Connections* 24 (3): 43–52.

Lake, David A., and Mathew McCubbins. 2006. "The Logic of Delegation to International Organizations." In *Delegation and Agency in International Organizations*, edited by Darren C. Hawkins, David A. Lake, Daniel Nielsen, and Michael Tierney, 341–68. New York: Cambridge University Press.

Larsen, Egon. 1978. *A Flame in Barbed Wire*. London: Frederick Muller.

Levitt, Barbara, and James G. March. 1988. "Organizational Learning." *Annual Review of Sociology* 14: 319–40.

Liddick, Donald R., Jr. 2001. "Political Fund-raising, Patron-Client Relations, and Organized Criminality: Two Case Studies." *Journal of Contemporary Criminal Justice* 17 (4): 346–57.

Liebowitz, Stan. 2002. *Re-thinking the Network Economy*. New York: Amacom.

Lin, Nan. 2001. *Social Capital: A Theory of Social Structure and Action*. Cambridge: Cambridge University Press.

Lipson, Charles. 1991. "Why Are Some International Agreements Informal?" *International Organization* 45 (4): 495–538.

Lohmann, Susanne. 1994. "The Dynamics of Informational Cascades: The Monday Demonstrations in Leipzig, East Germany, 1989–91." *World Politics* 47 (1): 42–101.

Lu, C. 2000. "The One and Many Faces of Cosmopolitanism." *Journal of Political Philosophy* 8: 5.

Lukes, Steven. 1974. *Power: A Radical View*. London: Macmillan.

———. 1977. *Power: A Radical View*. 2nd ed. London: Macmillan.

Lupia, Arthur, and Mathew D. McCubbins. 1998. *The Democratic Dilemma: Can Citizens Learn What They Need To Know?* Cambridge: Cambridge University Press.

Lupsha, Peter A. 1996. "Transnational Organized Crime versus the Nation-State." *Transnational Organized Crime* 2 (1): 21–48.

Macrae, Joanna, ed. 2002. *The New Humanitarianisms: A Review of Trends in Global Humanitarian Action*. London: Overseas Development Institute.

Macrae, Joanna, Sarah Collinson, Margie Buchanan-Smith, Nicola Reindorp, Anna Schmidt, Tasneem Mowjee, and Adele Harmer. 2002. *Uncertain Power: The Changing Role of Official Donors in Humanitarian Action*. HPG Report 12. London: Overseas Development Institute.

Mahonen, Petri. 2000. "The Standardization Process in IT—Too Slow or Too Fast." In *Information Technology Standards and Standardization: A Global Perspective*, edited by Kai Jacobs, 35–47. Hershey, Penn.: IGI Publications.

Manger, Mark S. 2007. "Plugged into the Network? A Longitudinal Social Network Analysis of Preferential Trade Agreements." Paper presented at the annual meeting of the International Political Economy Society, Stanford, November 9–10.

Mansfield, Edward D., and Jon C. Pevehouse. 2000. "Trade Blocs, Trade Flows, and International Conflict." *International Organization* 54 (4): 775–808.

Maoz, Zeev. 2001. "Democratic Networks: Connecting National, Dyadic, and Systemic Levels-of-Analysis in the Study of Democracy and War." In *War in a Changing World,* edited by Zeev Maoz and A. Gat, 143–82. Ann Arbor: University of Michigan Press.

——. 2006. "Network Polarization, Network Interdependence, and International Conflict, 1816–2002." *Journal of Peace Research* 43 (4): 391–411.

Maoz, Zeev, Lesley G. Terris, Ranan D. Kuperman, and Ilan Talmud. 2005. "International Relations: A Network Approach." In *New Directions for International Relations: Confronting the Method-of-Analysis Problem,* edited by Alex Mintz and Bruce Russett, 35–64. Lanham, Md.: Lexington Books.

Marin, Bernd, and Renate Mayntz, eds. 1991. *Policy Networks: Empirical Evidence and Theoretical Considerations.* Frankfurt: Campus Verlag.

Marsh, David, and Martin Smith. 2000. "Understanding Policy Networks: Towards a Dialectical Approach." *Political Studies* 48: 4–21.

Martin, Andy, Carolyn Culey, and Suzy Evans. 2006. "Make Poverty History: 2005 Campaign Evaluation Executive Summary." London: Firetail.

Marwell, Gerald, and Pamela Oliver. 1993. *The Critical Mass in Collective Action.* Cambridge: Cambridge University Press.

Mastrofski, Stephen, and Gary Potter. 1987. "Controlling Organized Crime: A Critique of Law Enforcement Policy." *Criminal Justice Policy Review* 2 (3): 269–301.

Mathiason, John, Milton Mueller, Hans Klein, Mark Holitscher, and Lee McKnight. 2004. "Internet Governance: The State of Play." Syracuse, N.Y.: Internet Governance Project. Available at http://www.internetgovernance.org. Accessed April 4, 2008.

Matthew, Jessica. 1997. "Power Shift." *Foreign Affairs* 76 (1): 51–66.

Mattli, Walter, and Tim Buthe. 2003. "Setting International Standards: Technological Rationality or Primacy of Power" *World Politics* 56: 1–42.

Mazur, Jay. 2000. "Labor's New Internationalism." *Foreign Affairs* 79 (1): 79–93.

Mazzetti, Mark. 2007. "Qaeda Is Seen as Restoring Leadership." *New York Times,* April 2.

McAdam, Doug. 2003. "Beyond Structural Analysis: Toward a More Dynamic Understanding of Social Movements." In *Social Movements and Networks: Relational Approaches to Collective Action,* edited by Mario Diani and Doug McAdam, 281–98. Oxford: Oxford University Press.

McDougall, Robert. 2002. "Remarks to the Canada–Japan Seminar." Department of Foreign Affairs and International Trade, Ottawa, Canada, November 23.

McGloin, Jean Marie. 2005. "Policy and Intervention Considerations of a Network Analysis of Street Gangs." *Criminology and Public Policy* 4 (3): 607–36.

McIllwain, Jeffrey Scott. 1998. "An Equal Opportunity Employer: Opium Smuggling Networks in and around San Diego during the Early Twentieth Century." *Transnational Organized Crime* 2 (4): 31–54.

Mearsheimer, John J. 2001. *The Tragedy of Great Power Politics.* New York: W. W. Norton.

Médecins Sans Frontières (MSF) Holland. 2005. "Darfur 2004: A Review of MSF-H's Responsiveness and Strategic Choices." Amsterdam, January.

Merton, Robert K. 1968. *Social Theory and Social Structure.* New York: Free Press.

Meyer, Kathryn, and Terry Parssinen. 1998. *Webs of Smoke: Smugglers, Warlords, Spies, and the History of the International Drug Trade.* Lanham, Md.: Rowman and Littlefield.

Milgram, Stanley. 1967. "The Small World Problem." *Psychology Today* 2: 60–67.

——. 1975. *Obedience to Authority: An Experimental View.* New York: Harper and Row.

Ministry of Foreign Affairs, Canada. 2005. "Missile Proliferation and the Missile Technology Control Regime." Available at http://www.dfait-maeci.gc.ca/arms/missile-en.asp. Accessed April 4, 2008.

Mitrany, David. 1933. *The Progress of International Government.* William Dodge Lectures, Yale University. New Haven, CT: Yale University Press.

——. 1943. *A Working Peace System.* London: Martin Robertson.

Mizruchi, Mark S. 1989. "Similarity of Political Behavior among Large American Corporations." *American Journal of Sociology* 95 (2): 401–24.

Moore, Ray, and Donald Robinson. 2005. *Partners in Democracy.* New York: Oxford University Press.

Moravcsik, Andrew. 1998. *The Choice for Europe.* Ithaca: Cornell University Press.

Morgenthau, Hans Joachim. 1948. *Politics among Nations: The Struggle for Power and Peace.* New York: Alfred A. Knopf.

Morselli, Carlo. 2001. "Structuring Mr. Nice: Entrepreneurial Opportunities and Brokerage Positioning in the Cannabis Trade." *Crime, Law, and Social Change* 35 (3): 203–44.

Mueller, Milton. 1989. "The Switchboard Problem: Scale, Signaling, and Organization in Manual Telephone Switching, 1878–1898." *Technology and Culture* 30 (3): 534–60.

———. 2002a. "Competing DNS Roots: Creative Destruction or Just Plain Destruction?" *Journal of Network Industries* 3 (3): 313–34.

———. 2002b. *Ruling the Root: Internet Governance and the Taming of Cyberspace.* Cambridge: MIT Press.

———. Forthcoming. *The Global Politics of Internet Governance.*

Mutua, Makau. 2001. "Human Rights International NGOs: A Critical Evaluation." In *NGOs and Human Rights: Promise and Performance,* edited by Claude E. Welch. Philadelphia: University of Pennsylvania Press.

Naím, Moisés. 2003. "The Five Wars of Globalization." *Foreign Policy* (January–February): 29–37.

National Research Council (NRC). 2005. *Signposts in Cyberspace.* Washington, D.C.: NAS Press.

Nelson, P. 1997. "Conflict, Legitimacy, and Effectiveness: Who Speaks for Whom in Transnational NGO Networks Lobbying the World Bank?" *Nonprofit and Voluntary Sector Quarterly* 26: 4.

Nemeth, Roger J., and David A. Smith. 1985. "International Trade and World System Structure: A Multiple-Network Analysis." *Review* 8 (4): 517–60.

Newman, Mark, Albert-László Barabási, and Duncan J. Watts, eds. 2006. *The Structure and Dynamics of Networks.* Princeton: Princeton University Press.

Noam, Eli. 2001. *Interconnecting the Network of Networks.* Cambridge: MIT Press.

Ohmae, Kenichi. 1995. *The End of the Nation-State.* New York: Simon and Shuster.

Oliver, Pamela E., and Daniel J. Myers. 2003. "Networks, Diffusion, and Cycles of Collective Action." In *Social Movements and Networks: Relational Approaches to Collective Action,* edited by Mario Diani and Doug McAdam, 173–203. Oxford: Oxford University Press.

Padgett, John F. 2001. "Organizing Genesis, Identity, and Control: The Transformation of Banking in Renaissance Florence." In *Networks and Markets,* edited by James E. Rauch and Alessandra Casella, 211–57. New York: Russell Sage Foundation.

Padgett, John F., and Christopher K. Ansell. 1993. "Robust Action and the Rise of the Medici, 1400–1434." *American Journal of Sociology* 98 (6): 1259–1319.

Pande, Savita. 1999. "Missile Technology Control Regime: Impact Assessment." *Strategic Analysis* 23 (6).

Pape, Robert A. 2005. *Dying to Win: The Strategic Logic of Suicide Terrorism.* New York: Random House.

Parnas, David L. 1972. "On the Criteria to Be Used in Decomposing Systems into Modules." *Communications of the ACM* 15 (12): 1053–58.

Persson, Torsten, and Guido Tabellini. 2005. *The Economic Effects of Constitutions.* Cambridge: MIT Press.

Picciotto, Sol. 1997. "Fragmented States and International Rules of Law." *Social and Legal Studies* 6 (2): 259–79.

———. 2000. "North Atlantic Cooperation and Democratizing Globalism." In *Transatlantic Regulatory Cooperation: Legal Problems and Political Prospects,* edited by George Bermann, Matthias Herdegen and Peter Lindseth, 495–519. Oxford: Oxford University Press.

Picciotto, Sol, and Renate Mayne. 1999. *Regulating International Business: Beyond Liberalization.* London: Macmillan.

Podolny, Joel M., and Karen L. Page. 1998. "Network Forms of Organization." *Annual Review of Sociology* 24: 57–76.

Pollack, Mark. 2005. "The New Transatlantic Agenda at Ten: Reflections on an Experiment in International Governance." *Journal of Common Market Studies* 43 (5): 899–919.

Pollack, Mark, and G. Schaffer, eds. 2001. *Transatlantic Governance in the Global Economy.* Lanham, Md.: Rowman and Littlefield.

Portes, Alejandro. 1998. "Social Capital: Its Origins and Applications in Modern Sociology." *Annual Review of Sociology* 41: 1–24.

Powell, Walter W. 1990. "Neither Market nor Hierarchy: Network Forms of Organization." *Research in Organizational Behavior* 12: 295–336.

——. 1996. "Inter-Organizational Collaboration in the Biotechnology Industry." *Journal of Institutional and Theoretical Economics* 152 (1): 197–215.

Powell, Walter W., and Stine Grodal. 2005. "Networks of Innovators." In *The Oxford Handbook of Innovation,* edited by Jan Fagerberg, David C. Mowery, and Richard R. Nelson, 56–85. New York: Oxford University Press.

Power, Jonathan. 1981. *Amnesty International, the Human Rights Story.* New York: McGraw-Hill.

R Development Core Team. 2007. R: A Language and Environment for Statistical Computing (2.6.1). R Foundation for Statistical Computing, Vienna. Available at http://www.R-project.org.

Raab, Jörg, and H. Brinton Milward. 2003. "Dark Networks as Problems." *Journal of Public Administration Research and Theory* 13 (4): 413–39.

Raban, Jonathan. 2005. "The Truth about Terrorism." *New York Review of Books,* January 13, 22–26.

Randle, M. 2004. "Jubilee 2000: The Challenge of Coalition Campaigning." Centre for the Study of Forgiveness and Reconciliation, Coventry University.

Rauch, James E. 1998. "Networks versus Markets in International Trade." *Journal of International Economics* 48: 7–35.

Rauch, James, and Alessandra Casella, eds. 2001. *Networks and Markets.* New York: Russell Sage Foundation.

Raustiala, Kal. 2002. "The Architecture of International Cooperation: Transgovernmental Networks and the Future of International Law." *Virginia Journal of International Law* 43 (1): 1–92.

Reinicke, Wolfgang H. 1998. *Global Public Policy: Governing without Government?* Washington, D.C.: Brookings Institution Press.

——. 1999. "The Other World Wide Web: Global Public Policy Networks." *Foreign Policy* 117: 44–57.

Reuter, Peter. 1983. *Disorganized Crime: The Economics of the Visible Hand.* Cambridge: MIT Press.

Rice, Condoleezza. 2005. "Remarks on the Second Anniversary of the Proliferation Security Initiative." May 31. Available at http://www.state.gov/secretary/rm/2005/46951.htm. Accessed April 4, 2008.

Richani, Nazih. 2002. *Systems of Violence: The Political Economy of War and Peace in Colombia.* Albany: State University of New York Press.

Richardson, Michael. 2006. *The PSI: An Assessment of Its Strengths and Weaknesses, with Some Proposals for Shaping Its Future.* Singapore: Institute of Southeast Asian Studies

Rieff, David. 2002. *A Bed for the Night: Humanitarianism in Crisis.* London: Vintage.

Rogers, Everett M. 1995. *The Diffusion of Innovations.* New York: Free Press.

Roldán, Mary. 1999. "Colombia: Cocaine and the 'Miracle' of Modernity in Medellín." In *Cocaine: Global Histories,* edited by Paul Gootenberg, 165–82. New York: Routledge.

Rosenau, James N. 1988. "Patterned Chaos in Global Life: Structure and Process in the Two Worlds of World Politics." *International Political Science Review* 9 (4): 327–64.

———. 1990. *Turbulence in World Politics: A Theory of Change and Continuity.* Princeton: Princeton University Press.

———. 1992. "Governance, Order and Change in World Politics." In *Governance without Government: Order and Change in World Politics,* edited by James Rosenau and E. Czempiel, 1–29. Cambridge: Cambridge University Press.

———. 2000. "Change, Complexity, and Governance in a Globalizing Space." In *Debating Governance: Authority, Steering, and Democracy,* edited by Jon Pierre, 167–200. Oxford: Oxford University Press.

Rosendorf, Peter, and Helen Milner. 2001. "The Optimal Design of International Trade Institutions: Uncertainty and Escape." *International Organization* 55 (4): 829–57.

Rossem, Ronan Van. 1996. "The World System Paradigm as General Theory of Development: A Cross-National Test." *American Sociological Review* 61 (3): 508–27.

Roston, Michael. 2004. "Polishing Up the Story on the PSI." *In the National Interest.* Online weekly. Available at http://www.inthenationalinterest.com/Articles/Vol3Issue23/Vol3Issue23Roston.html. Accessed April 4, 2008.

Roy, Olivier. 2004. *Globalized Islam: The Search for a New Umma.* London: Hurst and Company.

Russett, Bruce, John R. Oneal, and David R. Davis. 1998. "The Third Leg of the Kantian Tripod for Peace: International Organizations and Militarized Disputes, 1950–85." *International Organization* 52 (3): 441–67.

Rustow, Dankwart A. 1970. "Transitions to Democracy: Toward a Dynamic Model." *Comparative Politics* 2 (3): 337–63.

Sabel, Charles. 1993. "Constitutional Ordering in Historical Context." In *Games in Hierarchies and Networks,* edited by Fritz Scharpf, 65–123. Boulder, Colo.: Westview Press.

Sageman, Marc. 2004. *Understanding Terror Networks.* Philadelphia: University of Pennsylvania Press.

SAIC. Strategies Group. 2001. "Assessment of Preventive Threat Reduction: A Report Prepared for the Advanced Systems and Concepts Office, Defense Threat Reduction Agency, Ft. Belvoir, Virginia." February 8.

Salazar, Alonzo, J., and Ana María Jaramillo. 1996. *Medellín: Las subculturas del narcotráfico.* Bogotá: CINEP.

Salter, Arthur. 1921. *Allied Shipping Control.* Oxford: Clarendon Press.

———. 1933 [1919]. "The Organization of the League of Nations." In *Sir Arthur Salter: The United States of Europe and Other Papers,* edited by W. Arnold-Forster. London: Allen and Unwin.

Scharpf, Fritz W. 1993a. Introduction to *Games in Hierarchies and Networks: Analytical and Empirical Approaches to the Study of Governance Institutions,* edited by Fritz W. Scharpf. Boulder, Colo.: Westview Press.

———, ed. 1993b. *Games in Hierarchies and Networks: Analytical and Empirical Approaches to the Study of Governance Institutions.* Boulder, Colo.: Westview Press.

Schelling, Thomas C. 1978. *Micromotives and Macrobehavior.* New York: W. W. Norton.

Schott, Jeffrey J. 2004. "Free Trade Agreements: Boon or Bane of the World Trading System?" In *Free Trade Agreements: U.S. Strategies and Priorities,* edited by J. J. Schott, 3–33. Washington, D.C.: Institute for International Economics.

Scott, John. 2000. *Social Network Analysis: A Handbook.* 2nd ed. London: Sage Publications.

Shapiro, Carl, and Hal R. Varian. 1999. *Information Rules: A Strategic Guide to the Network Economy.* Boston: Harvard Business School Press.

Shaw, Robert, 1997. "Internet Domain Names: Whose Domain Is This?" In *Coordinating the Internet,* edited by Brian Kahin and James H. Keller, 107–34. Cambridge: MIT Press.

Shiman, Daniel, and Jessica Rosenworcel. 2002. "Assessing the Effectiveness of Section 271 Five Years after the Telecommunications Act of 1996." In *Communications Policy and Information Technology,* edited by Lorrie Faith Cranor and Shane Greenstein, 183–216. Cambridge: MIT Press.

Shy, Oz. 2001. *The Economics of Network Industries.* Cambridge: Cambridge University Press.

Sikkink, Kathryn. 1998. "Transnational Politics, International Relations Theory, and Human Rights." *PS: Political Science and Politics* 3: 516–23.

Simmons, Beth A., and Zachary Elkins. 2004. "The Globalization of Liberalization: Policy Diffusion in the International Political Economy." *American Political Science Review* 98 (1): 171–89.

Singer, J. David, Stuart Bremer, and John Stuckey. 1972. "Capability Distribution, Uncertainty, and Major Power War, 1820–1965." In *Peace, War, and Numbers,* edited by Bruce Russett, 19–48. Beverly Hills, Calif.: Sage Publications.

Slaughter, Anne-Marie. 1997. "The Real New World Order: The State Strikes Back." *Foreign Affairs* 76 (5): 183–97.

——. 2000. "Agencies on the Loose? Holding Government Networks Accountable." In *Transatlantic Regulatory Cooperation: Legal Problems and Political Prospects,* edited by George Bermann, Matthias Herdegen, and Peter Lindseth. Oxford: Oxford University Press.

——. 2004a. *A New World Order.* Princeton: Princeton University Press.

——. 2004b. "Disaggregated Sovereignty: Towards the Public Accountability of Global Government Networks." *Government and Opposition* 39 (2): 159–90.

Slim, Hugo. 2002. "By What Authority? The Legitimacy and Accountability of Non-Governmental Organizations." Geneva: International Council on Human Rights Policy.

Smith, David A., and Douglas R. White. 1992. "Structure and Dynamics of the Global Economy: Network Analysis of International Trade, 1965–1980." *Social Forces* 70 (4): 857–93.

Smith-Doerr, Laurel, and Walter W. Powell. 2005. "Networks and Economic Life." In *The Handbook of Economic Sociology,* edited by Neil J. Smelser and Richard Swedberg, 379–402. Princeton: Princeton University Press.

Snyder, David, and Edward L. Kick. 1979. "Structural Position in the World System and Economic Growth, 1955–1970: A Multiple-Network Analysis of Transnational Interactions." *American Journal of Sociology* 84 (5): 1096–1126.

Sphere. 2000. *Humanitarian Charter and Minimum Standards in Disaster Response.* Geneva.

Spiro, P. 1995. "New Global Communities: Non-Governmental Organizations in International Decision-Making Institutions." *Washington Quarterly* 18 (1): 45–56.

Stein, Arthur. 1982. "Coordination and Collaboration: Regimes in an Anarchical World." *International Organization* 36 (2): 299–324.

Stein, Janice Gross. 2007. "Humanitarian Organizations: Accountable Why, to Whom, for What, and How?" In *Humanitarianism in Question: Politics, Power, and Ethics,* edited by Michael Barnett and Tom Weiss. Ithaca: Cornell University Press.

Strange, Susan. 1996. *The Retreat of the State.* Cambridge: Cambridge University Press.

Sunstein, Cass. 1996. "Social Norms and Social Roles." *Columbia Law Review* 18: 903–68.

TeleGeography. 2000. *TeleGeography 2001.* Washington, D.C.: TeleGeography.

Terry, Fiona. 2002. *Condemned to Repeat? The Paradox of Humanitarian Action.* Ithaca: Cornell University Press.

Tetlock, Philip E. 1991. "Learning in U.S. and Soviet Foreign Policy: In Search of an Elusive Concept." In *Learning in U.S. and Soviet Foreign Policy,* edited by George W. Breslauer and Philip E. Tetlock, 20–61. Boulder, Colo.: Westview Press.

Thompson, Grahame F. 2003. *Between Hierarchies and Markets: The Logic and Limits of Network Forms of Organization.* New York: Oxford University Press.

Thoumi, Francisco E. 1995. *Political Economy and Illegal Drugs in Colombia.* Boulder, Colo.: Lynne Rienner.

Trondal, Jarle. 2004. "Two Faces of Internationalization of Administrative Policy: Between Government Innovation and Transgovernmental Imitation." Unpublished manuscript, Centre for European Studies, Agder, Norway.

Tucker, Jonathan, ed. 2001. "The Chemical Weapons Convention: Implementation Challenges and Solutions." Washington, D.C.: Monterey Institute of International Studies. Available at http://cns.miis.edu/pubs/reports/pdfs/tuckcwc.pdf. Accessed April 4, 2008.

United Nations. Division for Social Policy and Development. 2005. *Report on the World Social Situation: The Inequality Predicament.* Available at http://www.un.org/esa/socdev/rwss/rwss.htm. Accessed April 4, 2008.

U.S. Department of State. Bureau of International Security and Nonproliferation. 1993. "Missile Technology Control Regime." January 7.

———. 2003a. "Proliferation Security Initiative: Statement of Interdiction Principles." Fact sheet, September 4.

———. 2003b. "Proliferation Security Initiative: Chairman's Conclusions at the Fourth Meeting." October 10.

———. 2003c. "Missile Technology Control Regime." Fact sheet, December 23.

———. 2004. "Missile Technology Control Regime Questions and Answers." Fact sheet, August 2.

Van Calster, Patrick. 2006. "Revisiting *Mr. Nice:* On Organized Crime as Conversational Interaction." *Crime, Law, and Social Change* 45 (4–5): 337–59.

Vick, Karl. 2007. "Al-Qaeda's Hand in Istanbul Plot." *Washington Post,* February 13, A01.

Volden, Craig, and Michael Cohen. 2006. "The Diffusion of Successful Welfare Policies." Paper presented at the meetings of the European Consortium for Political Research.

Walker, Jack L. 1969. "The Diffusion of Innovation among American States." *American Political Science Review* 63: 880–99.

Wallerstein, Immanuel. 1974. "The Rise and Future Demise of the World Capitalist System: Concepts for Comparative Analysis." *Comparative Studies in Society and History* 16 (4): 387–415.

Waltz, Kenneth N. 1979. *Theory of International Politics.* New York: McGraw-Hill.

Wasserman, Stanley, and Katherine Faust. 1994. *Social Network Analysis: Methods and Applications.* Cambridge: Cambridge University Press.

Watts, Duncan J. 1999. *Small Worlds: The Dynamics of Networks between Order and Randomness.* Princeton: Princeton University Press.

———. 2003. *Six Degrees: The Science of a Connected Age.* New York: W. W. Norton.

———. 2004. "The 'New' Science of Networks." *Annual Review of Sociology* 30: 243–70.

Watts, Nicole F. 2004. "Institutionalizing Virtual Kurdistan West: Transnational Networks and Ethnic Contention in International Affairs." In *Boundaries and Belonging,* edited by Joel S. Migdal, 121–47. Cambridge: Cambridge University Press.

Wayland, Sarah. 2004. "Ethnonationalist Networks and Transnational Opportunities: The Sri Lankan Tamil Diaspora." *Review of International Studies* 30: 405–26.

Webber, Mark, Stuart Croft, Jolyon Howorth, Terry Terriff, and Elke Krahmann. 2004. "The Governance of European Security." *Review of International Studies* 30: 3–26.

Weinberg, Jonathan. 2002. "ICANN, 'Internet Stability,' and the New Top Level Domains." In *Communications Policy and Information Technology: Promises, Problems, Prospects,* edited by Lorrie Faith Cranor and Shane Greenstein, 3–24. Cambridge: MIT Press.

Welch, Claude E. 2001. "Amnesty International and Human Rights Watch: A Comparison." In *NGOs and Human Rights: Promise and Performance,* edited by Claude E. Welch. Philadelphia: University of Pennsylvania Press.

Wendt, Alexander. 1999. *Social Theory of International Politics.* Cambridge: Cambridge University Press.

Westney, D. Eleanor. 1987. *Imitation and Innovation: The Transfer of Western Organizational Patterns to Meiji Japan.* Cambridge: Harvard University Press.

Weyland, Kurt Gerhard. 2004. *Learning from Foreign Models in Latin American Policy Reform.* Washington, D.C.: Woodrow Wilson Center Press.

Whytock, Christopher. 2005. "A Rational Design Theory of Transgovernmentalism: The

Case of E.U.–U.S. Merger Review Cooperation." *Boston University International Law Journal* 23 (1): 1–53.

Williams, Phil. 2001. "Transnational Criminal Networks." In *Networks and Netwars: The Future of Terror, Crime, and Militancy,* edited by John Arquilla and David Ronfeldt, 61–97. Santa Monica, Calif.: RAND.

Wines, Michael. 2005. "When Doing Good Aids the Devil." *New York Times,* December 25, WK5.

Winston, Morton E. 2001. "Assessing the Effectiveness of International Human Rights NGOs." In *NGOs and Human Rights: Promise and Performance,* edited by Claude E. Welch. Philadelphia: University of Pennsylvania Press.

Wolf, Martin. 2004. *Why Globalization Works.* New Haven: Yale University Press.

Yanacopulos, Helen. 2004. "The Public Face of Debt." *Journal of International Development* 16: 10.

Yanacopulos, Helen, and M. Baillie Smith. 2007. "The Ambivalent Cosmopolitanism of International NGOs." In *The Challenge of Development Alternatives: Can NGOs Make a Difference?,* edited by A. Bebbington, S. Hickey, and D. Mitlin. London: Zed Publishers.

Young, H., A. M. Osman, Y. Aklilu, R. Dale, B. Badri, and A. J. A. Fuddle. 2005. *Darfur 2004: Livelihoods under Siege.* December. Available at http://www.Unsudanig.org/emergencies/Darfur/assessments/data/UnderSiege.pdf.

Zahab, Mariam Abou, and Olivier Roy. 2004. *Islamist Networks: The Afghan-Pakistan Connection.* New York: Columbia University Press.

Zanini, Michele, and Sean J. A. Edwards. 2001. "The Networking of Terror in the Information Age." In *Networks and Netwars: The Future of Terror, Crime, and Militancy,* edited by John Arquilla and David Ronfeldt, 29–60. Santa Monica, Calif.: RAND.

Zaring, David. 1998. "International Law by Other Means: The Twilight Existence of International Financial Regulatory Organizations." *Texas International Law Journal* 33 (2): 281–330.

Zhang, Sheldon, and Ko-Lin Chin. 2002. "Enter the Dragon: Inside Chinese Human Smuggling Organizations." *Criminology* 40 (4): 737–67.

Index

Page numbers in italics refer to figures and tables.